German Period	US Period	Style	
Renaissance	Early Colonial	Gothic	(to c1670)
Renaissance/ Baroque (c1650–1700)		Baroque (c1620–1700)	Walnut period (c1670–1735)
	William & Mary		
Baroque (c1700–1730)	Dutch Colonial	Rococo (c1695–1760)	
	Queen Anne		Early mahogany period (c1735–1770)
Rococo (c1730–1760)	Chippendale (from 1750)		
Neo–classicism (c1760–1800)		Neo–classical (c1755–1805)	Late mahogany period (c1770–1810)
	Early Federal (1790–1810)		
Empire (c1800–1815)	American Directoire (1798–1804)	Empire (c1799–1815)	
	American Empire (1804–1815)		
Biedermeier (c1815–1848)	Late Federal (1810–1830)	Regency (c1812–1830)	
Revivale (c1830–1880)	Victorian	Eclectic (c1830–1880)	
Jugendstil (c1880–1920)		Arts & Crafts (c1880–1900)	
	Art Nouveau (c1900–1920)	Art Nouveau (c1900–1920)	

How to use this book

It is our aim to make this book easy to use. In order to find a particular item, consult the contents list on page 5 to find the main heading – for example, Arms & Armour. Having located your area of interest, you will find that sections have been sub-divided alphabetically. If you are looking for a particular factory, designer or craftsman, consult the index which starts on page 291.

---

116   SILVER & PLATE · BOXES & CASES

Boxes & Cases

The look without the price

Silver snuff box, with engraved decoration, maker's mark indistinct, Birmingham 1800, 2in (5cm) wide, ⅞oz.
£300–360 / €440–520
$550–660 WW ⚒

If the maker's marks on this snuff box were more distinguishable it could have achieved nearer £450 / €650 / $820.

Britannia standard
Britannia standard silver is of a higher quality than sterling silver. It was introduced in 1697 to prevent silversmiths using melted-down coinage as a source of metal, and it was stamped with a figure of Britannia.

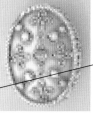

◀ **Britannia standard silver-gilt pill box,** set with gems, Birmingham 1910, 2in (5cm) wide.
£190–220
€270–310
$340–400 G(L) ⚒

Find out more in
Miller's Silver & Plate Buyer's Guide, Miller's Publications, 2002

Miller's compares...

A. Silver-gilt snuff box, by Taylor & Perry, the engine-turned cover with a crest, Birmingham 1833, 3¼in (8.5cm) wide, 3¼oz.
£300–360 / €440–520
$550–660 WW ⚒

B. Silver-gilt squeeze-action snuff box, by C.L. Rawlings and W. Summers, with engine-turned decoration, London 1831, 3½in (9cm) wide, 3oz.
£800–900 / €1,150–1,300
$1,450–1,650 BEX ⊞

Item A is a standard example of a snuff box whereas Item B has a working squeeze-action mechanism, attractive shape and is in good condition. All this accounts for the higher value of Item B.

The look without the price
highlights later items produced 'in the style of' earlier counterparts. It illustrates how you don't have to spend a fortune to have the original look.

Information box
covers relevant collecting information on factories, makers, fakes and alterations, period styles and designers.

Price guide
these are based on actual prices realized shown in £sterling with a €Euro and US$ conversion. Remember that Miller's is a price guide not a price list and prices are affected by many variables such as location, condition, desirability, whether it is a dealer ⊞ or auction ⚒ price (see the source code below) and so on. Don't forget that if you are selling it is quite likely you will be offered less than the price range. Price ranges for items sold at auction tend to include the buyer's premium and VAT if applicable. The exchange rate used in this edition is 1.82 for $ and 1.47 for €.

Find out more in
directs the reader towards additional sources of information.

Source code
refers to the Key to Illustrations on page 286 that lists the details of where the item was photographed. The ⚒ icon indicates the item was sold at auction. The ⊞ icon indicates the item originated from a dealer.

Miller's compares
explains why two items which look similar have realized very different prices.

Caption
provides a brief description of the item. It explains, where possible, why an item is valued at a particular price.

Introduction

One of the great benefits of working for a premier London auction house is the privilege of rubbing shoulders with some of the world's leading authorities on fine and decorative art. Some produce after-sale reports pointing out the highs and lows of the auction alongside an analysis of the results. I try to soak up as many of these details as possible – simply to stay on the ball. It is often said that six months out of this business and the chances are that you have already lost the plot.

This is where *Miller's Buying Affordable Antiques Price Guide* can help redress the balance. It is compiled by a team of experts, all of whom have carefully reviewed the ups and downs of the past year and have selected images that mirror their understanding as to what might be considered not only affordable but relatively undervalued.

The furniture scene continues to offer incredible value for money as a result of brown furniture failing to attract attention from both home and overseas buyers for yet another year. I never cease to be amazed that it is still possible to buy an 18th-century oak coffer or a George III mahogany chest of drawers in sound condition for as little as £500 / €720 / $900. However, as in previous years, rare and top-quality furniture continues to command no shortage of would-be owners prepared to dig deep into seemingly bottomless pockets.

The same criteria would appear to apply to most of the antiques market, with buyers of English ceramics proving to be very fickle, if recent auction results are anything to go by. The demand for Royal Worcester seems to have become limited to the most important examples painted by Baldwyn or pierced by Owen, with the remainder more readily available to those of us with lesser means. Blush ivory is one such casualty worth considering, as are figures modelled by James Hadley. The same would appear to hold true of blue and white 18th-century First Period Worcester and Dutch Delft, where bidding has become highly selective, making it possible to pick up certain blue and white 18th-century plates for as little as £40 / €60 / $75. The not-so-humble Victorian Staffordshire figure offers yet another area worthy of further inspection, with many collectors attending auctions intent on a specific purchase while ignoring much on offer at very low opening bids.

Collectors of 18th-century glass have been spoiled in recent years as a result of several important collections finding their way onto the auction scene. The result is that good, if somewhat standard, opaque and air-twist stem wine glasses can often still be snapped up for as little as £300 / €430 / $540. Bristol blue decanters dating from the late 18th century must be worth a second look when offered at £200 / €300 / $360 for a pair, even if the gilding is less than pristine. Classic 19th-century paperweights from Baccarat, Clichy and St Louis also represent value for money with prices for the majority of millefiori weights almost unchanged from a decade or more ago.

Possibly the bargain of the moment, however, has to be the late 19th- and early 20th-century silver tea set. Prices have plunged by more than half to as little as £150 / €220 / $270. The same would appear to apply to all useful wares of the same vintage whereas novelty silver continues to find no shortage of bidders.

This Guide is the compass to point you in the right direction towards an antiques and collectors' market that I personally consider to be open season for those seeking value for money.

Eric Knowles, FRSA

Types of Wood

Bird's-eye maple ▶

Bird's-eye maple, or American sugar maple, describes the very attractive figuring in maple. It was popular for veneers during the Regency period, and was also used in Victorian and Edwardian bedroom suites. The wood of the maple is whitish, and responds well to polishing. Bird's-eye maple is also popular today for picture frames.

◀ Burr walnut

Burr walnut is the term used for walnut with knotty whorls in the grain where injuries occurred on the trunk or roots of the tree. It was often used in decorative veneers. Walnut is a close-grained hardwood, the colour varying between light golden brown to dark grey-brown in colour with dark streaks, often with a rich grain pattern.

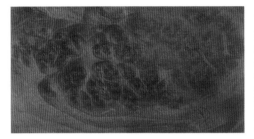

Calamander ▶

Calamander is a member of the **ebony** family and derives from Ceylon. Popular in the Regency period, it is light brown in colour, striped and mottled with black, and was used for veneers and banding. Calamander was also used in the manufacture of small decorative boxes. Ebony is close-grained, black in colour, and is resistant to decay.

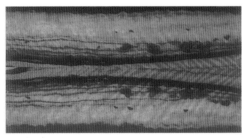

◀ Elm

The English variety of elm is hard and durable, but liable to warp, and prone to woodworm. Chairs were made from elm from the Georgian period, and the seats of Windsor chairs were elm from the 18th century. The wych elm has a particularly attractive grain and polishes well. **Burr elm** was used for veneers and cabinet-work in the early 18th century.

Kingwood ▶

Kingwood is related to rosewood, which was first imported to Britain from Brazil in the late 17th century. It is a rich brown with purplish tones, giving it an alternative name of violet wood. Also known as princewood, it was used as a veneer or for parquetry decoration, particularly in France. From c1770 it was used for crossbanding and borders.

Oak ▶

Oak is a slow-growing tree, taking between 150 and 200 years to reach maturity. The wood is hard and pale in colour, but darkens to a rich brown with age and polishing. Furniture made from oak is usually heavy and solid, and simple in design. From the middle of the 17th century oak was used mainly for the carcases of furniture and drawer linings, but became popular again in the late 19th century with the Arts and Crafts movement.

Satinwood ▶

Satinwood was used widely for veneers and inlaid decoration, the pale colour making it particularly suitable for painting. The grain varies from plain to rich figuring, the latter having a more transparent grain under polish or varnish. Cabinet-makers of the 19th century preferred the West Indian variety, which is darker than the East Indian variety, and was used as a veneer in fine furniture from c1765. It was rarely used in the solid, and not for chairs until c1800. The Eastern type, imported in the late 18th century, was pale yellow and used mainly for crossbanding.

◄ Mahogany

Mahogany is a close grained hardwood, native to northern and central South America and the West Indies. It varies in colour from dark brown to red, and sometimes has a spotted effect. Furniture made from mahogany became very popular with cabinet-makers in Britain from the mid-18th century, followed by France and the rest of Europe. African mahogany, which is lighter in weight, was used from the 1800s onwards.

◄ Rosewood

Rosewood is a very dark brown hardwood, with an almost black wavy grain. The name comes from the scent released when the wood is cut. Rosewood was used for inlaid decoration in the 17th century, and for veneer, but was not used for making solid furniture until the early 19th century. It was also used for decorative banding and small panels from the late 18th century.

◄ Sycamore

Sycamore is a European wood related to the North American maple, and is as strong as oak. It is hard, milky-white, with a fine even grain with natural lustre. In medieval times furniture was made in solid sycamore, and from the late 17th century it was used in floral marquetry on walnut furniture. When quarter-sawn the figuring is known as **fiddleback**, as it was often used in the manufacture of violins. Sycamore treated with iron oxide or stained green or grey was known as **harewood.**

Furniture

At present the top end of the antique furniture market continues to realize strong prices. As ever, a piece that is beautifully made, by a well-known craftsman and with an interesting provenance always achieves a high market value. However, these pieces are perhaps more appropriately placed in the art market category than antiques.

For those wishing to furnish a home with quality antique furniture, the buying and selling of antiques generally, and furniture in particular, continues to be slow for a variety of reasons: the continued slow-down in retailing, the current passion of interior designers for glass, chrome and pale timber furniture, and, arguably, the fact that prices for traditional antiques soared three or four years ago and put off a large number of potential new buyers.

The result of these combined factors is that fewer buyers are chasing more items and that prices of antique furniture now compare favourably with those of quality modern furniture. Generally speaking dealers have by now cut their losses and are prepared to offer competitive prices, and this trend is also being reflected in auctioneers' hammer prices. Overall now is a good time to purchase middle-of-the-road antiques, as with a little time spent researching the market for your required piece, there are good buys to be made.

Age no longer seems to be a determining factor in how much the market values a piece of furniture. Popular factors would appear to be timber, style and design. Timbers such as walnut or rosewood (solid or veneered) continue to be in demand, while mahogany is generally out of favour. With prices at a sensible level, oak, elm, ash and even pine country pieces are enjoying something of a renaissance, while yew-wood has never lost its appeal.

Popular at present are clean, symmetrical lines such as those found in early Georgian, Regency and early 20th-century furniture. The busier styles of the late Georgian and the Victorian eras are struggling in the current climate of minimalist decorative style, although good carved furniture, natural or gilded, has maintained a solid presence in the market.

Another key factor in determining the market value of antique furniture is whether it is functional and suited to current lifestyles. With the prevailing fashion for fitted bedroom furniture, wardrobes and chests of drawers have dropped further in price although by comparison a good matching pair of bedsde cabinets has not. The computer age has deprived the bureau of its useful purpose in the home, so despite the secret drawers and excellent storage it provides the bureau is, at present, redundant and therefore is a good buy should you particularly want one. The market value of any type of chair is without doubt dictated by how much restoration is required, as usually a chair will need to have, or will have had, some form of repair in order to make it fully usable.

We are confident that in this section you will find a wide selection of furniture, from the classic modern to the historical rarity, and we hope that this broad range will in turn help you to widen your understanding of antique furniture in our current sensitive market.

Raj Bisram

Beds & Cradles

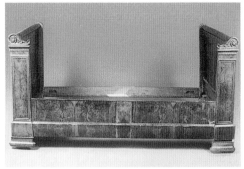

Rope bed, with wood supports, c1830, 49½in (125.5cm) wide. This is a very reasonable price for such an item. This piece sold in America, but if it had been sold in the UK it could have achieved up to £200 / €290 / $360.
£45–50 / €65–75
$85–100 JAA ⚒

French Empire walnut sleigh bed, with carved decoration, 19thC, 51in (129.5cm) wide. It is unusual to find such an item in walnut. This bed sold on the American market and achieved a good price. If it had been sold in the UK it could have achieved up to £500 / €720 / $940.
£260–310 / €370–440
$480–570 JAA ⚒

Miller's compares...

A. Victorian walnut swinging cradle, with pierced slats, applied mouldings and an iron hanger to each end, one leg repaired, 41in (104cm) wide.
£100–115 / €145–170
$180–210 JDJ ⚒

B. Mahogany cradle, the arched top with foliate carved decoration, 19thC, 32¼in (82cm) wide.
£300–360 / €430–520
$540–650 DN(BR) ⚒

Victorian oak three-piece bedroom suite, comprising bed, dresser and commode, with carved decoration, American, c1900. This suite sold in America where such items command higher prices than they would in the UK, where they are currently out of style.
£530–630 / €770–910
$970–1,150 JAA ⚒

Although Item A is a swinging cradle and Item B is a rocking cradle, they are both decorative and should have achieved roughly the same price. Item B was sold in the UK where there is currently a stronger market than in the US, which is why it achieved a higher price than Item A, which was sold in America.

▶ **Victorian mahogany four-poster bed,** restored, 61in (155cm) wide. This bed has been restored and given new drapes and a canopy. However, if it had been in original condition, it could have achieved nearer £1,200 / €1,750 / $2,150.
£720–860 / €1,050–1,250
$1,300–1,550 SWO ⚒

Benches

◄ **Oak bench,** with later carving and alterations, 18thC, 52½in (133.5cm) wide. Oak items are currently fashionable and the later additions to this bench have been tastefully completed and have not reduced the value.
£450–540 / €650–780
$820–980 WL ⚒

Locate the source

The source of each illustration in Miller's can be found by checking the code letters below each caption with the Key to Illustrations, pages 286–290.

◄ **Late Victorian walnut hall bench,** 54in (137cm) wide. Larger pieces of furniture have become less fashionable due to the small room sizes of contemporary homes. This bench was designed for a large house and therefore it has a limited market.
£880–1,050 / €1,250–1,450
$1,550–1,850 SWO ⚒

► **Walnut hall bench,** with simulated bamboo handles and turned supports, c1870, 36in (91.5cm) wide. This is a rare bench, with good colour and quality craftsmanship. Original benches of this design are hard to find, hence the high value of this item. Reproductions can be found at a third of the price.
£850–950
€1,250–1,400
$1,600–1,800 LGr ▦

Bookcases & Shelves

Miller's compares...

A. Victorian mahogany bookcase, the two glazed doors above a frieze drawer and two further panelled doors, 35in (89cm) wide.
£150–180 / €220–260 $280–330 CHTR ✦

B. Edwardian mahogany bookcase, the two glazed doors above two drawers and two further panelled doors, 34¾in (88.5cm) wide.
£780–930 / €1,100–1,300 $1,400–1,650 SWO ✦

Item A is a small bookcase with simple design that sold for a very reasonable price. Item B, however, is a more decorative and detailed bookcase with inlaid marquetry and elegant beading. Both bookcases are of a popular size but Item B would make a good focal point in a room and this has attracted buyers, hence the higher price.

Ebonized waterfall bookcase, with a pierced brass gallery and brass handles, 19thC, 31in (78.5cm) wide. This is a very reasonable price for such an item. It could have achieved as much as £500 / €720 / $910.
£340–400 / €490–580 $620–720 BWL ✦

Edwardian mahogany bookcase, with satinwood banding and inlaid stringing, with adjustable shelves, 35½in (90cm) wide. Bookcases are always in demand and pieces with adjustable shelving are more desirable because of their adaptability.
£350–420 / €510–600 $630–760 WW ✦

◄ **Victorian oak bookcase,** with adjustable shelves, 48in (122cm) wide.
£400–480 / €580–690 $720–870 SWO ✦

Victorian walnut bookcase, the burr-walnut top above a moulded frieze and three adjustable shelves, 50in (127cm) wide.
£420–500 / €610–720 $760–910 DN 🔨

Mahogany campaign bookcase, unfolding to reveal two glazed doors, 19thC, 36in (91.5cm) high. Campaign furniture is currently in demand and this has increased the value of such items.
£430–510 / €620–740 $780–930 BWL 🔨

Set of Victorian carved walnut hanging shelves, with four graduated serpentine shelves, 49in (124.5cm) wide. This is a very good price for such a beautifully carved and interesting set of shelves. They could easily have achieved £1,000 / €1,450 / $1,800.
£600–720 / €870–1,050 $1,100–1,300 WILK 🔨

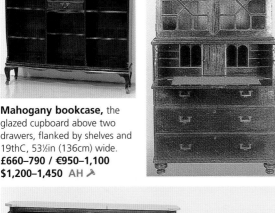

◄ **Military-type secretaire bookcase,** the two glazed doors enclosing adjustable shelves, the chest with secretaire drawer enclosing a fitted interior, above three further drawers, 19thC, 39in (99cm) wide. The recessed handles on this chest enable it to be packed away more easily for travelling. It was a good buy at auction.
£700–840 / €1,000–1,200 $1,300–1,550 Mit 🔨

Mahogany bookcase, the glazed cupboard above two drawers, flanked by shelves and 19thC, 53½in (136cm) wide.
£660–790 / €950–1,100 $1,200–1,450 AH 🔨

Victorian mahogany bookcase, the shelves flanked by turned columns, 57in (145cm) wide. Items made of mahogany are popular and have the advantage of being lower in price than those made in walnut.
£750–900 / €1,100–1,300 $1,400–1,650 SWO 🔨

◄ **Pair of Victorian mahogany bookcases,** with marble tops above adjustable shelves, 54in (137cm) wide. Pairs of bookcases always command a high price but these could have sold for more, making them a good buy at auction.
£900–1,050 / €1,300–1,500 $1,650–1,900 HYD 🔨

Chairs

Regency mahogany open armchair and side chair, repaired, the armchair with later upholstery, c1810. Pairs of open armchairs are more desirable than individual chairs such as these – which are a reasonable price for two mahogany chairs. It is important to consider the cost of reupholstering to one's own taste as this can add substantially to the overall cost of the item.
£100–120 / €145–170
$200–230 Hal 🔨

▶ **Inlaid mahogany dining chair,** c1780. This simple style of chair is currently popular.
£150–165 / €220–250
$270–300 QA ⊞

Elm armchair, with a wheel back, 19thC.
£105–125 / €150–180
$200–240 BeFA 🔨

Pair of Chippendale-style mahogany elbow chairs, with pierced splats and drop-in seats, 18thC. This is a very good price for two elbow chairs of this style and quality.
£130–155 / €190–220
$240–280 DMC 🔨

Victorian lacquered chair, inlaid with mother-of-pearl and painted with flowers. This chair has very attractive decoration and could probably have been expected to achieve more at auction. It is important to remember that central heating may cause damage to lacquered items.
£150–180 / €220–260
$270–320 WILK 🔨

◀ **Pair of cherrywood side chairs,** with rush seats and turned stretchers, 19thC.
£150–180 / €220–260
$270–330 DN 🔨

Victorian inlaid mahogany rocking chair, with upholstered seat, back and arms. When purchasing a chair, remember that having it resprung will also mean that the chair will have to be reupholstered. It is important to take into account this added cost when placing a bid at auction.
£150–180 / €220–260
$270–320 AMB 🔨

◄ **Pair of elm side chairs,** the spirally fluted stick back above an upholstered seat, Dutch, 19thC. These chairs were previously owned by Sibyl Colefax and John Fowler. A good provenance such as this will always add value to an item.
£170–200 / €250–290
$310–360 DN ⚒

Child's walnut armchair, with upholstered seat, back and arms, one leg repaired, 19thC. There is high demand for children's furniture. This armchair could have achieved nearly £250 / €360 / $450 if it had been in perfect condition.
£180–210 / €250–300
$320–380 WW ⚒

Child's mahogany rocking chair, 19thC. The rockers on this chair were probably added later, thus reducing its value.
£200–240 / €290–350
$360–430 AH ⚒

Pair of Victorian walnut armchairs, with carved decoration and button-back upholstery. This style of chair is currently unfashionable. Now would be a good time to buy while prices are still low.
£200–240 / €290–350
$360–430 DA ⚒

Find out more in

Miller's Antiques Price Guide, Miller's Publications, 2005

Pair of Regency mahogany armchairs, with rope-twist backs and panelled seats. This is a reasonable price for a pair of armchairs – they were a good buy at auction.
£220–260 / €320–380
$400–470 DN(HAM) ⚒

Walnut upholstered wingback armchair, early 20thC. The upholstery on this chair is in need of some attention which will add to its cost.
£240–280 / €340–400
$430–510 CHTR ⚒

George III Chippendale-style mahogany armchair, legs retipped. This is a fair price for a chair with this type of repair.
£250–300 / €360–430
$460–540 L&E ⚒

Victorian mahogany upholstered armchair, on cabriole legs. This classic chair, upholstered in a neutral fabric, could have made nearer £700 / €1,000 / $1,250.
£260–310 / €380–450
$470–560 TRM(E) ⚒

Gothic revival armchair, with leather upholstery, c1840. This chair was sold in the US. If it had been sold in the UK, where there is a market for this style, it could have achieved £400 / €580 / $730.
£260–310 / €380–450
$470–560 SK ⚒

◄ **Edwardian mahogany upholstered salon wing chair.** This chair would be a good investment, even after the cost of reupholstery has been taken into account .
£280–330 / €410–480
$510–600 DA ⚒

Early Victorian mahogany chair, on turned and reeded legs, with button-back upholstery.
£280–330 / €410–480
$510–600 WilP ⚒

► **George IV mahogany upholstered wing armchair,** on turned legs. This is a reasonable price for a classic chair. It could have achieved £400–500 / €580–720 / $730–910 on a better day.
£280–330 / €410–480
$510–600 DN ⚒

Mahogany armchair, with later button-back upholstery, on cabriole legs, c1860.
£320–380 / €460–550
$580–690 Hal ⚒

Set of five Victorian rosewood balloon-back dining chairs,
with upholstered stuff-over seats, on cabriole legs. Had this been a
set of six chairs rather than five they could have achieved
£600–900 / €870–1,300 / $1,100–1,650.
£350–420 / €510–610
$640–760 DN(BR) 🔨

► **Gothic revival
oak hall chair,**
with ebony-inlaid
decoration, c1870.
£360–400
€520–580
$650–720 ANO ⊞

◄ **Victorian elm and ash
smoker's bow elbow chair,**
with turned supports and
baluster legs. This beautifully
decorated chair could be used
as a desk chair.
£380–450 / €550–650
$690–810 Mal(O) 🔨

Inlaid mahogany armchair, c1900.
£360–400 / €520–580
$650–720 QA ⊞

◄ **Pair of late
Victorian walnut
armchairs,** with
button-back
upholstery, on turned
legs. Although these
chairs look
comfortable, the cost
of replacing the worn
upholstery would be
quite substantial.
£400–460
€560–660
$710–840 WW 🔨

**Victorian mahogany
spoonback armchair,** carved
with flowers, scrolls and tendrils,
with button-back upholstery.
This is a good price if you like
this style of decoration.
£400–460 / €580–660
$710–840 DN(BR) 🔨

◄ Set of six oak dining chairs, with barley-twist supports and bobbin-turned stretchers, late 19thC, with two similar chairs. These chairs were a good buy, and selling the two non-matched chairs would be a way of recouping some of the purchase price, thus increasing the bargain.
£400–460
€560–660
$710–840 DMC ✗

Late Victorian chair, with later upholstery.
£420–470 / €610–680
$760–860 WiB ⊞

► Yew-wood and elm Windsor armchair, with a lyre back and crinoline stretcher, late 18thC. Yew is a popular wood and usually commands high prices. This chair is a very reasonable price and could have been expected to achieve nearer £1,000 / €1,450 / $1,800. Crinoline stretchers and makers' names add value to such pieces.
£420–500
€610–720
$760–910 GIL ✗

Mahogany elbow chair, c1815.
£430–480 / €620–690
$780–870 Lfo ⊞

◄ Painted and parcel-gilt elbow chair, with a cane seat, early 19thC. It is hard to find quality painted furniture such as this. This example is a good price.
£450–540
€650–780
$820–980 DN ✗

Upholstery

Reupholstery is common and does not reduce the value, as original fabric rarely survives in good condition. However, old upholstery such as needlework is desirable.

Miller's compares...

A. Inlaid mahogany armchair, c1900.
£450–500 / €650–720
$820–910 QA ⊞

B. Inlaid mahogany armchair, c1900.
£540–600 / €780–870
$980–1,100 QA ⊞

Both Item A and Item B are attractive chairs. Item B, however, has a more delicate back and an embroidered seat, making it a more desirable purchase, which is why it sold for more than Item A.

Near pair of William IV walnut open carvers/armchairs, repaired and reupholstered, c1835. Although these chairs have been repaired and reupholstered, they are made of walnut, and this desirable wood has added to their value.
£450–540 / €650–780
$820–980 Hal ⚚

Oak armchair, with leather upholstery and brass studs, early 20thC. Worn leather is currently fashionable and has added to the appeal and value of this gentleman's chair.
£480–570 / €690–820
$870–1,050 DN ⚚

Mahogany reclining library chair, with adjustable back and pull-out foot rest, mid-19thC. Chairs of this type were patented by George Minter, of Soho, London.
£480–570 / €690–820
$870–1,050 HOK ⚚

Victorian mahogany armchair, with leather upholstery and brass studs, on turned legs.
£500–600 / €720–870
$910–1,100 DN ⚚

Set of six mahogany dining chairs, with leather seats, 19thC. These simple chairs were sold in Ireland. If sold in the UK, where they would find a ready market, they could have achieved over twice this price.
£520–620 / €750–900
$950–1,100 JAd ⚒

◄ **Set of nine ebonized and gilt-painted chairs,** with turned supports and cane seats, 19thC.
£500–600 / €720–870
$910–1,100 BWL ⚒

Mahogany library chair, stamped 'Straham & Co', c1835. This attractive chair is in good condition, hence the high price.
£520–580 / €750–840
$950–1,050 DEB ⊞

Carved mahogany armchair, c1870.
£580–650 / €840–940
$1,050–1,200 CRU ⊞

Mahogany elbow chair, reupholstered, c1835.
£590–650 / €860–950
$1,050–1,200 LGr ⊞

Rosewood nursing chair, c1850. This is an attractive chair with an unusual shape and back.
£610–680 / €880–980
$1,100–1,250 MTay ⊞

Walnut armchair, c1775.
£620–690 / €900–1,000
$1,100–1,250 GGD ⊞

Sets/pairs

Unless otherwise stated, any description which refers to 'a set' or 'a pair' includes a guide price for the entire set or the pair, even though the illustration may show only a single item.

Pair of low chairs, with upholstered seats and backs, on painted turned legs, French, late 19thC.
£620–740 / €900–1,050
$1,150–1,350 DN ⚹

◄ **Set of six mahogany dining chairs,** comprising four side chairs and two carvers, 19thC.
£620–740 / €900–1,050
$1,150–1,350 BWL ⚹

Child's mahogany highchair, comprising a bergère and a table, c1775. This is a good example of its type – these highchairs are sought after.
£670–750 / €970–1,100
$1,100–1,300 WAA ⊞

Regency mahogany rocking chair, with leather upholstery.
£630–700 / €900–1,000
$1,150–1,300 MLL ⊞

Children's chairs

An enormous variety of special chairs for children were made from the beginning of the 19th century. Examples include high chairs that could be separated to form a chair and a play table, or fold into a walker. Many surviving pieces were made in the late 19th and early 20th centuries for less affluent homes. These later children's chairs are often attractive and can be obtained for very modest sums, although it should be noted that they no longer comply with EC safety regulations.

Carved wood tub chair, with a hinged compartment below a drop-in seat, Continental, 19thC. Although this chair achieved a fair price, commodes in general have currently lost their appeal.
£700–780 / €1,000–1,150
$1,250–1,400 SWO ⚲

Victorian gentleman's rosewood armchair, with foliate-carved decoration, on cabriole legs, together with a lady's chair.
£760–900
€1,100–1,300
$1,400–1,650 DMC ⚲

◀ **Set of six Victorian Gothic-style oak dining chairs,** the arched backs with pointed crests, with solid seats and straight moulded legs.
£780–930
€1,150–1,350
$1,400–1,650
DN ⚲

Pair of George IV mahogany hall chairs, on turned supports.
£800–960 / €1,200–1,400
$1,450–1,750 L ⚲

Late Victorian Hepplewhite-style mahogany elbow chair, with inlaid decoration and later upholstery.
£810–900 / €1,150–1,300
$1,450–1,650 LGr ⊞

◀ **Mahogany armchair,** c1800.
£810–900
€1,150–1,300
$1,450–1,650
GGD ⊞

Walnut armchair, with pictorial leather upholstery, the arm terminals carved in the form of putti, finials replaced, Italian, 19thC. This is an ornate, good-quality piece at a very reasonable price.
£810–900 / €1,150–1,300
$1,450–1,650 LGr ⊞

Chests & Coffers

Oak coffer, the hinged cover above a carved frieze, early 18thC, 44in (112cm) wide. The simple decoration and small size of this coffer make it a desirable piece of furniture for today's smaller homes. It was a good buy as it could possibly have sold for £600 / €870 / $1,100.
£240–280 / €350–400
$440–510 HYD ⚒

The look without the price

Oak boarded chest, with carved and moulded decoration, on later supports, 17thC, 44in (112cm) wide.
£260–310 / €380–450
$470–560 WW ⚒

This 17th-century chest is very attractive but the later additions have adversely affected the price. Had it been completely original, this chest could have sold for £1,500 / €2,200 / $2,750.

◄ **Wooden chest,** with painted decoration, Swiss, 18thC, 51in (129.5cm) wide. This marriage chest might have been more popular with UK or Continental bidders than with those in the US, where it was sold.
£320–380 / €460–550
$580–690 SK ⚒

Miller's compares...

A. Coffer, the front with three panels, 18thC, 46¾in (119cm) wide.
£320–380 / €460–550
$580–690 L&E ⚒

B. Oak chest, moulded with geometric panels, late 17thC, 49¼in (125cm) wide.
£620–740 / €890–1,050
$1,150–1,350 WW ⚒

Item A is a plain chest whereas item B is older, has geometric mouldings and scrolled brackets, all of which appeal to collectors and account for it being a higher price than Item A.

Panelled oak coffer, the plank top above carved panels, 18thC, 38¼in (97cm) wide.
£350–420 / €510–610
$640–760 CHTR 🔨

Pine chest, Continental, c1890, 44in (112cm) wide.
£450–500 / €650–730
$820–910 COF ⊞

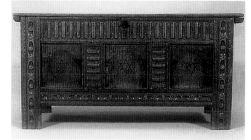

Oak chest, the plank top enclosing a lidded candlebox, the moulded frieze above three panels inlaid with stars, late 17thC, 49½in (125.5cm) wide. *This is a very reasonable price for a chest with such attractive decoration.*
£480–570 / €700–830
$870–1,050 WW 🔨

Locate the source

The source of each illustration in Miller's can be found by checking the code letters below each caption with the Key to Illustrations, pages 286–290.

Panelled oak coffer, with a carved frieze, 17thC, 56¾in (144cm) wide.
£350–420 / €510–610
$640–760 GTH 🔨

Painted wood blanket chest, the interior fitted with a till and a secret compartment, now missing, American, Pennsylvania or New York, late 18thC, 42in (106.5cm) long. *Painted furniture such as this, especially when it is of American origin, is currently finding a very ready market in the US, hence the high price of this blanket chest.*
£460–550 / €670–790
$840–1,000 S(NY) 🔨

Boarded oak chest, with iron hinges, early 17thC, 44in (112cm) wide. *This chest was a good buy at auction. It could have achieved £600–720 / €870–1,000 / $1,100–1,300.*
£480–570 / €700–830
$870–1,050 Hal 🔨

◄ **Oak coffer,** the panelled top above a carved frieze, 18thC, 36½in (92.5cm) wide. This coffer has a good patina, a feature which always appeals to collectors.
£480–570
€700–830
$870–1,050 DMC ⚒

Louis 16th-style chest, inscribed 'Anna Maria Margreita Schulte', dated 1802, 49¼in (125cm) wide. Domed chests are more popular with European collectors.
£550–660 / €800–940
$1,000–1,200 DORO ⚒

Boarded oak chest, the panelled sides with incised decoration, on a later stand, 17thC, 30in (76cm) wide. With its unusual carving this chest could have made more, but the later stand has held the price down.
£550–660 / €800–940
$1,000–1,200 Hal ⚒

► **Oak coffer,** with a carved frieze, dated 1690, 38¼in (97cm) wide.
£580–690
€840–1,000
$1,050–1,250
CHTR ⚒

Oak mule chest, the three geometric moulded panels above two short drawers, carved with foliate decoration, 56in (142cm) wide. The problem of retrieving items from the bottom of large coffers was solved by the addition of drawers at the base. This type of coffer is often known as a mule chest.
£550–660 / €800–940
$1,000–1,200 HYD ⚒

Oak chest, the three panels flanked by carved flower garlands, German, 18thC, 55¼in (140.5cm) wide.
£720–860 / €1,050–1,250
$1,300–1,550 S(Am) ⚒

Padouk-wood chest, inlaid with brass, the hinged cover enclosing a pierced sliding panel concealing three small drawers, Anglo-Indian, early 19thC, 29in (73.5cm) wide. This chest has very attractive brass-inlaid decoration and this accounts for the higher price.
£850–1,000 / €1,200–1,450
$1,500–1,800 DMC ⚒

Chests of Drawers

Cherrywood chest of drawers, American, c1840, 46in (117cm) wide. This chest of drawers was sold in the US but would have been more sought after in the UK where it could have achieved three times this amount.
£85–100 / €125–145
$150–180 DuM 🖾

Victorian pitch pine chest of drawers, with two short over three long drawers, 43in (109cm) wide.
£110–130 / €160–190
$200–240 CHTR 🖾

George III oak chest of drawers, with graduated long drawers flanked by reeded pilasters, 38½in (98cm) wide. Although this chest has damaged brasswork it is possible to restore it by having new handles and escutcheons cast.
£160–190 / €240–280
$290–350 CHTR 🖾

The look without the price

Georgian oak chest of drawers, with two short over three long drawers, 37in (94cm) wide.
£170–200 / €250–300
$300–360 WilP 🖾

This pale oak chest is a practical and attractive piece of furniture at an affordable price. However, had it been made of mahogany, rather than oak, its value would be doubled.

Late Regency figured mahogany chest of drawers, the quartered reeded pilasters with tulip-carved capitals, 42½in (108cm) wide. This is an attractive chest and proves there are still bargains to be had at auction.
£190–220 / €280–330
$350–410 DD 🖾

▶ **Mahogany chest of drawers,** with two short drawers above three long drawers, 19thC, 42in (106.5cm) wide.
£200–240
€290–350
$360–430 PF 🖾

◄ **Victorian mahogany chest of drawers,** with five small and three long graduated drawers, 40½in (103cm) wide.
£220–260 / €320–380
$400–470 WilP ⚒

► **Victorian mahogany chest of drawers,** with two short and three long drawers, 38½in (98cm) wide. This chest of drawers is very good value.
£230–270 / €340–400
$420–500 JAd ⚒

Mahogany bowfronted chest of drawers, with two short over three long drawers, early 19thC, 43¼in (110cm) wide.
£240–280 / €350–410
$440–520 AMB ⚒

Painted pine chest of drawers, with four drawers, Eastern European, c1890, 39in (99cm) wide.
£270–300 / €390–440
$490–540 NWE ⊞

The look without the price

Feather-banded walnut chest of drawers, the crossbanded top above three drawers, with later brass handles and escutcheons, reconstructed, damaged, early 18thC, 43½in (110.5cm) wide.
£300–360 / €440–520
$540–650 Hal ⚒

This is probably the base of a linen press or a chest-on-chest. Had it been an original chest of drawers and in good condition it could have achieved nearer

£1,000 / €1,450 / $1,800 at auction. However it serves as an attractive functional piece of furniture more suited to the modern home.

Miller's compares...

A. George III mahogany chest of drawers, with two short over three long graduated drawers, 42½in (108cm) wide.
£300–360 / €440–520 $540–650 CHTR ➶

B. George III mahogany chest of drawers, with two short over three long drawers flanked by fluted and quartered columns, raised on shaped bracket feet, 41in (104cm) wide.
£750–900 / €1,100–1,300 $1,400–1,650 Hal ➶

The shaped feet, canted edges, fluted pilasters and the overall quality of Item B are preferable to the more basic design of Item A. These factors account for the higher price of Item B.

Mahogany and boxwood-strung chest of drawers, the two frieze drawers inlaid with conch shells, above two short and three long drawers with ivory escutcheons and brass handles, c1820, 45¼in (115cm) wide.
£340–400 / €490–580 $620–730 WL ➶

Kingwood commode, with gilt-metal mounts and line-inlaid decoration, the marble top above four long drawers, French, late 19thC, 39½in (100.5cm) wide.
£400–480 / €580–700 $730–870 RTo ➶

◀ **Mahogany bowfronted chest of drawers,** crossbanded in satinwood and kingwood, with boxwood and ebony stringing, early 19thC, 45in (114.5cm) wide. This is a fair price for a chest of drawers that is showing signs of wear and tear and is in need of restoration, the cost of which must be taken into account when buying such items.
£350–420 / €510–610 $640–760 CHTR ➶

Chests of drawers

The majority of chests of drawers produced from the late 18th century onwards were practical pieces of furniture. Although some were made of solid mahogany, most were veneered on oak or pine, and their quality can vary widely.

The standard arrangement was either four long drawers of graduated depth or two short drawers over three graduated long drawers. Some pieces were also fitted with a brushing slide.

Bowfronted chests, which were introduced around 1800, remained in production throughout the 19th century. They were a popular alternative to straight-fronted examples.

Mahogany campaign chest of drawers, with two short over three long drawers, 19thC, 39in (99cm) wide.
£450–540 / €650–780 $820–980 HYD ➶

Victorian walnut Wellington chest, with a locking bar and six drawers, 20in (51cm) wide. Wellington chests are very sought after and this example sold for a very reasonable price.
£500–600 / €730–870
$910–1,100 G(L) 🔨

William IV mahogany bowfronted chest, with two short and three long drawers, flanked by turned pilasters, on turned feet, 45in (114.5cm) wide.
£550–660 / €800–960
$1,000–1,200 JAd 🔨

Find out more in

Miller's Late Georgian to Edwardian Furniture Buyer's Guide, Miller's Publications, 2003

George III mahogany chest of drawers, with two short over three long drawers, 39in (99cm) wide. This chest of drawers has a good colour and was a reasonable buy at auction.
£520–620 / €750–900
$950–1,100 HYD 🔨

George III mahogany serpentine chest of drawers, with later handles, feet missing, 41½in (105.5cm) wide. The cost of repairs and replacing the feet and the handles on this chest would be substantial, but once restored it could command nearly four times as much.
£530–630 / €770–910
$960–1,150 E 🔨

Victorian mahogany secretaire chest, the gadrooned frieze above a crossbanded fall-front opening to reveal a sycamore-veneered interior, interior veneer possibly later, possibly Scottish, 50¾in (129cm) wide.
£600–720 / €870–1,050
$1,100–1,300 DN 🔨

George III mahogany chest of drawers, with four long graduated drawers, 34in (86.5cm) wide.
£530–630 / €770–910
$960–1,150 MAL 🔨

Mahogany chest of drawers, the crossbanded top above two short and four long drawers, early 19thC, 41in (104cm) wide. This chest has an unusual arrangement of drawers.
£550–660 / €800–960
$1,000–1,200 DN 🔨

Mahogany chest of drawers, the four long graduated drawers with bone escutcheons, early 19thC, 37½in (95.5cm) wide.
£620–740 / €900–1,050
$1,150–1,350 WW 🔨

Brass-mounted Consular-style miniature fruitwood commode, with three long drawers, French, 1850–75, 18½in (47cm) wide.
£630–740 / €910–1,100
$1,150–1,350 NOA 🪓

Marquetry chest of drawers, Continental, 19thC, 26in (66cm) high. Marquetry is not currently in fashion. If you like this style of decoration, now would be a good time to buy as prices are low.
£680–820 / €1,000–1,200
$1,250–1,500 BWL 🪓

◄ George III mahogany chest of drawers, with chequered stringing, c1800, 34in (86.5cm) wide.
£720–860 / €1,050–1,250
$1,300–1,550 S(O) 🪓

► Regency mahogany bowfronted chest of drawers, with two short over three long drawers, 1800–25, 42in (106.5cm) wide.
£740–880 / €1,050–1,250
$1,350–1,600 NOA 🪓

George III mahogany chest of drawers, with three long drawers, with later additions, 43½in (110.5cm) wide.
£740–880 / €1,050–1,250
$1,350–1,600 NOA 🪓

Walnut chest of drawers, with three crossbanded short drawers over three long graduated drawers, with brass handles and engraved brass escutcheons, c1700, 38½in (98cm) wide.
£750–900 / €1,100–1,300
$1,350–1,600 GTH 🪓

Oak chest of drawers, the four long drawers with moulded panels and bobbin-turned applied mouldings, damaged, late 17thC, 38in (96.5cm) wide. Sympathetic restoration could more than double the value of this chest of drawers.
**£780–930 / €1,150–1,350
$1,400–1,650** E 🔨

Mahogany chest of drawers, with two short over three long drawers, 1860, 48in (122cm) wide.
**£790–880 / €1,150–1,300
$1,450–1,600** MTay ⊞

▶ **George I oak and walnut crossbanded chest of drawers,** with two short and three long drawers, 36½in (92.5cm) wide. It is possible that this chest of drawers was fought over by two bidders, which would account for its high price.
**£850–1,000
€1,250–1,450
$1,550–1,800**
HYD 🔨

George III mahogany chest of drawers, with two short over three long drawers, 38in (96.5cm) wide.
**£900–1,050 / €1,300–1,550
$1,600–1,900** HYD 🔨

◀ **George III mahogany chest-on-chest,** with satinwood crossbanding and boxwood and ebony stringing, the upper section with three short and three long drawers flanked by canted corners with satinwood veneer, above a base with a slide and three long drawers, some later stringing and inlay, 40½in (103cm) wide.
**£900–1,050 / €1,300–1,550
$1,600–1,900** DN 🔨

George III mahogany chest of drawers, with two short and three long oak-lined drawers and with brass handles, flanked by fluted quarter pilasters, 39½in (100.5cm) wide.
**£920–1,100 / €1,350–1,600
$1,700–2,000** DMC 🔨

Cupboards & Cabinets

Mahogany wall cabinet, with two panelled doors, 19thC, 16in (40.5cm) high.
£40–45 / €60–70
$75–85 BeFA ⚲

▶ **Late Victorian mahogany inlaid bedside cabinet,** the cupboard door with boxwood inlay, on applewood legs, 30½in (77.5cm) high.
£110–130 / €160–190
$200–240 BeFA ⚲

Victorian cedarwood wall cabinet, with two panelled doors enclosing shelves, 29½in (75cm) high.
£135–160 / €195–230
$250–300 BeFA ⚲

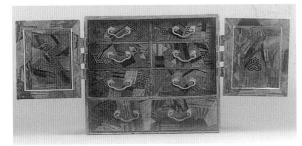

Inlaid wood table cabinet, the two doors opening to reveal six short drawers, above a long drawer, Japanese, early 20thC, 17½in (44.5cm) wide.
£150–180 / €220–260
$280–330 PFK ⚲

▶ **Victorian coromandel stationery cabinet,** with a fitted interior and brass mounts, 13in (33cm) wide.
£250–300
€370–440
$460–550 AMB ⚲

Mahogany cigar cabinet, c1910, 18in (45.5cm) high. Cigar cabinets are desirable to collectors and carry a premium.
£220–250 / €320–360
$400–450 WiB ▦

For more examples of Cigar boxes see Boxes (pages 238–243)

Walnut side cabinet, the glazed door enclosing three shelves, with gilt-metal mounts, 29½in (75cm) wide.
£260–310 / €380–450
$470–560 CHTR ✗

Victorian inlaid walnut side cabinet, with a glazed door and ormolu mounts, 30¼in (77cm) wide.
£300–360 / €440–520
$550–660 WilP ✗

Mahogany bedside cabinet, c1890, 32in (81.5cm) high.
£300–340 / €440–490
$550–620 QA ⊞

▶ **Inlaid mahogany bedside cabinet,** c1900, 29in (73.5cm) high.
£310–350 / €450–510
$560–630 QA ⊞

Victorian walnut cabinet, the front inlaid with panels of floral marquetry, the glazed door enclosing a plush-lined interior, with gilt-metal mounts, 31in (78.5cm) wide.
£360–430 / €520–620
$660–780 GAK ✗

Louis XV-style walnut bedside cabinet, with a marble top, c1900, 35in (89cm) high.
£360–400 / €520–580
$660–730 SWA ⊞

◀ **Chinese export lacquered table cabinet,** the two panelled doors enclosing six drawers, with gilt decoration of flowers, figures and buildings, c1900, 26½in (67.5cm) wide. This distinctive piece would appeal to collectors. It has intricate decoration and good-quality workmanship and could have sold for twice this price.
£440–520 / €640–750
$800–950 SWO ✗

George III corner cupboard, the two panelled doors enclosing a hanging space and later pegs, above a crossbanded frieze drawer between canted corners, damaged, c1800, 41in (104cm) wide.
£480–570 / €700–830
$870–1,050 Hal 🔨

To find out more about antique furniture see the full range of Miller's books at
www.millers.uk.com

The look without the price

Seventeenth century-Flemish-style oak cupboard-on-stand, the upper section with two panelled doors flanked by fluted columns, the base with two short drawers, on turned legs, 41in (104cm) wide.
£500–600
€730–870
$910–1,100
HYD 🔨

If this were an original 17th-century Flemish piece, it could be worth as much as £2,000–4,000 / €2,900–5,800 / $3,600–7,300. However, it still serves as an eye-catching piece of furniture at a more affordable price.

Chestnut armoire, French, 18thC, 53½in (136cm) wide.
£520–620 / €750–900
$950–1,100 DN 🔨

Mahogany clothes press, the two panelled doors above two short and two long drawers, with later brass handles, early 19thC, 51½in (131cm) wide.
£520–620 / €750–900
$950–1,100 DN 🔨

George III mahogany night cupboard, the hinged top with later fitted cutlery trays above a dummy drawer with a tambour-fronted cupboard and a drawer, 26in (66cm) wide.
£550–660 / €800–960
$1,000–1,200 HYD 🔨

Victorian figured walnut and kingwood-banded pier cabinet, with gilt-metal mounts, the glazed door enclosing a velvet-lined shelf, losses to veneer, 31½in (80cm) wide.
£550–660 / €800–960
$1,000–1,200 DN(BR) 🔨

Victorian burr-walnut writing desk/music cabinet, the two marquetry-inlaid cupboard doors enclosing pigeonholes and a drawer above a sliding writing surface, over a glazed door enclosing three shelves, 24in (61cm) wide.
£550–660 / €800–960
$1,000–1,200 DN(BR) 🔨

Cedarwood cabinet, with a moulded top above panelled doors with iron escutcheons, Italian, 17thC, 36in (91.5cm) wide. This style of cabinet has a limited appeal and demand is therefore low, hence the price.
£600–720 / €870–1,050
$1,100–1,250 Mal(O) 🔨

◀ **Satinwood cabinet,** with two glazed doors below a shelf, c1900, 39in (99cm) high.
£630–700 / €900–1,000
$1,100–1,250 QA ⊞

Mahogany breakfront serpentine display cabinet, the cupboard inlaid with harewood and boxwood floral decoration and enclosing a shelf above a dummy drawer and a recess, flanked by two glazed doors enclosing glass shelves, on six cabriole legs, c1910, 52in (132cm) wide. The large size of this display cabinet would limit the potential number of buyers – it would be difficult to accommodate in a flat or small house.
£600–720 / €870–1,050
$1,100–1,300 Hal 🔨

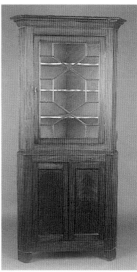

George III mahogany corner cupboard, with a glazed door enclosing shelves, above two panelled doors, 41in (104cm) wide.
£700–840 / €1,000–1,200
$1,250–1,500 L 🔨

Regency mahogany stationery cabinet, the two panelled doors opening to reveal a fitted interior, 30in (76cm) wide. This is an unusual piece of furniture with many uses which could account for its high price.
£710–790 / €1,050–1,200 $1,300–1,450 DOA ⊞

George III oak and elm cupboard-on-stand, the upper section with two panelled doors over three dummy drawers, the base with three short drawers, 50in (127cm) wide. This cupboard sold for well below its estimate – probably because of its large size and chunky style.
£700–840 / €1,000–1,200 $1,250–1,500 LAY ⚒

▶ **George III Hepplewhite-style gentleman's mahogany wardrobe,** the panelled boxwood- and ebony-strung doors with dummy drawers, above a long drawer, 51in (129.5cm) wide.
£800–960 / €1,200–1,400 $1,450–1,750 DMC ⚒

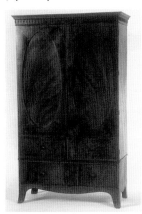

Mahogany tambour-fronted bedside cabinet, Dutch, c1820, 18in (45.5cm) wide. This style of bedside cabinet always appeals and therefore demand, and prices, are high.
£810–900 / €1,150–1,300 $1,450–1,650 GGD ⊞

Oak smoker's cupboard, dated 1894, 13in (33cm) high.
£810–900 / €1,150–1,300 $1,450–1,650 SAT ⊞

Art Nouveau inlaid mahogany display cabinet, the mirror-inset back with inlaid decoration, above three glazed doors and two further inlaid doors, 54in (137cm) wide.
£900–1,050 / €1,300–1,550 $1,600–1,900 DMC ⚒

Oak cabinet, the two panelled doors with moulded and carved decoration, c1800, 64¼in (163cm) wide.
£960–1,150 / €1,400–1,650 $1,750–2,100 DORO ⚒

Find out more in

Miller's Art Nouveau & Art Deco Buyer's Guide, Miller's Publications, 2001

Desks & Writing Tables

◀ **Edwardian mahogany bureau,** with blind-fret decoration, the fall-front with a pierced gallery and shelves above and a drawer and bookshelves below, 29in (73.5cm) wide. It is unusual to find a bureau with a gallery. This is an unusual and interesting piece.
£85–100
€125–145
$155–180 AMB ⚒

Rosewood bonheur du jour, with two drawers above a fall-front enclosing a fitted interior, over a frieze drawer, on cabriole legs, 19thC, 39¾in (101cm) wide.
£200–240 / €290–350
$360–430 CHTR ⚒

Brass-bound walnut writing slope, c1870, 17in (43cm) wide. This slope has the original key which adds to the value.
£210–240 / €300–350
$380–440 MB ⊞

Teak writing slope, inlaid with bone, overlaid with white metal embossed with foliate and animal decoration, inscribed 'Presented to the Hon'ble Sir Lancelot Hare K.C.S. Lieutenant Governor of Eastern Bengal and Assam', dated 1908, 15in (38cm) wide. This slope would be of interest to collectors of military or Indian antiques. Now is a good time to buy Indian items as they are currently in vogue and prices could rise.
£260–310 / €380–450
$470–560 DMC ⚒

Mahogany and ebony-strung bureau, the fall-front enclosing pigeonholes and short drawers, above two short and two long graduated drawers, side cracked, altered, 19thC, 29in (73.5cm) wide. This bureau has good proportions, a feature which enabled it to hold its price, despite being cracked. Cracks are caused by the dry air created by central heating.
£350–420 / €510–610
$640–760 Hal ⚲

▶ **George II mahogany bureau bookcase,** the upper section with a moulded cornice above two glazed doors, the bureau with a fall-front enclosing a fitted interior with a baize-lined writing surface, over four long graduated drawers, on bracket feet, 36in (91.5cm) wide. Bureau bookcases are always popular, and this piece has good proportions.
£520–620 / €750–900
$950–1,150 HYD ⚲

Mahogany bureau, the crossbanded top above a fall-front with a fitted interior, above four long graduated drawers, early 19thC, 36in (91.5cm) wide. This bureau has a good patina and the unusual frieze and splayed legs are attractive features.
£400–480 / €580–700
$730–870 DMC ⚲

George III mahogany bureau, the fall-front enclosing a fitted interior with a satinwood-veneered front and rosewood banding, over four long graduated drawers, 42in (106.5cm) wide. Bureaux are currently unpopular with contemporary home-owners who may require a piece of furniture that can accommodate a computer. This example has particularly well figured wood and it has sold for a very reasonable price.
£400–480 / €580–700
$730–870 WW ⚲

Desks and bureaux

The bureau is probably the most practical type of desk for the modern home. Designed to stand against a wall, it occupies less floor space than a freestanding desk and has the storage capacity of a medium-sized chest of drawers. There are various designs to choose from, such as fall-front bureaux, davenports and bonheurs de jour, all of which offer different combinations of pigeonholes and drawers together with a writing surface. Writing tables offer much less storage space but, along with kneehole desks, are currently in demand because of their ability to accommodate a home computer.

Writing desk, by James Shoolbred & Co, decorated with blind-fret carving, with a stationery compartment, flanked by two side drawers with gilt-brass galleries, the breakfront top with a tooled leather insert above a central frieze drawer and four short drawers, 19thC, 42in (106.5cm) wide. This ornate desk would be of interest to collectors of Shoolbred furniture. The proportions are good and it has the original handles, which make it more desirable and therefore more valuable.
£600–720 / €870–1,050
$1,100–1,300 WILK ⚲

Plum pudding mahogany bureau, with gilt-metal mounts, the marble top with a pierced gallery above two drawers, the cylinder enclosing a leather writing surface, above two drawers, late 19thC, 31½in (80cm) wide. The plum pudding mahogany is very attractive and adds appeal to this otherwise standard cylinder bureau.
£620–740 / €900–1,050 $1,150–1,350 DN

Mid-Victorian burr-walnut davenport, the stationery compartment enclosed by a hinged lid, above a writing slope with a serpentine front enclosing a well, over four drawers opposing four dummy drawers, on cabriole legs, 37½in (95.5cm) high. Although currently an unpopular form of desk due to its inability to accommodate a computer, this davenport has a good patina and an attractive serpentine front, and would be a good buy.
£720–860 / $1,050–1,250 $1,300–1,550 RTo

Sheraton revival satinwood lady's desk, painted in neo-classical style with ribbon ties and floral swags, the fall enclosing a fitted stationery recess, flanked by two hinged part-glazed doors centred with portraits, with later metal feet, 24¾in (63cm) wide. This is an attractive and unusual item of furniture as it is a desk and a screen. It represents a very reasonable buy at auction. The unusual design would make it appealing to interior designers and the small proportions would make it suitable for contemporary homes with restricted space.
£650–780 / €940–1,100 $1,200–1,400 DN

A japanned writing table, decorated in gilt with figures and landscapes, the leather-inset top above a frieze drawer, on cabriole legs with gilt-metal sabots, late 19thC, 29¼in (74.5cm) high. Japanned furniture is always popular with American collectors.
£700–840 / €1,000–1,200 $1,250– 1,550 DN

Mahogany kneehole desk, the crossbanded top above a long drawer over a kneehole cupboard and six short drawers, 18thC, 32in (81.5cm) wide. Small examples of furniture, such as this, are always in demand and as a result tend to fetch higher prices than larger, more unwieldy pieces.
£780–930 / €1,150–1,350 $1,450–1,700 Mal(O)

◄ **Mahogany _secrétaire à abattant_,** with a frieze drawer over a fall-front enclosing a fitted interior with a pull-out galleried writing slide, above three long drawers, Continental, c1825, 44in (112cm) wide. This item is probably German. It has a galleried writing slide which is unusual on such a piece, and this has added to its desirability and value.
£800–960 / €1,200–1,400 $1,450–1,750 G(L)

Mirrors & Frames

Carved and sawn walnut mirror, plate replaced, c1725, 15½in (39.5cm) wide. This is an attractive walnut mirror at an affordable price.
£260–310 / €380–450
$480–570   NOA ⚒

Gilt-metal girandole, the two-branch frame cast with leaves, French, late 19thC, 10¾in (27.5cm) wide. This style is rather ornate for current tastes, but the candle sconces are a desirable feature.
£300–360 / €440–520
$550–660   DN ⚒

▶ **Wooden box mirror,** c1780, 19¾in (50cm) high. This George III mirror has a good patina and its original plate. Old glass can be restored and it is better to do this than replace it with a new piece, as original glass is desirable and adds to the value of the mirror.
£420–470 / €610–680
$760–860   F&F ⊞

Miller's compares...

A. Pier mirror, the inverted breakfront cornice decorated with balls to a diaper frieze, the plate flanked by Egyptian-head pilasters, paint and plate later, 19thC, 32in (81.5cm) high.
£140–165 / €200–240
$250–300   WW ⚒

B. Regency gilt wall mirror, with a *verre églomisé* landscape frieze, the plate flanked by fluted pilasters with Corinthian capitals, 33in (84cm) high.
£370–440 / €540–640
$670–800   BWL ⚒

Both Item A and Item B are currently highly sought-after mirrors and therefore desirable purchases. However, Item A is in need of some repair and this has kept its auction value low. With restoration it could possibly be worth more than twice this price. However, Item B is a desirable gilt mirror that is in good condition, and this accounts for its higher price.

Beech mirror, with a bevelled plate, c1900, 41in (104cm) wide. This mirror was possibly originally part of a dressing table. The bevelled glass is an attractive feature.
£450–500 / €650–730
$820–910   COF ⊞

Giltwood convex mirror, surmounted by an eagle flanked by acanthus scrolls, the frame set with spheres, with an ebonized reeded inner frame and a foliate base, 19thC, 25½in (65cm) wide. Convex mirrors are currently out of fashion and this is reflected in the price. They were making twice this price a few years ago, so now would be a good time to buy.
£550–660 / €800–960
$1,000–1,200 DN 🔨

Renaissance-style painted and gilt carved mirror, with original plate, Italian, c1900, 26½in (67.5cm) wide. This attractive mirror was sold in America, where it probably has more appeal, as it achieved a fairly high price.
£560–670 / €810–970
$1,000–1,200 NOA 🔨

To find out more about antique furniture see the full range of Miller's books at
www.millers.uk.com

Victorian mahogany cheval mirror, the frame on pierced and scroll-mounted end supports, 35½in (90cm) wide. Cheval mirrors are highly sought after. This one sold for a very reasonable price – it could have achieved £800–1,200 / €1,150–1,450 / $1,450–2,150.
£600–720 / €870–1,050
$1,100–1,300 CHTR 🔨

Mahogany cheval mirror, the plate within a reeded frame, with baluster and bamboo-turned supports, 19thC, 30in (76cm) wide. Although this item is in need of some restoration, the demand for this style of mirror is reflected in the high price it achieved at auction.
£700–840 / €1,000–1,200
$1,250–1,500 PF 🔨

Regency mahogany cheval mirror, with ebonized line inlay, the plate with a brass handle rising on sashes, 65½in (166.5cm) high.
£720–860 / €1,050–1,250
$1,300–1,550 WW 🔨

Regency-style giltwood and gesso convex mirror, 19thC, 22½in (57cm) wide. This is a well-carved piece. This mirror has very fine carving, a feature which enabled it to command such a price.
£780–930 / €1,150–1,350
$1,400–1,700 S(O) 🔨

Sofas & Settees

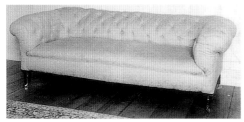

Late Victorian chesterfield sofa, with button-back upholstery, on turned legs, 80in (203cm) wide. When buying upholstered furniture the price of reupholstery should be taken into consideration. This sofa represents good value at this price.
£150–180 / €220–260
$270–320 GTH ⚷

Mahogany and bird's-eye maple Empire-style sofa, attributed to Thomas Day, the rolled arms veneered with a stylized dolphin/snake, on scroll feet, slight damage, some veneer missing, American, 1801–61, 93in (236cm) wide. This unusual sofa would probably be quite uncomfortable to sit on – which is probably why it sold for a reasonable price.
£380–450 / €550–650
$690–820 JDJ ⚷

▶ **Biedermeier wooden sofa,** c1830, 78¾in (200cm) wide. The demand for Biedermeier furniture has slowed down recently, particularly in Germany where this piece was sold. In a buoyant market this sofa could have made three to four times this price.
£380–450 / €550–650
$690–720 DORO ⚷

The Chesterfield

In 1773, the fourth Earl of Chesterfield commissioned the cabinet-maker Robert Adam to design a piece of furniture that would permit a gentleman to sit with his back straight to avoid what he referred to as 'odd motions, strange postures and ungenteel carriage'.

Louis XV-style giltwood day bed, the rail and apron carved with rosettes, foliage and ribbons, on ring-turned fluted supports, 19thC, 54in (137cm) long.
£350–420 / €510–610
$640–760 GAK ⚷

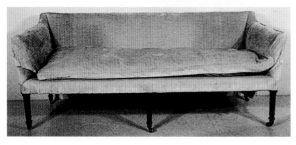

◀ **Sofa,** on six ring-turned tapering legs with brass cups and casters, with later upholstery, c1830, 76in (193cm) wide.
£550–660 / €800–960
$1,000–1,200 Hal ⚷

Victorian carved and pierced walnut-framed cameo-back settee, with buttoned upholstery. This is a very decorative piece of furniture, and this is reflected in its value.
£670–800 / €970–1,150
$1,200–1,450 DMC 🔨

Edwardian mahogany-framed bergère lounge suite, with double cane sides, the supports carved with stiff acanthus on claw feet, unholstery worn, 55¼in (140.5cm) wide. Bergère furniture with double caning is of better quality, more desirable and therefore more valuable than single-caned examples.
£750–900 / €1,100–1,300
$1,400–1,650 DD 🔨

Louis XVI-style carved and stained beechwood sofa, French, c1875, 56in (142cm) wide.
£820–980 / €1,200–1,400
$1,500–1,800 NOA 🔨

The look without the price

George I-style giltwood settee, with carved scrolled arms, on cabriole legs, 66in (167.5cm) wide.
£800–960 / €1,150–1,400
$1,450–1,750 Mal(O) 🔨

This is an attractive piece of furniture at a reasonable price. A genuine George I giltwood settee could command a four- or five-figure sum.

Stands

Edwardian mahogany folding cake stand, with bobbin-turned supports, 36in (91.5cm) high.
£35–40 / €50–60
$65–75 BeFA

Oak stick stand, c1875, 27in (68.5cm) wide. Arts and Crafts is a very collectable area at the moment and items can command a heavy premium. This stick stand would be a good investment piece.
£85–95 / €125–140
$155–175 SAT ⊞

Mahogany boot stand, 19thC, 26in (66cm) wide. This is quite an unusual boot stand and it also has its original tray, a feature which will have added to its value.
£280–330 / €410–480
$510–600 SWO

Victorian walnut and brass reading stand, the cast-iron base with cabriole legs and paw feet, enamelled label 'John Carter maker 6A New Cavendish St, London', 14½in (37cm) wide. Reading stands are still used today, and this example still retains the maker's label, which adds to its desirability.
£300–360 / €440–520
$550–660 DN

Mahogany and parquetry-inlaid watch stand, the raised back with painted glass windows, each flanking an aperture and a painted door, above a bowfronted base with four drawers, 19thC, 16in (40.5cm) wide. These stands are very collectable by collectors of both pocket watches and watch stands. This example is an unusual style, which has contributed to its desirability and value.
£500–600 / €730–870
$910–1,100 WW

Federal figured maple, cherrywood and birchwood candlestand, American, possibly New Hampshire, 14½in (37cm) wide. Cherrywood is very desirable as it is an unusual wood that is not often found in the UK. The good colour of this piece has contributed to its high price.
£790–940 / €1,150–1,350
$1,450–1,700 S(NY)

Stools

Painted wood footstool, with a rush seat, on turned stretcher supports, c1875, 15in (38cm) wide. This Arts and Crafts footstool is unusual in that it has been painted. It would make a good investment piece.
£120–140 / €170–200
$220–260 Mal(O) ➢

▶ **Victorian rosewood piano stool,** by Brooke Ltd, the upholstered seat with rise and fall action, on turned supports and stretchers. Although the antique furniture market is currently in the doldrums, piano stools are still sought after. The fact that this piece is made of rosewood and has a maker's name has contributed to the price.
£210–250 / €300–360
$380–460 BWL ➢

▶ **Louis XV-style carved beechwood footstool,** upholstered in damask, French, c1875, 16in (40.5cm) wide.
£170–200
€250–290
$310–360 NOA ➢

Adjustable beech piano stool, by J. & J. Kohn, with a cane seat, c1880, 16in (40.5cm) diam. Bentwood furniture is collectable and sought-after.
£300–330 / €430–480
$540–600 TDG ⊞

Late Victorian inlaid mahogany stool, 22in (56cm) wide.
£300–360 / €440–520
$550–660 WilP ➢

Mahogany revolving music stool, c1800, 21in (53.5cm) high.
£700–780 / €1,000–1,150
$1,250–1,400 GEO ⊞

Tables & Side Furniture

Edwardian mahogany occasional table, with a shaped top, pierced side supports and a shaped undertier with bobbin rails to front and back, 27in (68.5cm) wide. This is an unusual and attractive table.
£70–80 / €100–115
$125–145 DA 🔨

Mahogany Sutherland table, with ring-turned pilaster double end standards united by a baluster stretcher, some restoration near wings, 35½in (90cm) wide. The restoration on this table should not be detrimental to its value as wear near hinges is common. Sutherland tables are becoming increasingly popular because they can be folded against a wall and will fit easily into a small house or flat. This table sold for a very reasonable price; it could have achieved twice this value if there had been two competitive bidders at auction.
£85–95 / €125–140
$155–175 Hal 🔨

Victorian mahogany library table, the moulded top above two end frieze drawers, 54in (137cm) wide. The top of this table has faded and this, together with its large size, accounts for the low price it achieved at auction.
£140–165 / €200–240
$250–300 PF 🔨

Oak side table, with a frieze drawer, 30in (76cm) wide. This table sold for a very reasonable price which may be due to its condition. However, once restored, it could be worth considerably more.
£170–200 / €250–290
$310–360 PF 🔨

Oak side table, the plank top above a long drawer with a shaped apron, late 17thC, 26½in (67.5cm) wide. This early side table appears to have been stripped and this accounts for its low selling price. This was a good buy at auction as it is well worth restoring, which would increase its value.
£170–200 / €250–290
$310–360 PF 🔨

◀ **Late Victorian carved mahogany chiffonier,** the mirrored back with a shelf, the base with three drawers over three cupboards and a recess, 59in (150cm) wide. Large, dark pieces of furniture such as this are currently out of vogue, hence the low price of this chiffonier. The demand for this type of furniture is currently so low that some pieces are being broken up and the decorative panels are being used to make 'new' items in styles that are more in demand.
£200–240 / €290–350
$360–430 CHTR 🔨

Lacquered bamboo table, Chinese, 19thC, 28in (71cm) wide. Lacquer tables such as this are sought after by interior designers. They tend to fetch more money in London and other large cities than in the provinces.
£210–240 / €300–350
$380–440 QM ⊞

The look without the price

Victorian 17thC-style oak sideboard, with a flute-moulded drawer above a pot board on turned and moulded supports, with a panelled back, upper section missing, on bun feet, 52in (132cm) wide.
£240–280 / €350–410
$440–510 PF ↗

This Victorian sideboard is large and has heavy carving. A genuine 17th-century piece would have much finer carving and be able to command ten times this amount.

Locate the source

The source of each illustration in Miller's can be found by checking the code letters below each caption with the Key to Illustrations, pages 286–290.

Edwardian mahogany Sutherland table, with satinwood crossbanding and inlay, 24in (61cm) wide. The satinwood crossbanding and inlay is a good indication that this is a quality piece, which makes this table more desirable and therefore more valuable.
£220–260 / €320–380
$400–470 DD ↗

Early Victorian rosewood card table, with a fold-over top, on a baluster column with four carved scroll supports, 8¾in (22cm) wide.
£250–300 / €360–430
$460–550 AMB ↗

Victorian mahogany side table, with two drawers over a shelf, on turned supports, 48in (122cm) wide. This is a multi-functional table that would lend itself to many uses within the home.
£260–310 / €380–450
$470–560 WilP ↗

Edwardian mahogany display table, the glazed hinged top enclosing a velvet-lined interior, on six cabriole legs united by curved stretchers and a shelf, 20½in (52cm) diam. This style of table is currently popular with collectors who are buying them to use as display tables for their collections.
£300–360 / €440–520
$550–660 PF ⚘

Victorian mahogany chiffonier, with a scrolled pediment above a shelf on turned column supports, the base with two panelled cupboard doors, 45in (114.5cm) wide.
£280–330 / €410–480
$510–600 CHTR ⚘

Flame mahogany work table, the hinged top enclosing a fitted interior, repaired, 22in wide (56cm) wide. This was a good investment buy as it is an attractive piece of furniture with good proportions. It could have sold for more at auction.
£300–360 / €440–520
$550–660 DN(BR) ⚘

Miller's compares...

A. Walnut tilt-top table, on a turned column, 19thC, 53in (134.5cm) diam.
£320–380 / €460–550
$580–690 E ⚘

B. Victorian rosewood breakfast table, the top with a moulded edge on a turned and fluted column, 53in (134.5cm) diam.
£620–740 / €900–1,050
$1,150–1,350 HYD ⚘

Item A is probably veneered and has possibly been reduced in height. Item B is made of solid timber, is a more pleasing shape and is overall a better quality table, all of which make it a more desirable piece with a higher value than Item A.

◄ **Inlaid card table,** with a central frieze drawer, on carved end supports, c1840, 49¾in (126.5cm) wide.
£340–410
€500–600
$620–740
DORO ⚘

Card Tables

The tops of some card tables have projecting dished corners to hold candlesticks. Alternatively, some have pull-out slides fitted into spalyed corners. Cloth-lined receptacles were also provided for counters.

Early Victorian rosewood card table, the fold-over top enclosing an inset baize, above a carved frieze, slight losses to veneers, 35¾in (91cm) wide. This table has good proportions and taking its condition into consideration was a reasonable buy at auction.
£350–420 / €510–610
$640–760 DN(BR) ✗

Liberty Arts & Crafts mahogany table, with a frieze drawer above a shelf, 29in (73.5cm) wide. Liberty Arts & Crafts items usually command an impressive premium on today's market. This table sold for a reasonable price.
£400–480 / €580–700
$730–870 APO ⊞

Victorian burr-walnut two-tier table, with ebony crossbanding and boxwood stringing, the supports with three fluted columns united by a turned stretcher, 30¼in (77cm) wide.
£360–430 / €520–620
$660–780 AMB ✗

The look without the price

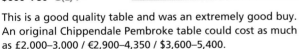

Edwardian Chippendale-style mahogany Pembroke table,
the serpentine leaves with ropetwist mouldings, over a real and a dummy drawer, 36in (91.5cm) wide.
£360–430 / €520–620
$660–780 G(L) ✗

This is a good quality table and was an extremely good buy. An original Chippendale Pembroke table could cost as much as £2,000–3,000 / €2,900–4,350 / $3,600–5,400.

Victorian mahogany breakfront sideboard,
the foliate-carved and moulded back above a drawer and three panelled doors, 59½in (151cm) wide.
£380–450 / €550–650
$690–820 DMC ✗

◀ **George III mahogany writing table,** with a fitted drawer, 35½in (90cm) wide. This multi-functional item could also be used as a dressing table.
£380–450 / €550–650
$690–820 LHA ✗

▶ **Regency satinwood side cabinet,** with a drawer above two doors with pleated silk panels, 25in (63.5cm) wide.
£380–450 / €550–650
$690–820 G(B) ✗

William IV figured mahogany card table, the hinged top on a carved column, 31½in (80cm) wide. William IV furniture is always sought after. This piece has very fine carving – known as tulip carving – and pleasing proportions.
£400–480 / €580–700
$730–870 RTo 🔨

Regency mahogany folding card table, with a swivel top, 36in (91.5cm) wide. This is a good-quality veneered table. It sold for a fair price but will increase in value, so was a good investment.
£400–480 / €580–700
$730–870 E 🔨

Arts and Crafts oak occasional table, c1900, 24in (61cm) diam.
£400–450 / €580–650
$730– 820 APO ⊞

Mahogany drop-leaf table, mid-19thC, 41½in (105.5cm) wide.
£410–490 / €590–710
$750–890 NOA 🔨

Victorian walnut writing table, the replaced leather-inset top above two frieze drawers, damaged, paper label for Edwards & Roberts, London, 48in (122cm) wide. Writing tables are always popular and achieve high prices. The benefit of a maker's label is desirable and top makers' names command high prices. Although this example has woodworm in one leg it is easily treatable and does not detract from value.
£420–500 / €610–730
$760–910 WW 🔨

Miller's compares...

A. Victorian mahogany three-tier buffet, with a three-quarter gallery on turned and block supports with gadrooned finials, 34½in (87.5cm) wide.
£400–480 / €580–700
$730–870 DA 🔨

B. William IV mahogany three-tier buffet, with three-quarter galleries, the end supports with lancet finials and scroll brackets, 45½in (115.5cm) wide.
£600–720 / €870–1,050
$1,100–1,300 DN 🔨

Buffets are highly sought-after pieces of furniture. Item A has good, classical lines, but Item B is of an unusual design, and this makes it the more valuable of the two examples.

◄ **Fruitwood wine table,** the plank tilt top on two end supports with a swinging support, French, mid-19thC, 46in (117cm) diam.
£440–520
€640–750
$800–950 NOA 🔨

Miller's compares...

A. Regency mahogany Pembroke table, the twin flap top above a frieze drawer with later handles, with gadroon-capped fluted legs, feet replaced by brass roller casters, 28¾in (73cm) wide.
£440–520 / €640–750
$800–950 WW 🔨

B. Mahogany Pembroke table, with a bowed end and cockbeaded drawer opposing a dummy drawer, c1785, 33in (84cm) wide.
£650–780 / €940–1,100
$1,200–1,400 WL 🔨

Mid-Victorian rosewood occasional table, with a bird's-eye maple marquetry chessboard top, above a crenellated frieze applied with turned pendant finials, on a spiral fluted column with three leaf-carved scrolled legs, 19¼in (49cm) wide. This is a very desirable small table with the advantage of a chessboard inlay, which adds to its decorative appeal and value.
£450–540 / €650–780
$820–980 DN(BR) 🔨

Item A and Item B are both good-quality tables. Item A is made of flame mahogany, which is always desirable, but Item B is of an earlier date, and this is what accounts for its higher value.

Regency mahogany breakfast table, the tilt top on a baluster and leaf-turned column, 52in (132cm) wide. This table, which has an unusual and attractive column, was a very good buy on the day.
£450–540 / €650–780
$820–980 HYD 🔨

Georgian mahogany pillar table, the top on a birdcage mechanism, 26in (66cm) diam. Tilt-top tables are extremely useful pieces of furniture; this one sold for a reasonable price.
£460–550 / €670–800
$840–1,000 BWL 🔨

◄ **George II mahogany tea table,** the fold-over top above a frieze with brass escutcheons, 30in (76cm) diam. This is a good-quality table in a sought-after style. It is in good condition and has sold at a reasonable price.
£460–550 / €670–800
$840–1,000 HYD 🔨

George IV mahogany and rosewood-banded tilt-top breakfast table, the top with a reeded edge, the crossbanding divided by brass stringing, 58in (147.5cm) wide.
£480–570 / €700–830
$870–1,050 JAd 🔨

George III mahogany drop-leaf table, the hinged top over a drawer and two dummy drawers, on tapered legs, 21in (53.5cm) wide. It is unusual to find a drop-leaf table with only one leaf. This is a very useful piece of furniture.
£520–620 / €750–900
$950–1,100 G(L) 🔨

Oak breakfront side cabinet, by Christopher Pratt of Bradford, the raised back with a bracket shelf over bevelled mirror recesses with turned and carved pillars, over three panelled and carved cupboard doors, flanked by four drawers to one side, a leaded glazed door to the other, c1900, 82in (208.5cm) wide. This large piece of furniture is of a style that is currently out of vogue, so if you like this look, now is the time to buy.
£520–620 / €750–900
$950–1,100 AH 🔨

Breakfast table, with geometrical marquetry inlay, c1840, 40¼in (102cm) diam.
£550–660 / €800–960
$1,000–1,200 DORO 🔨

George III manchineel-wood drop-leaf occasional table, the top above a single frieze drawer with brass handles, 24in (61cm) wide.
£550–660 / €800–960
$1,000–1,200 HYD 🔨

George IV mahogany card table, 36in (91.5cm) wide. This table has good proportions and has sold at a reasonable price.
£580–690 / €840–1,000
$1,050–1,250 L 🔨

◄ **William IV mahogany side table,** the top with a gallery and a moulded edge, above two long and two short drawers flanking an arched recess, 42¼in (107.5cm) wide. Side tables are often used as dressing tables or desks. This practicality makes them desirable and increases their value.
£580–690 / €840–1,000
$1,050–1,250 DN 🔨

George II walnut side table, the top decorated with crossbanding, above a drawer, 30in (76cm) wide.
£580–690 / €840–1,000
$1,050–1,250 L 🔨

◄ **Victorian burr-walnut Sutherland table,** the serpentine drop sides on turned and carved columns united by a stretcher, 36in (91.5cm) wide. This Sutherland table is unusual in that the top swivels to provide extra support when the leaves are extended.
£580–690 / €840–1,000
$1,050–1,250 HYD 🔨

George III mahogany bowfronted sideboard, the central drawer above an arched recess and cupboard, flanked by two short drawers over a deep drawer and cupboard, 63in (160cm) wide. This small sideboard has good colour and patina, and bowfronted furniture is very popular. It was a good buy as it could have fetched £1,000 / €1,450 / $1,800.
£600–720 / €870–1,050
$1,100–1,300 DMC 🔨

◄ **William and Mary-style walnut and marquetry side table,** the top with a marquetry panel and moulded and gilt border, above two short drawers, 39in (99cm) wide.
£600–720 / €870–1,050
$1,100–1,300 HYD 🔨

Victorian ebony and walnut marquetry drop-leaf table, the fitted frieze drawer with brass mounts, 22in (56cm) wide. Although ebony is currently out of vogue, this table has held its value because it is made of walnut and has inlay.
£620–740 / €900–1,050
$1,150–1,350 JAd 🔨

Mahogany chiffonier, with maple crossbanding, the shelf on two supports over a frieze drawer and two panelled doors, on modified bracket feet, 19thC, 35¾in (91cm) wide.
£640–760 / €930–1,100
$1,200–1,400 G(B) 🔨

Regency satinwood and rosewood crossbanded occasional table, the canted top with a shell patera, 21¾in (55.5cm) wide. This table has good proportions and the use of satinwood has increased its desirability and, therefore, its value.
£650–780 / €940–1,100
$1,200–1,400 RTo 🔨

George I walnut side table, the crossbanded top above a single long and two small drawers flanking a shaped frieze, 30in (76cm) wide. Red walnut is unusual and this table was a good buy at auction. With two keen bidders on the day it could have made more than three times this price.
£650–780 / €940–1,100
$1,200–1,400 HYD 🕱

► **Sheraton revival demi-lune side cabinet,** with painted decoration, the door enclosing a drawer and a recess, late 19thC, 33½in (85cm) wide. The Sheraton revival occured during the Edwardian era as a reaction to the heaviness of Victorian furniture.
£680–810
€990–1,150
$1,250–1,450 DN 🕱

Victorian rosewood work table, the drop flaps with telescopic supports, above a fitted drawer and work well, on a spiral-turned and shaped underframe, 22in (56cm) wide. This table is useful as it could double as a side table.
£750–900 / €1,100–1,300
$1,400–1,650 G(B) 🕱

► **Brass-inlaid tea table,** the frieze mounted with a brass eagle, one foot damaged, early 19thC, 31in (78.5cm) wide.
£750–900 / €1,100–1,300
$1,400–1,650 BWL 🕱

◄ **Regency brass-mounted mahogany chiffonier,** the back with a shelf on scrolled and turned supports, above a line-inlaid top with a frieze drawer with a Venus and putti brass mount, above two panelled cupboard doors enclosing adjustable shelves, flanked by brass line-inlaid pilasters, losses and restoration, 38½in (98cm) wide.
£720–860
€1,050–1,250
$1,300–1,550
DN(BR) 🕱

Giltwood centre table, the foliate hardstone-inlaid marble top with an interlaced strapwork border, 19thC, 18in (45.5cm) wide. Giltwood should only be professionally cleaned. A light dusting should be adequate in the home.
£770–920 / €1,100–1,350 $1,400–1,650 DMC ⚹

Victorian figured walnut dining table, the top with marquetry inlay, on a carved baluster column and triform base, 42in (106.5cm) diam. This table fetched twice the estimate at auction. This was probably because it has good figuring and is of a larger size than most tables of this type.
£950–1,100 / €1,400–1,550 $1,750–2,000 Mal(O) ⚹

► **Burr-elm and kingwood break bowfronted side cabinet,** French, c1910, 62½in (159cm) wide. Burr-elm is an unusual wood, and this useful piece of furniture was a good buy at auction.
£960–1,150 / €1,400–1,650 $1,750–2,050 S(O) ⚹

William IV rosewood card table, the top with a moulded edge above a frieze drawer, flanked by turned rails and carved end supports, 35¾in (91cm) wide.
£920–1,100 / €1,350–1,600 $1,700–2,000 DN ⚹

► **Mahogany table,** the marble top above a frieze on three supports united by a triform stretcher, on block feet, French, c1840, 26in (66cm) diam. This is a very useful, multi-functional table and this adds to its value.
£950–1,100 / €1,400–1,550 $1,750–2,000 DN ⚹

◄ **Paper-mâché tilt-top table,** with mother-of-pearl inlay, c1880, 18in (45.5cm) diam. Restoration of papier-mâché is a difficult process and should only be undertaken by professionals.
£790–880 / €1,150–1,300 $1,450–1,600 MTay ⊞

Henry II-style walnut buffet, the shelves with spindle galleries above a marble top, over two doors and a display space, possibly French, c1890, 49in (124.5cm) wide.
£810–900 / €1,150–1,300 $1,450–1,650 SWA ⊞

Whatnots & Butlers' Trays

◄ **Mahogany butler's tray,** on a stand, tray cracked, 19thC, 31in (78.5cm) wide. Butlers' trays are always in demand, but this example is cracked and this has been reflected in the price it achieved at auction.
£150–180
€220–260
$270–330 Hal ⚘

Rosewood serpentine five-tier whatnot, surmounted by a carved stylized shield, with a mirrored back, 19thC, 26½in (67.5cm) wide. This highly decorative whatnot is most unusual. It was a good buy, as with two keen bidders it could have made three times this price.
£200–240 / €290–350
$360–430 E ⚘

Miller's compares...

A. George IV mahogany three-tier whatnot, with ring-turned acorn finials and turned supports above a base with a cupboard door over a drawer, 16¼in (41.5cm) wide.
£520–620 / €750–900
$950–1,150 DN ⚘

B. Rosewood three-tier whatnot, with turned supports, above a base with a drawer, 19thC, 18¼in (46.5cm) wide.
£750–900 / €1,100–1,300
$1,400–1,650 G(B) ⚘

Item A, a whatnot-cum-cupboard, is a rather heavy piece of furniture. Item B is much more delicate and is also made of rosewood, which is a more desirable wood than mahogany. It is for these reasons that Item B achieved a higher price than Item A.

Three-tier *étagère*, the carved top above three tiers on carved spiral-twist and S–scroll supports, on spiral-twist legs, 1860–70, 45in (114.5cm) wide. The delicate proportions of this *étagère* make it an attractive buy and account for its value.
£680–810 / €990–1,150
$1,250–1,450 DORO ⚘

Miscellaneous

Edwardian mahogany tray, with an inlaid shell motif and brass handles, 22in (56cm) wide.
£150–170 / €220–250
$270–310 DEB ⊞

Fruitwood canterbury, with bobbin-turned divisions and supports, on turned legs with horn casters, French, 19thC, 18½in (47cm) wide. The design of this canterbury is not very practical and this accounts for the low price.
£250–300 / €360–440
$460–550 DN 🔨

George III mahogany two-tier dumb waiter, the shelves with reeded borders, damaged, 42in (106.5cm) high. This dumb waiter has a cracked top which has probably accounted for the low price. When buying two-tier dumbwaiters it is advisable to check that a tier has not been removed from a three-tier example, as this would lower the price.
£200–240 / €290–350
$360–440 HYD

Victorian rosewood pole screen, with a needlework panel, on a spiral-twist column, 58in (147.5cm) high.
£220–260 / €320–380
$400–470 BeFA 🔨

Regency mahogany canterbury, with three divisions, on turned legs, 22in (56cm) wide.
£380–450 / €550–650
$690–820 G(L) 🔨

Victorian walnut canterbury, the inlaid top with a brass rail, on turned supports, the base with pierced fretwork and a drawer, feet missing, 24½in (62cm) wide.
£480–570 / €700–830
$870–1,050 CHTR 🔨

Early Victorian rosewood canterbury, the shelf and base with fretwork panels, above a drawer, on turned feet, damaged, 21½in (54.5cm) wide. Although this piece is damaged, it is made of rosewood and has good-quality fretwork, both of which have contributed to its value.
£580–690 / €840–1,000
$1,050–1,250 AMB 🔨

Ceramics

Now, more than at any other time in recent memory, enthusiasts can form an interesting collection of ceramics at prices to suit even the smallest budget. Over the last year the most noticeable trend is that collectors are saving their money and concentrating on buying the rarest and best examples from ceramic factories. This means that the more commonly seen examples of models from a factory can be acquired very reasonably, even in good condition. For example, Royal Worcester blush ivory porcelain wares can be acquired for as little as £40–50 / €60–70 / $75–90 for an example that would have sold for £120 / €175 / $220 a few years ago.

You can start a collection with more modest pieces and, as your eye and taste become more confident, you can consider saving up for the more expensive and scarce examples. Decorative ceramics such as French and English Sèvres-style porcelain can be bought for a fraction of the price of a genuine piece but create the same look. It may also be possible to acquire wares from markets that are slightly weaker in Britain; for example, 18th-century Italian maiolica wares are generally more affordable in this country than their home market. The more readily found examples of such 19th-century decorative ceramics as majolica and Dresden flower-decorated porcelain have dropped in price over the last year. In contrast, prices have risen for the more academic, early and rare examples such as blue and white porcelain, where new research is currently being undertaken into identifying the wares of the early English factories. Significant discoveries have been made and as a result many pieces have been reattributed. Examples from factories such as Isleworth, Limehouse,

Vauxhall and Lund's Bristol, as well as early wares from Worcester, Chelsea and Bow, are currently fetching record prices, with rare pieces commanding four- and five-figure sums. It is difficult to pick up inexpensive or even damaged examples from these early factories.

Similar research into English pottery has led to high prices for rare and unusual examples of slipware, delft, salt-glazed stoneware and creamware. An early polychrome-decorated English delft plate can command anything from £5,000–10,000 / €7,200–14,600 / $9,100–18,200. However, it is still possible to pick up a bargain. For example, a small English delft plate decorated with a chinoiserie design and dating from 1750–60 can be found for as little as £80–100 / €115–145 / $145–180, and a late salt-glazed stoneware piece with *famille rose* decoration, in good condition, can be purchased for £200–500 / €290–720 / $360–910.

The main market for Staffordshire figures now seems to be the US, where rare figures and exotic subjects are in particular demand. Early English pottery is also sought after there and can fetch very high prices.

Ceramics is one of the collecting areas where damage dramatically reduces value. If you are willing to accept the odd chip or crack then you can find real bargains, whether at auction or from a dealer. Restoration, depending on how well it has been executed, will also devalue ceramics. So, if you are looking for a return on your investment then avoid heavily restored or badly damaged pieces. However, if you just like the look of a piece then do not let damage or restoration stop you buying it.

Daniel Bray

Baskets & Boxes

Miller's compares...

A. Porcelain box, German, c1910, 3½in (9cm) diam.
£40–45 / €60–70
$75–85 DuM ➚

B. Meissen-style porcelain box and cover,
with gilt-metal mounts, the interior painted with a vase
of flowers, Continental, c1820, 3¼in (8.5cm) diam.
£200–240 / €290–350
$360–430 Hal ➚

Item A could possibly by Dresden but the
ornate design is currently out of fashion.
Item B, however, is an earlier box in a

sought-after style that appeals to collectors
and therefore commands a higher price.

Worcester basket, with pierced decoration, the exterior
applied with flowerheads, slight damage, marked, c1770,
7½in (19cm) diam. Had this basket been in perfect
condition it could have achieved £400 / €580 / $730.
£260–310 / €380–450
$470–560 PF ➚

To find out more about antique ceramics see the
full range of Miller's books at
www.millers.uk.com

The look without the price

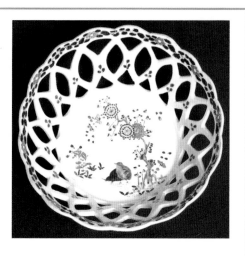

Bow basket, decorated with Two Quails pattern, c1758, 6in (15cm) diam.
£470–530 / €680–770
$860–960 JUP ⊞

This English porcelain basket is decorated with Kakiemon-style painting and would appeal to Bow collectors. However, an original Japanese Kakiemon piece would be very desirable and could command a five-figure sum.

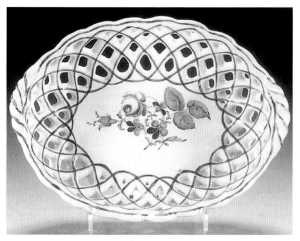

Pearlware cosmetic box and cover, painted with leaves and flowers, damaged, early 19thC, 4¾in (12cm) diam. The damage to this item has not affected the price as it is a rare piece.
£450–540 / €650–780
$820–980 WW ⚒

Bayreuth faïence basket, marked, 1761–88, 7¼in (18.5cm) wide.
£720–860 / €1,050–1,250
$1,300–1,550 S(O) ⚒

The look without the price

Metal-mounted porcelain snuff box, painted with figures in 18thC costume playing back-gammon, German, 1850–1900, 3¼in (8.5cm) wide.
£840–1,000 / €1,200–1,450
$1,550–1,850 S(O) ⚒

This snuff box depicts an 18th-century pastime, a subject which is popular with collectors. However, had it been an 18th-century piece it could have commanded over £2,000 / €2,900 / $3,600.

Candlesticks

Pair of Sitzendorf candelabra, applied with roses and foliage, each support in the form of a lady and an infant, Austrian, late 19thC, 18½in (47cm) high. This is a very good price for these candlesticks if you like this style of decoration.
£210–250 / €300–360
$380–450 JAd ✎

Miller's compares...

A. Porcelain chamberstick, painted with vignettes of landscapes, 19thC, 5in (12.5cm) high.
£120–140 / €170–200
$210–250 WW ✎

B. Spode chamberstick, with gilt decoration, c1820, 1¾in (4.5cm) high.
£850–950 / €1,250–1,400
$1,550–1,750 DIA ⊞

Item A is by an unknown maker and was therefore sold on its decorative merits. Item B, on the other hand, is by a sought-after maker and is elaborately decorated with a gilt ground, which is why it has a higher value than Item A.

Find out more in

Miller's Ceramics Buyer's Guide, Miller's Publications, 2006

Pair of Samson candelabra, in the form of Ceres and Pan, applied and painted with flowers, one with slight damage, 19thC, 14¼in (36cm) high.
£290–340 / €420–500
$520–620 Bea ✎

▶ **Pair of Sèvres-style gilt-bronze-mounted porcelain candlesticks,** painted with figures, on marble bases, French, 1875–1900, 11½in (29cm) high. Although one would expect a set of this type to include a clock, these candlesticks – which were sold in the US – are a very reasonable price. Had they been sold in the UK, where they would be more sought after, they could have achieved £600–800 / €870–1,150 / $1,100–1,450.
£440–520 / €640–750
$800–960 NOA ✎

Imperial Porcelain Manufactory candlestick, with gilt decoration, slight damage, Russian, 15½in (39.5cm) high. Good Russian porcelain is currently fetching very high prices.
£630–750 / €910–1,100 $1,150–1,350 BUK(F) 🔨

◄ **Minton candelabra,** the support in the form of a lady in classical dress, stamped mark, dated 1868, 26½in (67.5cm) high. This a fair price for a single candelabra. A pair could have made over double this price.
£650–780 / €940–1,100 $1,200–1,450 E 🔨

Pair of Derby figural candlesticks, encrusted with flowers, c1760, 6in (15cm) high.
£720–860 / €1,050–1,250 $1,300–1,550 S(O) 🔨

◄ **Pair of Meissen wall brackets,** applied with cherubs, crossed swords marks, restored, German, 19thC, 15in (38cm) high.
£750–900 €1,100–1,300 $1,350–1,600 WW 🔨

► **Pair of Wemyss candlesticks,** decorated with cockerels, Scottish, c1900, 11¾in (30cm) high. Wemyss ware is very collectable.
£760–850 €1,100–1,250 $1,400–1,550 GLB ▦

Pair of Dresden figural candlestics of a man and a woman picking fruit, German, 19thC, 15in (38cm) high.
£800–960 / €1,100–1,300 $1,350–1,600 BWL 🔨

Cups, Mugs & Tea Bowls

Wedgwood tea cup and saucer, with hand-painted and gilded decoration, signed 'M. Smith', c1900, saucer 6in (15cm) diam. This tea cup and saucer would probably have been part of a set.
£55–65 / €80–95
$105–125 LGr

Paris porcelain cabinet cup and saucer, French, c1890, cup 3in (7.5cm) diam.
£65–75 / €95–105
$125–145 K&M

◀ **Child's ceramic mug,** transfer-printed with a deer-stalking scene, Scottish, 1860–80, 3in (7.5cm) high. Children's pieces are highly collectable and this mug has the added premium of being Scottish.
£80–90 / €115–130
$155–175 GAU

Mason's Ironstone mug, painted with butterflies and insects, the interior decorated with mythical beasts, c1840, 6½in (16.5cm) diam.
£100–120 / €145–170
$200–230 WL

◀ **Porcelain custard cup,** painted with flowers, French, c1740, 3½in (9cm) wide. This cup is probably missing its cover. If the cover had been present this item could have achieved three times this price.
£100–120 / €145–170
$200–230 WW

◄ **Ceramic mug,** printed with Far Pavilions or Speeding Sampan pattern, 1805–20, 6in (15cm) high.
£110–130
€160–190
$200–240 DN ✎

► **Pearlware mug,** printed and painted with a donkey race, damaged and restored, 19thC, 3in (7.5cm) high. This mug is decorated with a rare pattern which, despite the damage, has made it desirable and therefore more valuable.
£120–140 / €170–200
$210–250 WW ✎

Caughley tea bowl and saucer.

Caughley tea bowl and saucer, painted with birds in branches, 18thC.
£120–140 / €170–200
$210–250 G(L) ✎

◄ **Worcester mug,** printed with Fisherman pattern, crescent mark, 18thC, 3½in (9cm) high. Early pieces of Worcester can be found at reasonable prices if not decorated with a rare pattern.
£120–140
€170–200
$210–250 BWL ✎

► **Famille rose mug,** decorated with a gilt crest, 18thC, 5in (12.5cm) high.
£170–200
€250–300
$310–370 WW ✎

Creamware mug, printed and painted with the Arkwright Arms, inscribed 'Within the Ark, Safe Forever', slight damage, late 18thC, 4¾in (12cm) high.
£190–220 / €280–330
$350–420 WW ✎

Ceramic loving cup, the exterior printed with a locomotive and four wagons, the interior decorated with an applied frog and a lizard, damaged, 19thC, 5in (12.5cm) high.
£190–220 / €280–330
$350–420 LAY ⚖

Mason's Ironstone mug, with gilt decoration, the handle in the form of a snake, early 19thC, 8¼in (21cm) high.
£200–240 / €290–350
$360–430 HOLL ⚖

Porcelain libation cup, probably by Bow, moulded with Chinese animals, c1760, 6¼in (16cm) diam. This is possibly a Bow replica of a Chinese libation cup, in the *blanc-de-Chine* style. An original piece would have been made around 1710.
£200–240 / €290–350
$360–430 RTo ⚖

Creamware beaker, printed with Tea Party pattern, inscribed 'Kindly take this gift of mine, The gift and giver I hope is thine; And tho' the value is but small. A loving heart is worth it all', restored, late 18thC, 3½in (9cm) high. Although further restoration is needed on this beaker, it is decorated with an early pattern and offers good value for money.
£190–220 / €280–330
$350–420 WW ⚖

Locate the source

The source of each illustration in Miller's can be found by checking the code letters below each caption with the Key to Illustrations, pages 286–290.

Grainger's Worcester loving cup, painted with a view of Worcester, printed mark, c1840, 6in (15cm) high.
£200–240 / €290–350
$360–430 SWO ⚖

Stoneware mug, commemorating the Duke of Wellington, slight damage, early 19thC, 3¼in (8.5cm) high. Although there are many stoneware items commemorating Wellington on the market, this is a rare design that would appeal to collectors.
£200–240 / €290–350
$360–440 WW ✣

Pair of mugs, one transfer-printed with a thatched cottage and a church, the other with horses and a windmill, early 19thC, 5in (12.5cm) high.
£200–240 / €290–350
$360–440 DA ✣

Chamberlain's Worcester coffee can and saucer, decorated with an Imari pattern, c1810, saucer 5½in (14cm) diam.
£220–250 / €320–360
$400–450 G&G ▦

◀ **Porcelain cup and saucer,** with gilt decoration, Austrian, 1805, saucer 5¼in (13.5cm) diam.
£250–300
€360–430
$460–550
DORO ✣

Derby tea bowl and saucer, with gilded and painted decoration, marked, c1800, saucer 5in (12.5cm) diam.
£270–300 / €390–440
$490–550 ReN ▦

Set of seven Marieberg custard cups and covers, 18thC, 3¼in (8.5cm) high.
£280–330 / €410–480
$510–600 BUK ✣

▶ **Bow mug,** painted with Chinese figures, slight damage, painter's mark, c1760, 3½in (9cm) high.
£300–360 / €440–520
$550–660 WW ✣

Creamware mug, with engine-turned banded decoration, early 19thC, 5in (12.5cm) high.
£320–380 / €460–550
$580–690 PFK ⚲

Minton cup and saucer, decorated with playing cards, c1870, cup 3in (7.5cm) diam. This unusual printed and hand-painted piece would probably appeal to someone with an interest in the subject or those who collect teacups purely for their decorative appeal.
£320–360 / €460–520
$580–660 JOR ⊞

Porcelain cup and saucer, with gilt decoration, painted with a four-leaf clover, Austrian, 1825, saucer 5¼in (13.5cm) diam.
£340–410 / €500–600
$620–750 DORO ⚲

► **Royal Crown Derby chocolate cup, cover and saucer,** painted with roses, with gilt decoration, dated 1905, 4¼in (11cm) high.
£360–430
€520–620
$660–780 HOLL ⚲

Minton trio, decorated with landscapes, 1830, saucer 6in (15cm) diam.
£360–400 / €520–580
$660–730 JAK ⊞

◄ **Staffordshire redware mug,** applied with a lion, unicorn, birds, flowers and leaves, restored, c1760, 4¾in (12cm) high. Despite having been restored this rare item fetched a good price. In perfect condition it could have achieved double this amount.
£440–520 / €640–750
$800–950 WW ⚲

Sèvres-style porcelain tea cup and saucer, painted with Chinese figures in a garden, with gilt decoration, marked 'LL', 'BB' and 'A', c1800. It is rare to find Sèvres-style porcelain produced by an English factory, and this would account for the value of this item.
£500–600 / €730–870
$910–1,100 WW ⚒

Creamware jug, painted with Masonic symbols, inscribed 'Love the Brotherhood', damaged, late 18thC, 5½in (14cm) high. The hand-painted decoration has added a premium to this special-interest mug. However, had it been in perfect condition it could have achieved nearly twice this price.
£480–570 / €640–750
$800–950 WW ⚒

> **For more examples of** Cups & Mugs see Silver (page 132–165)

Porcelain *écuelle*, cover and stand, possibly Meissen, painted with landscapes, castles, ships and figures, slight damage, German, early 19thC, saucer 7in (18cm) diam.
£500–600 / €730–870
$910–1,100 BWL ⚒

Worcester mug, painted with Walk in the Garden pattern, 1751–74, 6in (15cm) high.
£510–610 / €740–880
$930–1,100 BWL ⚒

◄ Porcelain cup and saucer, with gilt decoration, painted with a cockerel and an inscription, Austrian, 1808, saucer 5¼in (13.5cm) diam.
£550–660
€800–960
$1,000–1,200
DORO ⚒

Dishes & Bowls

Fife Pottery spongeware bowl, Scottish, c1850,
9½in (24cm) diam.
£60–70 / €85–100
$115–135 GAU ⊞

Doulton Lambeth stoneware bowl, by Florence
Barlow, signed, slight damage, dated 1879,
7½in (19cm) diam.
£55–65 / €80–95
$105–125 Pott ↗

▶ **Imari charger,**
late 19thC, 12in
(30.5cm) diam,
with three
graduated bowls.
£60–70 / €85–100
$115–135 GTH ↗

The look without the price

Majolica dish, moulded with trailing leaves,
19thC, 14½in (37cm) diam.
£30–35 / €45–50
$55–65 G(L) ↗

Nineteenth-century majolica wares by
unknown makers can be found for a
fraction of the price of a piece by a
named maker such as Minton.

Methven Pottery spongeware bowl, Scottish, Kirkcaldy, c1860, 8½in (21.5cm) diam.
£75–85 / €110–125
$145–165 GAU ⊞

Earthenware dessert dish, painted in enamels with a rural scene, impressed 'Turner', marked 'Absolom Yarm', restored, 18thC, 8¼in (21cm) wide. William and John Turner produced fine creamwares between 1770 and 1790 at Lane End in Longton, Staffordshire.
£100–120 / €145–170
$200–230 PF ↗

> **For more examples of**
> Bowls & Dishes see Silver (132–165)

◄ **Porcelain bowl,** possibly Liverpool, decorated with an Oriental harbour scene, damaged, 18thC, 9½in (24cm) diam.
£100–120 / €145–170
$200–230 PF ↗

Miller's compares...

A. Brown, Westhead & Moore footbath, transfer-printed with floral decoration, moulded registration mark for 1877, 20in (51cm) wide.
£110–130 / €160–190
$200–240 SWO ↗

B. Victorian pottery footbath, decorated with Florentine pattern, slight damage, 9½in (24cm) wide.
£420–500 / €610–730
$760–910 CHTR ↗

Item A is the larger of the two footbaths and is in better condition. However, Item B has a more pleasing shape, colour and design, and there is a large number of collectors of blue and white pottery. It is these factors that account for the higher price of Item B.

Bow dish, handpainted with flowers and shrubs, slight damage, c1760, 9¼in (23.5cm) wide.
£120–140 / €170–200
$210–250 DN ⚚

Pottery dessert dish, transfer-printed with a ruined tomb overlooking an Italian bay, 19thC, 11¼in (28.5cm) wide. This is rather unusual in that the transfer-ware pattern has not been continued to the edge of the dish.
£140–165 / €200–240
$250–300 HOLL ⚚

English delft pottery dish, decorated with a fence and flowers design, 18thC, 9in (23cm) diam. English delft decorated with floral patterns can be purchased at reasonable prices. Pieces with more unusual decoration command higher prices.
£140–165 / €200–240
$250–300 GTH ⚚

▶ **Pottery platter,** transfer-printed with Ponte Rotto pattern, 19thC, 16½in (42cm) wide.
£150–180
€220–260
$280–330 BWL ⚚

Pottery tureen, printed with Hollywell Cottage pattern, 19thC, 14in (35.5cm) wide. If this tureen had been complete with its original cover it could be worth over double this amount.
£160–190 / €230–270
$290–350 GAK ⚚

Dutch Delft tin-glazed pottery charger, decorated with cockerels and a branch, 18thC, 13½in (34.5cm) diam.
£150–180 / €220–260
$270–320 GTH ⚚

▶ **Lowestoft bowl,** painted with floral sprays, slight wear, c1770, 6in (15cm) diam.
£160–190 / €230–270
$290–350 WW ⚚

Miller's compares...

A. English delft bowl, probably Bristol, decorated with floral panels, damaged, c1760, 8in (20.5cm) diam.
£160–190 / €230–270
$290–350 WW 🔨

B. Delft bowl, painted with flowers and rockwork, 18thC, 9in (23cm) diam.
£320–380 / €460–550
$580–690 WW 🔨

Item A, with its grey background and looser style of painting is the less desirable of these two bowls. Item B is more

sophisticated – the painted decoration is sharper and more colourful and this accounts for its higher price.

◄ **Pair of Derby sauce tureens and covers,** painted with roses and gilt bands, one crazed and stained, c1820, 6¾in (17cm) wide.
£160–190
€230–270
$290–350
SWO 🔨

Staffordshire pottery dish and cover, in the form of a hen, c1875, 6½in (16.5cm) high.
£170–200 / €250–300
$310–370 DA 🔨

Porcelain soup bowl, cover and stand, with gilt decoration, c1850, 6¼in (16cm) high.
£180–210 / €260–310
$320–380 DORO 🔨

Staffordshire dish and cover, in the form of a hen, 19thC, 9in (23cm) wide.
£180–210 / €260–310
$320–380 SJH ⚒

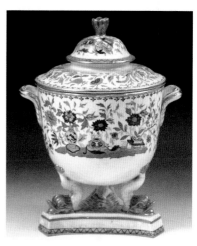

► **Ridgway ice pail and cover,** decorated with Oriental flowers, the three feet in the form of dolphins, damaged, c1825, 11¾in (30cm) high. This pail would have been printed in blue and then painted with enamels. A similar item that had been completely hand painted would achieve twice this price.
£200–240
€290–350
$360–430 SWO ⚒

◄ **Swansea pottery bowl,** decorated with Rampant Fern print, Welsh, c1830, 12in (30.5cm) diam.
£200–230 / €290–330
$360–410 WeW ⊞

Spode pottery meat platter, with matching drainer, transfer-printed with a rural scene, slight damage, impressed and painted marks, early 19thC, 18¾in (47.5cm) wide. It is unusual to find a platter with its original matching drainer.
£200–240 / €290–350
$360–430 F&C ⚒

Swansea pottery bowl, transfer-printed with Ladies with Baskets pattern, Welsh, c1830, 10in (25.5cm) wide.
£230–260 / €340–380
$420–470 WeW ⊞

► **Meissen dish,** painted with peacocks and poultry, the border with insects and flowers, German, 19thC, 16½in (42cm) wide. Tray-sized dishes such as this were usually part of a cabaret set. With its fine painting it should have achieved between £800–1,000 / €1,150–1,450 / $1,450–1,800.
£250–300 / €370–440
$460–550 BWL ⚒

◄ **Bow bowl,** decorated with The Cross-legged Fisherman pattern, c1760, 6in (15cm) diam.
£250–300
€370–440
$460–550 TEN 🔨

The look without the price

Vienna tureen and cover, painted with panels of flowers, with a lemon finial, cover restored, blue shield mark, c1780, 5½in (14cm) high.
£260–310
€380–450
$470–560
SWO 🔨

This tureen is not a particularly popular colour and it has been restored. However, Vienna tureens are rarer than Meissen examples, and had it been in good condition this piece could have achieved three times as much.

Chelsea-Derby dish, decorated with enamels and gilt in the Imari style, restored, marked, 18thC, 9in (23cm) diam. Had this dish been in original, perfect condition it could have achieved £800–1,000 / €1,150–1,450 / $1,450–1,800.
£250–300 / €370–440
$460–550 PF 🔨

Chelsea dish, painted with floral swags, puce anchor mark, c1765, 8¾in (22cm) wide.
£300–360 / €440–520
$550–660 WW 🔨

Wedgwood dish, decorated with waterlilies, c1810, 10in (25.5cm) wide.
£310–350 / €450–510
$560–640 SCO ⊞

Staffordshire pottery dish and cover, in the form of a hen, c1870, 13in (33cm) high.
£340–380 / €490–550
$620–690 HOW ⊞

Pottery bowl, the exterior printed with eight chinoiserie vignettes, the interior with *The York* and naval trophies, c1800, 11¼in (28.5cm) diam.
£350–420 / €510–610
$640–760 TEN ⚘

◄ **Worcester bowl,** with molded fluted decoration and painted with a parrot among flowers, 1760-70, 6in (15cm) diam,
£360–420
€510–610
$640–760 WW ⚘

► **Wemyss bowl,** decorated with a cockerel, inscribed 'Bon Jour', Scottish, c1905, 4in (10cm) diam.
£360–410 / €520–590
$660–750 GLB ⊞

Staffordshire spongeware dish, c1875, 14in (35.5cm) diam. These dishes are popular with American collectors.
£360–400 / €520–580
$660–730 HTE ⊞

English delft bowl, possibly Lambeth, damaged, 17thC, 13½in (34.5cm) diam.
£370–440 / €540–640
$670–800 BWL ⚘

English delft dish, painted with a floral decoration, slight damage, mid-18thC, 13in (33cm) diam.
£420–500 / €610–730
$760–910 WW ⚘

◄ **Chamberlain's Worcester dish,** depicting a view of Abbey House, Cirencester, c1815, 10in (25.5cm) wide.
£450–500
€650–730
$820–910 JAK ⊞

Delft bowl, painted in the baroque style with panels of flowers, slight damage, 1700–50, 11¾in (30cm) diam.
£500–600 / €730–870
$910–1,100 WW 🔨

Staffordshire stoneware punch bowl, painted with a lady and a servant, inscribed 'Mary Orm.' restored, c1760, 9in (23cm) diam. In original good condition this bowl would be worth £1,000 / €1,450 / $1,800.
£580–690 / €840–1,000
$1,050–1,250 DN 🔨

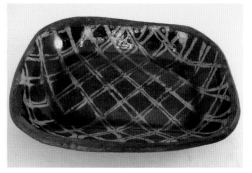

Slipware baking dish, probably Sussex, with trellis decoration, 18thC, 18in (45.5cm) wide. This is quite a rare item as Sussex and Kent are not particularly well known for their pottery production.
£500–600 / €730–870
$910–1,100 G(L) 🔨

◀ **Dutch Delft dish,** attributed to Pieter Adriaensz Kocks, decorated with birds of paradise and flowers, marked, early 18thC, 14in (35.5cm) diam.
£600–720
€870–1,050
$1,100–1,300
WILK 🔨

Miller's compares...

A. Platter, by Ralph Hall, from Select Views Series, depicting Gyrn, Flintshire, Wales, c1820, 17in (43cm) wide.
£630–700 / €910–1,000
$1,150–1,250 GN ⊞

B. Platter, from Antique Scenery Series, depicting North East view of Lancaster with bridge over River Lune, 1825–35, 21in (53.5cm) wide. The Antique Scenery Series is popular design produced in 1825–30 by an unknown maker.
£720–800 / €1,050–1,150
$1,300–1,450 GRe ⊞

Although Item A is the larger of these two platters, Item B has more pleasing decoration in that the central view covers a wider area of the plate, and it is this that gives it its value.

Bow dish, in the form of a leaf, c1770, 11½in (29cm) long.
£710–800 / €1,000–1,150
$1,300–1,450 GIR ⊞

Caughley bowl, painted with Lady with a Parasol pattern, slight damage, rim repaired, c1785, 5in (12.5cm) diam. This bowl is decorated with a rare pattern.
£710–800 / €1,000–1,150
$1,300–1,450 JUP ⊞

Wemyss honeycomb dish, cover and tray, decorated with bees and a beehive in an orchard, Scottish, c1900, 7½in (19cm) square. This dish is slightly unusual and the fact that it is complete with its cover and tray will attract collectors.
£730–820 / €1,050–1,200
$1,350–1,500 GLB ⊞

Dutch Delft dish, decorated with a dog, restored, c1700, 13½in (34.5cm) diam. An English delft piece from the same period would be worth double this amount.
£730–820 / €1,050–1,200
$1,350–1,500 G&G ⊞

Hispano-Moresque pottery bowl, damaged, Spanish, Manises, 1430–70, 5¼in (13.5cm) diam. This is a very rare bowl. Excessive restoration of pottery of this age and rarity is unwise as it reduces value.
£780–930 / €1,150–1,350
$1,400–1,750 S ⋗

The look without the price

Majolica dish, decorated with a man wearing a turban, marked, Italian, Santarelli, c1900, 12¼in (31cm) diam.
£960–1,150
€1,400–1,650
$1,750–2,100
S(O) ⋗

This is a copy of an earlier piece. An original 16th-century dish could be worth £8,000 / €11,600 / $14,500 or more.

Figures

◄ **Staffordshire figural spill vase,** entitled 'A Winter's Tale', depicting Jenny Marston as Perdita and Frederick Robinson as Florizel, c1850, 11¾in (30cm) high.
£75–85 / €110–125
$145–165 DA ♪

Pair of Staffordshire models of greyhounds, 19thC, 7½in (19cm) high. Although this is a fairly common Staffordshire piece it could have been expected to achieve double this price.
£110–130 / €160–190
$200–230 S(Am) ♪

Derby figural group of a woman and a hairdresser, slight damage, incised No. 84, c1770, 6¾in (17cm) high. Such pieces can be found at reasonable prices if the buyer is willing to accept slight damage.
£120–140 / €170–200
$220–250 DN ♪

Staffordshire figure of a putto, slight damage, c1810, 5¼in (13.5cm) high.
£135–150 / €195–220
$240–270 G&G ⊞

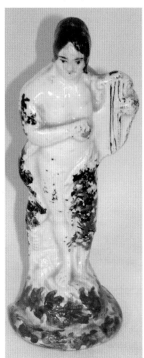

▶ **Prattware figure of Apollo,** c1790, 5¼in (13.5cm) high.
£135–150 / €195–220
$240–270 SER ⊞

Pair of Staffordshire models of spaniels and puppies, 19thC, 6¼in (16cm) high. Models of spaniels are common but the addition of puppies is unusual and this has increased the value of this pair.
£160–190 / €240–280
$290–350 SJH ♪

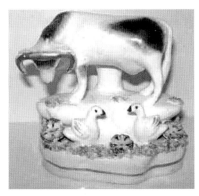

◀ **Staffordshire model of a cow and two ducks,** 19thC.
£160–190
€240–280
$290–350 SJH ➤

Pair of Vienna figures, of ladies and cherubs, slight damage, blue beehive mark, Austrian, late 19thC, 12in (30.5cm) high. Biscuit figures are more popular if they date from the 18th century. These figures would probably have also been produced with enamel decoration and would have cost significantly more.
£170–200 / €250–290
$310–360 DMC ➤

Meissen figure of Cupid, by Professor Heinriche Schwabe, slight damage, crossed swords mark, German, late 19thC, 8¼in (21cm) high. Meissen figures are currently coming down in price so now would be a good time to buy.
£180–210 / €250–300
$320–380 DN ➤

Copeland Parian figure of a bathing girl, after Owen Hale, entitled 'Riverside', impressed marks, c1885, 18½in (47cm) high. This is a common subject and the price of figures relates to their rarity.
£210–250 / €300–360
$380–450 Bea ➤

◀ *Blanc de chine* **figure of Guanyin,** impressed mark, c1800, 3½in (9cm) high.
£260–310 / €370–450
$470–560 SWO ➤

The look without the price

Porcelain figural group, of a lady and a harlequin, slight damage, 19thC, 6in (15cm) high.
£260–310 / €380–450
$470–560 BWL ➤

This is probably a Sampson copy of an early Meissen piece. An original 18th-century model would fetch a four- or even five-figure sum.

◀ **Staffordshire model of a lion,** slight damage, c1800, 3in (7.5cm) wide. Naïve-style models such as this do not fetch as much as examples that are more realistically portrayed.
£310–350
€450–510
$560–640 G&G ⊞

Meissen figure of a putto, slight damage, German, c1760, 3½in (9cm) high. Had this figure been in good condition it could have achieved twice this price.
£340–400 / €490–580
$620–730 DN ⚒

Miller's compares...

A. Meissen figural group of fruit pickers and a dog, damaged, crossed swords mark, incised 'C94', German, 19thC, 9¾in (25cm) high.
£300–360 / €440–520
$550–660 DN(BR) ⚒

B. Meissen figural group of a shepherdess and a gentleman, slight restoration, crossed swords mark, incised '447', German, late 19thC, 5½in (14cm) high.
£620–740 / €900–1,000
$1,150–1,350 DN ⚒

The price difference between these two Meissen figural groups is due to damage. Item A has substantial losses to the figures and the tree and this would be too expensive to restore. Item B on the other hand has a small amount of restoration that could be acceptable to a purchaser looking for an attractive group.

▶ **Copeland & Garrett earthenware model of a dog,** impressed mark 'New Faïence', one leg damaged, c1840, 11¾in (30cm) high. This model of a dog is rare, as is the mark and, although it is damaged, it should have achieved more at auction.
£360–430 / €520–620
$660–780 SWO ⚒

Worcester figure, entitled 'The Irish Girl', impressed mark 'Hadley', dated 1874, 6½in (16.5cm) high. This model was also produced in the white. James Hadley pieces are collected in their own right and this accounts for the high price.
£370–440 / €540–640
$670–800 Bea ⚒

Staffordshire figure of a barber, restored, 19thC, 6¼in (16cm) high. The restoration on this piece has probably had little bearing on its price. Figures depicting trades and musicians are sought after by collectors.
£380–450 / €550–650
$690–820 DA ✍

Meissen figure of a lute player, marked, German, c1900, 8in (20.5cm) high.
£380–450 / €550–660
$690–820 DORO ✍

Meissen figural group of two children, slight restoration, crossed swords mark, German, 19thC, 4¾in (12cm) high. Although this is an appealing figure, the restoration has reduced its value.
£380–450 / €550–650
$690–820 WW ✍

Miller's compares...

Meissen figure of Apollo, by J. J. Kändler, slight damage, crossed swords mark, incised '640', German, late 19thC, 10¾in (27.5cm) high. If unrestored or in original condition this figure could achieve £800–1,000 / €1,150–1,450 / $1,450–1,800.
£380–450 / €550–650
$690–820 DN ✍

A. Meissen figure of a winged putto, slight restoration, crossed swords mark, incised 'R123', German, late 19thC, 7in (18cm) high.
£400–480 / €580–700
$730–870 DN ✍

B. Meissen figure of cupid carrying a shoe, probably by Professor Schwabe, on a gilt and marbled plinth, crossed swords mark, numbered 'L117', '61' and '19', German, late 19thC, 6½in (16.5cm) high.
£900–1,050 / €1,300–1,500
$1,650–1,900 S(O) ✍

The expression on the face of Item A may have deterred potential buyers. As well as being more attractive, Item B has a more appealing base and has possible attribution to a named maker, which accounts for its higher price.

Pair of Worcester figures of Eastern musicians, by James Hadley, signed, printed mark, 1887, 12½in (32cm) high.
£400–480 / €580–700
$730–870 TEN ⚒

Minton Parian figure of Miranda, 1880, 16in (40.5cm) high.
£450–500 / €650–730
$820–910 JAK ⊞

Staffordshire pearlware figural group of Abraham, Isaac and the angel, restored, c1820, 7½in (19cm) high. Religious figures are currently selling well, especially on the American market.
£420–500 / €610–730
$760–910 WW ⚒

Staffordshire figure, by Walton, entitled 'Widow of Zarephath', 1810–20, 11in (28cm) high.
£440–490 / €640–710
$800–890 TYE ⊞

Pair of Staffordshire models of zebras, c1860, 6in (15cm) high.
Zebras are a more unusual subject matter and may carry a premium.
£490–550 / €710–800
$890–1,000 HOW ⊞

◄ **Meissen figure of a young girl,** with gilt decoration, German, 18thC, 5½in (14cm) high.
£500–600 / €730–870
$910–1,100 HYD ⚒

► **Whieldon-style model of a dog,** c1760, 3in (7.5cm) high.
£540–600 / €780–870
$980–1,100 TYE ⊞

◀ **Pair of Staffordshire models of spaniels,** c1850, 6in (15cm) high. It is important to check models that have legs exposed as these are susceptible to damage.
£580–650 / €840–940
$1,050–1,200 HOW ⊞

Pair of Minton majolica models of magpies, after the Meissen originals, impressed marks, c1870, 21in (53.5cm) high. Although these are unusual models, the colouring may not be to everyone's taste.
£580–690 / €840–1,000
$1,050–1,250 SWO ⚒

Copeland parian figure, entitled 'Innocence', c1847, 17in (43cm) high.
£670–750 / €970–1,100
$1,200–1,350 JAK ⊞

Meissen figure of a girl, crossed swords mark of Marcolini, German, c1810, 6¾in (17cm) high. Marcolini-period figures often fetch less than mid-19thC examples as the modelling and painting are not of such good quality.
£650–780 / €940–1,100
$1,200–1,450 JNic ⚒

▶ **Meissen figure of a muse,** by J. C. Jücht, slight damage, crossed swords marks, inscribed 'L66', German, c1790, 10½in (26.5cm) high. The early date of this piece accounts for the high price of this figure. A 19thC example would sell for less.
£700–840 / €1,000–1,200
$1,250–1,500 WW ⚒

Pair of Staffordshire figural groups, c1855, 9in (23cm) high.
£720–800 / €1,000–1,150
$1,300–1,450 HOW ⊞

Flatware

Pair of Cantonese plates, decorated with figures and flowers, late 19thC, 9½in (24cm) diam.
£25–30 / €40–45
$50–55 GTH ⚘

Knight, Elkin & Co plate, entitled 'Hannibal passing the Alps', with transfer-printed decoration, c1840, 8in (20.5cm) diam.
£45–50 / €65–75
$85–95 LGr ⊞

Plate, probably by Leeds Pottery, transfer-printed with Winding Road pattern, slight damage, 1820–30, 9½in (24cm) diam.
£45–50 / €65–75
$85–95 DN ⚘

The look without the price

Charger, hand painted with a river scene, 19thC, 18in (45.5cm) diam.
£50–60
€75–85
$100–115
DA ⚘

This charger is based on late 18th-century Chinese Qianlong period design. If it were an original example it could command between £400–500 / €580–720 / $730–910.

Staffordshire miniature platter, transfer-printed with birds and flowers, c1840, 6in (15cm) wide.
£50–60 / €75–85
$100–115 DAN ⊞

▶ **Yorkshire Pottery plate,** depicting a view of Kirkstall Abbey, c1820, 10in (25.5cm) diam.
£55–65 / €80–95
$105–125
NAW ⊞

Child's plate, depicting a tea party, 1840, 5in (12.5cm) diam. Children's plates are very collectable.
£60–70 / €85–100
$115–135 GN ⊞

Soup plate, printed with Duke of Wellington pattern, 1815–30, 9½in (24cm) diam.
£70–80 / €100–115
$135–155 DN ⚒

◄ **Kirkcaldy Pottery plate,** Scottish, c1900, 9in (23cm) diam. This is a decorative plate and Scottish ceramics are collectable.
£70–80 / €100–115
$135–155 GAU ⊞

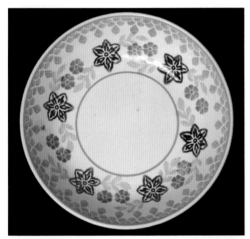

Swansea Pottery plate, depicting Holy Trinity Church, Barnstaple, 1835, 6in (15cm) wide. This plate would be worth more if it depicted a Welsh town such as Swansea.
£95–105 / €140–155
$170–190 WeW ⊞

◄ **Liverpool delft plate,** painted with floral decoration, slight damage, 18thC, 10in (25.5cm) diam. The damage has reduced the value of this plate by 30 per cent.
£100–120 / €145–175
$185–220 BWL ⚒

Delft plate, possibly London or Bristol, painted with flowers, slight damage, c1730, 8¾in (22cm) diam.
£105–120 / €150–175
$200–220 G&G ⊞

► **Pearlware nursery plate,** the border moulded with flowers, printed with a press gang scene, entitled 'The Recruits or Who'll Serve the King', damaged, c1795, 4½in (11.5cm) diam. Pieces depicting moments from history are popular with collectors.
£110–130
€160–190
$200–240 SAS ⚸

Set of four pearlware plates, transfer-printed with fishermen, early 19thC, 9¾in (25cm) diam.
£120–140 / €170–200
$210–250 HOLL ⚸

Plate, by Choisy le Roi, decorated with strawberries, French, c1880, 8in (20.5cm) diam.
£125–140 / €180–200
$220–250 MLL ⊞

Don Pottery plate, decorated with a view of the Obelisk at Catania, Sicily, c1820, 10in (25.5cm) diam.
£135–150 / €195–220
$240–270 GRe ⊞

► **Bristol delft plate,** painted with panels of chinoiserie houses, slight damage, c1770, 9in (23cm) diam.
£140–165
€200–240
$250–300 DN ⚸

Porcelain plate, possibly Swansea, painted with a bird, 18thC, 8in (20.5cm) diam.
£150–180 €220–260
$270–320 PF ✗

Delft charger, painted with Oriental figures, German, Frankfurt, 18thC, 15½in (39.5cm) diam.
£160–190 / €240–280
$290–350 HYD ✗

◀ **Four pottery plates,** transfer-printed with figures in chinoiserie landscapes, 19thC, 10in (25.5cm) diam.
£160–190 / €240–280
$290–350 BWL ✗

Creamware plate, with moulded and painted decoration, slight restoration, c1760, 5¼in (13.5cm) diam. The restoration may have discouraged potential bidders but this is a rare piece which was sought after at auction.
£160–190 / €240–280
$290–350 WW ✗

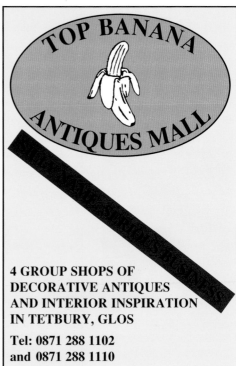

William Mason meat platter, depicting Richmond Bridge in Yorkshire, c1820, 10¼in (26cm) wide.
£175–195 / €250–280
$320–350 GN ⊞

Spode plate, transfer-printed with Death of a Bear from the Indian Sporting Series, c1810, 10in (25.5cm) diam. This is a desirable series and larger meat platters can achieve in excess of £1,000 / €1,450 / $1,800.
£180–200 / €260–290
$320–360 SCO ⊞

Plate, possibly Minton, painted with boats, c1860, 9in (23cm) diam.
£180–200 / €260–290
$320–360 JAK ⊞

Ynysmedw pottery plate, Welsh, c1860, 8in (20.5cm) diam. Welsh pottery pieces are collectable.
£185–210 / €270–300
$340–380 WeW ⊞

◄ **English delft dish,** painted with stylized flowers, restored, 18thC, 13in (33cm) diam. Without the restoration, this plate could have achieved over £400 / €580 / $730.
£195–230
€280–330
$350–410 WW 🔨

▶ **Nursery plate,** decorated with Masonic symbols, c1830, 4in (10cm) diam. Masonic designs add value to a piece as they are sought after by collectors.
£200–230 / €290–330
$360–410 GN ⊞

Child's plate, commemorating the birth of Albert Edward, Prince of Wales, c1841, 7in (18cm) diam. This rare commemorative plate has an interesting subject matter and is therefore collectable.
£200–240 / €290–350
$360–430 WW 🔨

Copeland cabinet plate, painted with a bouquet of roses, with ribbon-moulded rim, printed mark, c1870, 9in (23cm) diam.
£210–250 / €300–360
$380–450 Hal ⊞

Pair of Sèvres-style cabinet plates, painted with battle scenes, interlaced 'L' mark, c1900, 9½in (24cm) diam.
£210–250 / €300–360
$380–450 SWO 🔨

Chinese export soup plate, decorated with arms of Stradling of St Donats, slight damage, 18thC, 8¾in (22.5cm) diam. Despite bearing a previously unrecorded armorial that would have increased the value of this plate, the damage has kept the price down.
£220–260 / €320–380
$400–470 WW 🔨

▶ **Plate,** decorated with grazing rabbits, 1825–30, 7in (18cm) diam.
£220–250
€320–360
$400–450 GRe ⊞

▶ **Derby plate,** c1820, 10in (25.5cm) diam. A named view would add more value to this plate.
£220–250 / €320–360
$400–450 JAK ⊞

Dutch Delft plate, decorated with a peacock, De Claauw factory mark, 18thC, 9in (23cm) diam.
£220–250 / €320–360
$400–450 G&G ⊞

Minton plate, attributed to Joseph Smith, c1852, 9in (23cm) diam.
£220–250 / €320–360
$400–450 JAK ⊞

Staffordshire plate, transfer-printed with an 18thC-poem, c1835, 7in (18cm) diam. Earlier Staffordshire pieces would have been transfer-printed in black and would be more valuable.
£220–250 / €320–360
$400–450 ReN ⊞

Palissy-style plate, by Jose de Cuhna, Portuguese, c1860, 7in (18cm) diam. Palissy-style pieces are more desirable and more valuable if they are modelled with insects and reptiles rather than flowers.
£220–250 / €320–360
$400–450 BRT ⊞

◀ **Pair of porcelain plates,** decorated with mythological scenes, slight damage, Bohemian, late 19thC, 9½in (24cm) diam. These plates are well decorated and offer good value for money.
£250–300
€360–430
$460–550
DORO ⚒

Imari charger, decorated with a Taoist symbol and calligraphy, Japanese, Meiji period, 1868–1911, 18in (45.5cm) diam. The calligraphy on this plate might have helped increase its value.
£250–300 / €360–430
$460–550 NSal ⚘

▶ **Imari charger,** Japanese, Meiji period, 1868–1911, 18in (45.5cm) diam.
£270–320 / €390–460
$490–580 NSal ⚘

◀ **Delft plate,** decorated with flowers, restored, 18thC, 14in (35.5cm) diam. The good restoration to this plate has not detracted significantly from the value.
£260–310 / €380–450
$470–560 WW ⚘

Nursery plate, decorated with sign language instructions, the border moulded with the alphabet, c1840, 7in (18cm) diam.
£270–300 / €390–440
$490–550 GN ⊞

Wemyss plate, decorated with thistles, Scottish, c1905, 5½in (14cm) diam.
£270–300 / €390–440
$490–550 GLB ⊞

◀ **Pair of lustre plates,** painted with views of buildings, early 19thC, 8in (20.5cm) diam.
£300–360
€440–520
$550–660 G(L) ⚘

◀ **Creamware plate,** Italian, Naples, 1800–25, 10¾in (27.5cm) diam.
£310–370
€450–540
$560–670 S(P) ⚹

▶ **Maiolica plate,** slight damage, Italian, Naples, 1775–1800, 9½in (24cm) diam.
£310–370
€450–540
$560–670 S(P) ⚹

◀ **English delft plate,** probably Lambeth, painted with a galleon, damaged, 1740–60, 8¾in (22.5cm) diam. Although this plate is cracked, the illustration of a galleon has made it desirable.
£320–380 €460–550
$580–690 WW ⚹

Porcelain plate, painted by Samuel Alcock with flowers, c1820, 9in (23cm) diam.
£310–350 / €450–510
$560–640 JAK ⊞

Llanelli Pottery plate, painted by Shufflebotham with Wild Rose pattern, Welsh, c1900, 9½in (24cm) diam.
£310–350 / €450–510
$560–640 WeW ⊞

The look without the price

Set of six Longchamps majolica oyster plates, decorated with shells, French, c1890, 9in (23cm) diam.
£330–370 / €450–510
$560–640 MLL ⊞

English majolica pieces are often brighter in colour. A set of six Minton majolica plates could command £800–1,000 / €1,150–1,450 / $1,450–1,800.

Swansea pottery plate, painted by Thomas Pardoe, Welsh, c1800, 8in (20.5cm) diam. Renowned painters add value to porcelain.
£340–380 / €490–550
$620–690 WeW ⊞

▶ Pair of Copeland Spode cabinet plates, painted by H. Perry with exotic birds, printed mark, 1910, 9in (23cm) diam.
£360–380 / €460–550
$580–690 G(B) ✍

Pearlware plate, transfer-printed 'George', c1825, 6in (15cm) diam.
£360–400 / €520–580
$660–730 ReN ⊞

Porcelain plate, slight damage, Chinese, 18thC, 9in (23cm) diam. The unusual colours and design have enabled this plate to achieve a high price despite the damage.
£370–440 / €540–640
$670–800 S(P) ✍

The look without the price

Pair of Meissen cabinet plates, painted with birds, German, c1880, 9in (23cm) diam.
£360–400 / €520–580
$660–730 K&M ⊞

Early Meissen is more desirable than later pieces and if these plates had been 18th-century examples they could have made £600–800 / €870–1,150 / $1,100–1,450.

Wemyss plate, decorated with plums, impressed mark, Scottish, c1895, 8½in (21.5cm) diam.
£360–400 / €520–580
$650–720 RdeR ⊞

Chelsea plate, c1760, 8½in (21.5cm) diam.
£400–450 / €580–650
$730–820 AUC ⊞

Porcelain plate, Chinese, late 18thC, 9¾in (25cm) diam.
£410–490 / €600–720
$750–890 S(P) 🔨

Pair of porcelain plates, Chinese, c1750, 9in (23cm) diam.
£410–490 / €600–720
$750–890 S(P) 🔨

Doccia plate, restored, Italian, c1780, 9¼in (23.5cm) diam. This is a rare piece that is decorated in the Imari palette and is in a Continental silver shape.
£410–490 / €600–720
$750–890 S(P) 🔨

Pair of porcelain plates, slight damage, Chinese, 18thC, 9in (23cm) diam. These plates probably date from 1740 to 1750 and were possibly part of a larger set.
£410–490 / €600–720
$750–890 S(P) 🔨

Set of six Meissen plates, with gilt edges, decorated with
flowers, marked, German, 1750–1800, 9¾in (25cm) diam.
£410–490 / €600–720
$750–890 DORO ⚒

Doccia plate, Italian, c1810, 9¼in (23.5cm)
diam. This is a good, early example
from this factory.
£410–490 / €600–720
$750–890 S(P) ⚒

Wemyss plate, painted with buttercups, Scottish, c1900,
5in (12.5cm) diam.
£450–500 / €650–730
$820–910 RdeR ⊞

Royal Worcester plate, decorated with
swans, c1888, 8¾in (22cm) diam. This plate
is decorated in the manner of the Royal
Worcester painter Charles Baldwyn who is
famous for his designs incorporating swans.
Had this plate been signed it could have sold
for in excess of £1,000 / €1,450 / $1,800.
£500–600 / €730–870
$910–1,100 WW ⚒

▶ **Sèvres plate,**
hand-painted with
fruit and flowers,
French, 18thC, 10¼in
(26cm) diam. This is
a very reasonable
price for
a Sèvres piece.
£540–640
€780–930
$980–1,150 JAd ⚒

Doccia plate, Italian, c1810,
9½in (24cm) diam.
£540–640 / €780–930
$980–1,150 S(P) ⚒

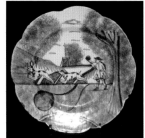

Dutch Delft plate, decorated with a fox and a parakeet, the rim with auspicious emblems, slight damage, c1750, 7¼in (18.5cm) diam. Chinese porcelain was often copied, and this is a tin-glazed pottery Dutch example. Small chips do not affect the price of Delft.
£500–550 / €720–800
$900–1,000 G&G ⊞

Dutch Delft plate, decorated with a hunter chasing a hare, c1750, 9in (23cm) diam. A European hunting scene on a plate is more desirable than a copy of a Chinese design, although polychrome decoration adds more value than does blue and white.
£500–550 / €720–800
$900–1,000 G&G ⊞

Porcelain plate, by Kornilov, the border with floral and gilt decoration, Russian, 1850s–60s, 9in (23cm) diam. Russian porcelain prices are currently buoyant due to interest from the home market.
£550–660 / €800–960
$1,000–1,200 BUK(F) ⚒

Llanelli pottery plate, painted by Aunt Sal, Welsh, c1900, 10in (25.5cm) diam.
£580–650 / €840–940
$1,050–1,200 WeW ⊞

Maiolica plate, restored, Italian, Turin, c1770, 9¾in (25cm) diam. This is an Italian market piece rarely seen in this country. Despite its restoration it sold at auction for a very reasonable price.
£580–690 / €840–1,000
$1,050–1,250 S(P) ⚒

► **Porcelain dish,** decorated with stylized flowers, Chinese, 18thC, 13¾in (35cm) diam. The dark cobalt blue used on this plate indicates that this dish was probably destined for export to the Italian market.
£700–840 / €1,000–1,200
$1,250–1,500 S(P) ⚒

Delft plate, decorated in sponged manganese with a tree in a flower pot, mid-18thC, 9in (23cm) diam. This is probably Bristol delft, and as such is a rare design.
£700–840 / €1,000–1,200
$1,250–1,500 WW 🖎

▶ **Pair of English delft plates,** London or Bristol, decorated with flowers and foliage, 1750–60, 8¼in (22cm) diam. Pairs of small plates are an affordable way to add to a collection, and flower designs are more common and therefore more reasonably priced
£720–800 / €1,000–1,150
$1,300–1,450 KEY ⊞

Sets/pairs

Unless otherwise stated, any description which refers to 'a set' or 'a pair' includes a guide price for the entire set or the pair, even though the illustration may show only a single item.

Porcelain plate, decorated with a vase of flowers, Chinese, 18thC, 15½in (39.5cm) diam.
£740–880 / €1,100–1,300
$1,350–1,600 S(P) 🖎

Four Rörstrand faïence plates, Swedish, 18thC, 8¾in (22cm) diam. As with many European ceramics of this date, the decoration on these plates imitates Chinese export blue and white porcelain.
£700–840 / €1,000–1,200
$1,250–1,500 BUK 🖎

The look without the price

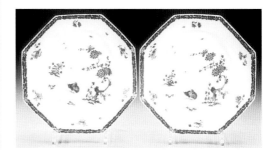

Pair of Bow plates, painted in the Kakiemon palette with Quail pattern, the border with foliage and gilt flowerheads, slight damage, c1760, 8¾in (22cm) diam.
£760–910 / €1,100–1,300
$1,400–1,650 S(O) 🖎

These plates are 18th-century copies. A pair of genuine Japanese Kakiemon plates would be worth at least ten times this price.

Savona maiolica plate, slight damage, Italian, 18thC, 7in (18cm) diam. The design on this plate is possibly taken from an engraving.
£780–930 / €1,150–1,350
$1,450–1,700 S(P) ⚹

▶ **Pilkington's Royal Lancastrian earthenware charger,** decorated by Richard Joyce with a galleon, impressed mark, 'JR' monogram within a square, date code for 1907, 10¼in (26cm) diam. This plate could have achieved a higher price if it had brighter glazing and been sold in the UK, rather than the US.
£790–940 / €1,150–1,350
$1,450–1,700 S(NY) ⚹

Minton meat platter, decorated with Windsor Castle pattern, from the English Scenery series, 1825–35, 21¼in (54cm) wide. The subject matter on this plate would appeal to American buyers.
£800–890 / €1,150–1,300
$1,450–1,600 GRe ⊞

Nantgarw porcelain plate, painted with flowers within a border moulded with foliate scrolls and painted with panels of flowers, fruit and birds, slight damage, impressed mark, Welsh, 1814–23, 8½in (21.5cm) diam. Nantgarw porcelain is rare. In perfect condition this plate could have made more than double this price.
£780–930 / €1,150–1,350
$1,450–1,700 S(O) ⚹

Maiolica plate, slight wear, Italian, Milan, 18thC, 9¼in (23.5cm) diam. This plate was sold in France, where there is more of a demand for Continental maiolica. If it had been sold in the UK it may not have fetched such a high price.
£820–980 / €1,200–1,400
$1,500–1,800 S(P) ⚹

Pair of Venice porcelain plates, decorated with flowers, slight wear, Italian, 1770–80, 9¼in (23.5cm) diam. Venice porcelain was not made for export and is rarely seen in the UK.
£820–980 / €1,200–1,400
$1,500–1,800 S(P) 🔨

Savona maiolica plate, decorated with two people in a landscape, blue mark, Italian, 18thC, 8¾in (22cm) diam.
The design on this plate was probably copied from an engraving.
£820–980 / €1,200–1,400
$1,500–1,800 S(P) 🔨

Four porcelain cups and saucers, decorated with peonies, slight damage, Chinese, 18thC, saucers 5¼in (13.5cm) diam.
£820–980 / €1,200–1,400
$1,500–1,800 S(P) 🔨

Worcester plate, painted in the Kakiemon palette with Sir Joshua Reynolds pattern, slight damage, c1770, 8¾in (22cm) diam.
£860–1,000 / €1,250–1,500
$1,550–1,850 S(O) 🔨

▶ **Pair of Lodi maiolica saucers,** Italian, restored, c1750, 6¼in (16cm) diam.
£910–1,050
€1,300–1,550
$1,600–1,900
S(P) 🔨

Jardinières

◀ **Bretby copperette jardinière,** slight damage, c1900, 7in (18cm) high.
£85–95
€125–140
$155–175 HUN ⊞

Doulton Lambeth jardinière, by Beatrice M. Durtnall, Emily Randell and Catherine Francis, decorated with foliage, 1891–1902, 11in (28cm) high. This piece was decorated by three lesser-known Doulton painters. Examples decorated by well-known designers attract higher prices.
£175–195 / €250–280
$310–350 CANI ⊞

◀ **Orchies majolica jardinière,** French, c1890, 11in (28cm) diam. Continental majolica is more affordable than examples by English factories such as Minton or George Jones.
£260–290 / €380–420
$470–530 MLL ⊞

▶ **Wemyss jardinière,** decorated with violets, Scottish, c1880, 3½in (9cm) diam.
£400–450
€580–650
$730–820 SDD ⊞

Wemyss jardinière, painted with cherries, slight damage, impressed marks, painted mark for T. Goode & Co, Scottish, late 19thC, 7in (18cm) high. Thomas Goode & Co, London, was one of the main retailers of Wemyss and their mark is often found on Wemyss ware.
£380–450 / €550–650
$690–820 DN ⚹

◀ **Minton majolica jardinière,** No. 3406, tube-lined with three peacocks, impressed mark, c1900, 27in (68.5cm) high. This type of ware with the Minton mark is known as 'Secessionist ware' and was influenced by the Viennese school of design of the same name.
£400–480 / €580–700
$730–870 TEN ⚹

Minton majolica jardinière, modelled with Vitruvian scroll and Greek key bands, with ribbon and laurel wreath handles, impressed mark for 1881, 14¼in (36cm) diam. Neo-classical majolica designs have become less popular compared to naturalistic designs by the best English makers.
£420–500 / €610–730
$760–910 DN(BR) ⚹

► **Wemyss jardinière,** decorated with roses, impressed mark, Scottish, 1880–1900, 8in (20.5cm) high.
£540–600 / €780–870
$980–1,100 RdeR ⊞

► **Coalport jardinière and stand,** decorated with Derby-style Imari panels and gilt dolphin handles, c1800, 6in (15cm) high. Early Coalport is desirable.
£480–570
€700–830
$870–1,050
SWO ⚹

Sèvres jardinière, decorated in the manner of Watteau with figures in a garden, the reverse with a panel of flowers, with a gilt-bronze beaded rim and lion-mask ring handles, on a gilt-bronze base, French, late 19thC, 11¼in (28.5cm) high.
£620–740 / €900–1,050
$1,150–1,350 NSal ⚹

► **Doulton Lambeth jardinière,** designed by John Broad, c1885, 6in (15cm) high. John Broad was a famous Doulton designer who specialized in cameo-effect medallions.
£810–900 / €1,150–1,300
$1,450–1,650 CANI ⊞

Jars & Canisters

◄ **Dutch Delft drug jar,** with a moulded spout and handle, inscribed 'S Fenicule', with a peacock-mask head and floral decoration, on a socle base, spout reduced, late 17thC, 8¾in (22cm) high. If this item had been an English delft example, it would have sold for a much higher price.
£190–220 / €280–320
$350–400 TRM(E) ⚒

Auction or dealer?

All the pictures in our price guides originate from auction houses ⚒ and dealers ⊞. When buying at auction, prices can be lower than those of a dealer, but a buyer's premium and VAT will be added to the hammer price. Equally, when selling at auction, commission, tax and photography charges must be taken into account. Dealers will often restore pieces before putting them back on the market. Both dealers and auctioneers can provide professional advice, so it is worth researching both sources before buying or selling your antiques.

Delft drug jar, inscribed 'U. Alb. Camp', early 18thC, 7½in (19cm) high. This is a common form of drug jar; it has a lot of damage, hence the low price.
£280–330 / €410–480
$510–600 HYD ⚒

Two porcelain tea canisters and covers, one by Volkstedt and painted with buildings in parkland, puce 'R' mark, slight wear, the other a Thuringian canister painted with birds on branches and flower sprigs, the cover with a rose finial, slight damage, German, 1770–90, larger 5¼in (13.5cm) high.
£840–1,000 / €1,200–1,450
$1,550–1,800 S(O) ⚒

Worcester tea canister, decorated with a wild flower spray, c1775, 5½in (14cm) high.
£720–800 / €1,000–1,150
$1,300–1,450 JUP ⊞

Jugs & Ewers

Pottery jug, French, c1890, 5in (12.5cm) high.
£40–45 / €60–65
$75–80 MLL ⊞

Savoie pottery jug, French, c1880, 6in (15cm) high.
£60–70 / €85–100
$110–125 MLL ⊞

Savoie pottery jug, French,
c1880, 7in (18cm) high.
£60–70 / €85–100
$110–125 MLL ⊞

Swansea Cambrian porcelain jug,
transfer-printed with Swiss Villa pattern, handle
missing, Welsh, 19thC, 12½in (32cm) high.
£80–90 / €115–130
$145–165 PF ⚒

**Moustier pottery jug and
cover,** French, c1880,
8in (20.5cm) high.
£90–100 / €130–145
$165–180 MLL ⊞

◄ **Gaming jug,** possibly Swansea, with
relief-moulded decoration, c1840,
7in (18cm) high. The Swansea attribution to
this jug has increased its value.
£90–100 / €130–145
$165–180 WeW ⊞

► **Stoneware jug,** relief-moulded with
Garibaldi mounted on a horse, restored,
Italian, c1864, 12in (30.5cm) high.
£95–110 / €140–160
$175–200 DN ⚒

Wedgwood black basalt cream jug, moulded with classical scenes, c1870, 5in (12.5cm) high.
£105–120 / €150–170
$190–210 SAT ⊞

Turner stoneware jug, moulded with grapevine sprigging above classical figures, the neck with a silver-plated rim, impressed mark, 1790–1810, 7in (18cm) high. Turner of Lane End, Staffordshire, produced fine white stonewares that are light in weight compared to those by other makers of the period.
£180–210 / €260–300
$330–380 DN ⚒

▶ **Two Staffordshire majolica guggle jugs,** c1870, 8in (20.5cm) high.
£180–200 / €260–290
$330–370 each BRT ⊞

▶ **Spode porcelain Hydra jug,** painted and gilt with flower sprays, slight damage, iron-red mark, c1821, 8¼in (21cm) high. Hydra refers to the design, which has an octagonal shape and a serpent handle.
£130–155
€185–220
$240–280 DN ⚒

Swansea pottery jug, Welsh, c1830, 6in (15cm) high.
£140–160 / €200–230
$250–290 WeW ⊞

Brannam Pottery jug, by James Dewdney, with incised fish decoration, the spout modelled as a fish head, incised signature and marks, slight damage, c1890, 14½in (37cm) high. This jug would have achieved more at auction had there been two keen collectors of Devon pottery bidding for it.
£220–260 / €320–380
$400–470 WW ⚹

◄ **Stoneware Bellarmine jug,** with an impressed mask on the neck and a lion rampant on the body, German, c1680, 8½in (21.5cm) high. Bellarmine is the bearded face or mask, generally found on the neck of a bottle, opposite the handle and below the bottom rim of the lip. The bottles are almost always salt-glazed and vary in height from about 4–22in (10–56cm); they were chiefly used in taverns as decanters between the cask and the table, although it is possible that they were also used as domestic storage jugs for acids, vinegar, oil and even mercury. The smaller examples were probably drinking mugs. Contemporary copies of these German Bellarmines were made in Fulham, London and are much rarer, fetching over £1,000 / €1,450 / $1,800.
£300–360 / €440–520
$550–660 SWO ⚹

Cream jug, transfer-printed with a pattern depicting fish curing in Alaska, c1820, 6in (15cm) wide.
£310–350 / €450–510
$560–640 GN ⊞

Worcester porcelain sparrow-beak jug and cover, moulded in low-relief with Chrysanthemum pattern, the cover with a flower finial, c1765, 5½in (14cm) high. Relief-moulded plain white jugs such as this example are worth less than those decorated in underglaze blue.
£320–380 / €460–550
$580–690 DN ⚹

► **Majolica ewer,** with an applied cherub playing panpipes above a satyr's mask, the body relief-moulded with scrolls of flowers and foliage, a recumbent griffin forming the base, the handle modelled in the form of a nymph, damaged, stamped marks, inscribed 'EO', 19thC, 21in (53.5cm) high. This is probably a German copy of a Minton ewer. However, it is badly damaged, which accounts for its low price.
£360–430 / €520–620
$660–780 WILK ⚹

Pair of maiolica ewers, decorated with classical scenes, restored, Italian, late 19thC, 26in (66cm) high. In perfect condition these ewers could fetch £1,200–1,600 / €1,700–2,300 / $2,150–2,900.
£430–510 / €620–740
$760–910 GH ⚹

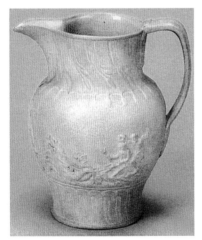

Commemorative caneware jug, the moulded body depicting Admiral Nelson and Neptune in a shell boat drawn by seahorses, the reverse with Britannia and a figure emblematic of victory, the front with a rear view of HMS *Victory*, slight damage, 1805–10, 7in (18cm) high. Nelson commemoratives were made in large numbers but are now rare, hence their sought-after status and value.
£500–600 / €720–870
$900–1,050 DN ⚹

Miller's compares...

A. Squire Toby jug, with hole for pipe, c1875, 10in (25.5cm) high.
£580–650 / €840–940
$1,050–1,200 JBL ⊞

B. Creamware Toby jug, decorated with translucent glazes, c1800, 10in (25.5cm) high.
£810–900
€1,150–1,300
$1,450–1,650 JBL ⊞

Item A is of a later date than Item B, but it has an unusual pattern on the waistcoat and trousers, making it desirable to collectors. However, Item B is in the Enoch Wood style and based on an early prototype. This has made it more desirable than Item A and therefore more valuable.

Bow sauce boat, painted in the Kakiemon palette, with a diaper border, slight damage, c1747, 8¼in (21cm) wide. As this is a rare piece the damage to the feet has not severely affected the price.
£600–720 / €870–1,050
$1,100–1,300 SWO ⚹

Worcester cream boat, transfer-printed with Obelisk Fisherman pattern, disguised numeral mark, c1780, 4⅓in (11cm) wide. A similar cream boat with a more common pattern would be worth half this price.
**£700–840 / €1,000–1,200
$1,250–1,550** WW 🔨

Derby sauce boat, painted with Oriental landscape scenes to each side and the interior base, handle missing, slight damage, large incised 'D' mark, Andrew Planche period, c1752, 3¾in (9.5cm) wide. This is an early Derby sauce boat with a rare factory mark. Despite the missing handle and the damage, it is still a valuable item.
**£840–1,000 / €1,200–1,450
$1,550–1,800** S(O) 🔨

▶ **Landlord Toby jug and cover,** originally the largest of a set of three, c1860, 13in (33cm) high. This is a very good example of a Landlord Toby jug.
**£850–950 / €1,250–1,400
$1,550–1,750** JBL ⊞

◀ **Creamware sauce boat,** modelled as a duck, decorated with underglaze colours, c1785, 7in (18cm) wide. The novelty form and use of underglaze colours has increased the value of this piece.
**£670–750 / €970–1,100
$1,200–1,350** AUC ⊞

Zsolnay pottery ewer, with reticulated sides, impressed mark, Hungarian, late 19thC, 13¾in (35cm) high. Although this is a rare piece of Zsolnay pottery it is more affordable than the Art Nouveau lustre ceramics produced by this factory, which sell in excess of £1,000 / €1,450 / $1,800.
**£840–1,000 / €1,200–1,450
$1,550–1,800** S(O) 🔨

Plaques

Porcelain plaque, depicting the head of a lady in period dress, German, c1880, 4in (10cm) diam, framed. Small German and French plaques such as this are common and affordable.
**£75–85 / €110–125
$135–155 DuM** ♟

Lustre wall plaque, inscribed 'Prepare to meet thy God', 19thC, 9in (23cm) wide. Religious themes are not very popular with collectors.
**£100–120 / €145–175
$180–220 WW** ♟

Porcelain plaque, painted with a basket of flowers within a raised gilt border and gilt dot decoration, 19thC, 9in (23cm) wide. The low price of this item suggests that it has been cut from a larger piece.
**£120–140 / €175–200
$220–250 SJH** ♟

◄ **Royal Copenhagen porcelain plaque,** painted with a vignette of the royal hunting lodge, Ermitage, within a gilt scroll-moulded frame, Danish, early 19thC, 4¾ x 5½in (12 x 14cm). The Danish market is stronger than the UK market for early Copenhagen pieces.
**£180–210 / €260–300
$330–380 DN(BR)** ♟

A Royal Doulton wall plaque, depicting a young fisherwife with a creel, printed mark, 14in (35.5cm) high. This plaque would have fetched more had it been signed by a Doulton Burslem artist
**£190–220 / €270–320
$350–400 PFK** ♟

Two Vienna-style porcelain plaques, depicting couples, signed 'Wildner', beehive marks, c1880, with gilt frames, 10 x 8in (25.5 x 20.5cm).
**£280–330 / €410–480
$510–600 TEN** ♟

► **Berlin porcelain plaque,** depicting a water nymph, impressed 'KPM' and sceptre mark, 19thC, 8¾ x 5¾in (22 x 14.5cm), in a giltwood frame.
**£430–510 / €620–740
$780–930 SK(B)** ♟

A Paris porcelain plaque, inscribed 'Bataille De Rocroy, 16 Mai 1643', signed 'Leber Von Schnetz', French, 19thC, 18in (45.5cm) diam. The value of plaques depend on the quality of the painting, the choice of scene and the colours used. This example is realistically priced.
£480–570 / €700–830
$880–1,050 SWO

Bohemian porcelain plaque, painted with The Death of the Lion King, after the fable by La Fontaine, in a yellow metal frame, 1850–1900, 4¾ x 6¼in (12 x 16cm). Scenes depicting characters from literature are desirable and sought after.
£580–690 / €850–1,000
$1,100–1,300 DORO

To find out more about antique ceramics see the full range of Miller's books at
www.millers.uk.com

▶ **Porcelain plaque,** impressed marks, German, late 19thC, 10 x 8½in (25.5 x21.5cm).
£960–1,150 / €1,400–1,650
$1,750–2,100 S(O)

The look without the price

Wedgwood black basalt plaque, depicting Josiah Wedgwood, c1891, 5in (12.5cm) high.
£540–600 / €780–870
$980–1,100 TYE

This plaque would appeal to collectors of Wedgwood because it depicts the factory's founder, and this has increased its value. Generally speaking, later Wedgwood plaques are worth much less than original late 18th-century examples.

Services

◄ **Sèvres part coffee service,** comprising 22 pieces, fleur-de-lys mark, coffee pot cover missing, 1825–50, coffee pot 10in (25.5cm) high.
£170–200 / €240–290
$310–370 NOA ⚒

Copeland Spode dessert service, with chinoiserie decoration, heightened with gold, 19thC.
£300–360 / €430–520
$550–660 CHTR ⚒

Ironstone dessert service, by Moore & Co, comprising 25 pieces, decorated with Poonah pattern, 1870–90.
£360–430 / €520–620
$660–780 HYD ⚒

► **Victorian porcelain dessert service,** comprising 15 pieces, impressed 'WW' mark, stand 7in (18cm) high.
£380–450
€550–650
$690–820
DN(BR) ⚒

◄ **Crown Derby tea and coffee service,** comprising 69 pieces, decorated with an Imari pattern, 19thC. Later Royal Crown Derby Imari wares are more desirable in the form of vases and miniature wares.
£400–480
€580–690
$730–870 WilP ⚒

Wedgwood dessert service, comprising 13 pieces, decorated with Sunflower patter, 1880, plates 8in (20.5cm) diam. This style of Wedgwood is also known as Greenware.
£490–550 / €710–800
$890–1,000 SAT ⊞

Meissen dinner service, comprising 12 plates and six soup dishes, German, Marolini period, 1774–1815. This is a very reasonable price for a Meissen service.
£590–700 / €860–1,000
$1,100–1,300 BUK ⚒

Porcelain tea service, comprising 32 pieces, painted with roses, slight damage, early 19thC.
£720–860 / €1,050–1,250
$1,300–1,550 RTo ⚒

Ridgway dessert service, comprising 26 pieces, comport damaged, c1835, 11½in (29cm) high. Ridgway frequently used a grey ground colour such as that shown here, but it is less popular than more colourful wares.
£520–620 / €750–900
$950–1,100 SWO ⚒

Doulton dessert service, comprising 18 pieces, printed marks, c1900. Doulton Burslem pieces achieve more if they are signed by the painter.
£640–760 / €920–1,100
$1,150–1,350 Bea ⚒

Find out more in

Miller's Antiques Checklist: Porcelain, Miller's Publications, 2001

Porcelain dessert service, comprising 19 pieces, painted by Edith Warner, marked, 1850–90. Edith Warner was an independent decorator who bought blank porcelain to paint with botanical studies.
£840–1,000 / €1,200–1,450
$1,550–1,800 S(O) ⚒

Stands

Jardinière stand, c1905,
25in (63.5cm) high.
£310–350 / €450–500
$560–640 DAD ⊞

J. & R. Riley cheese stand, decorated
with the arms of the Coventry Drapers,
1828, 11¾in (30cm) diam. Ceramic items
bearing arms related to livery companies are
sought after by collectors.
£660–740 / €960–1,000
$1,200–1,350 GN ⊞

Sèvres-style porcelain and brass writing stand, the two
containers in the form of globes, signed 'G. R. Avelot', French,
19thC, 13½in (34.5cm) wide.
£480–580 / €700–840
$870–1,050 BUK(F) ➴

Derby inkstand, painted mark, c1820, 11in (28cm) wide.
£610–680 / €880–980
$1,100–1,250 TYE ⊞

The look without the price

**Joseph
Holdcroft
majolica
cheese stand
and cover,**
moulded with
fish, c1870,
9½in (24cm) high.
£800–960
€1,200–1,400
$1,450–1,750
SWO ➴

Joseph Holdcroft produced good-quality majolica
wares which are more affordable than equivalent
pieces by Minton and George Jones. A George
Jones cheese dish of this size might achieve nearer
£2,500 / €3,600 / $4,550.

Tea & Coffee Pots

A Measham ware teapot, c1890,
7½in (19cm) high.
£105–120 / €150–170
$190–220 JBL ⊞

Carlton Ware Foxglove teapot, 1930s,
5in (12.5cm) wide.
£175–195 / €250–280
$310–350 BEV ⊞

Identifying original Measham ware

Measham was founded in the mid-19th century by William Mason who began by producing teapots made from the local straw-coloured clay that were then covered with a dark brown 'treacle' glaze. They were decorated with moulded, hand-coloured motifs including flowers and exotic birds and often with a plaque which was crudely stamped with a message such as 'Remember Me', 'A Present to a Friend' and 'God Bless Our Home'.

Original Measham pottery is now quite rare but it is possible to buy modern reproductions which are worth only a fraction of the cost of the real thing. On original pieces the motto is pressed into the surface of the clay and filled in with blue, or sometimes black, colouring. With reproductions the lettering is generally painted in black on the surface of the plaque although some items with pressed lettering have recently been produced. Another indication is that the clay is white rather than the genuine light straw colour. The decorative colours on original Measham are subtle and blend well, and the brown glaze is sometimes quite uneven but reproduction Measham has much more garish colours and the brown background is more consistent. By using these tests you can be 99 per cent sure whether or not you are buying genuine Measham. If in any doubt make sure you buy from a reputable dealer who can advise you.

Lowestoft teapot, painted with a Redgrave-style Cannonball pattern, damaged, c1780, 6¾in (17cm) high. This teapot would have achieved a much higher price had it been in perfect condition.
£220–260 / €310–370
$400–470 DN ⚒

Wedgwood jasper ware bachelor's teapot, slight damage, impressed mark, c1820, 9½in (24cm) high. Three-colour jasper wares from the early 19thC are more valuable than standard two-colour items.
£230–270 / €330–390
$420–490 BWL ⚒

Teapot, decorated with a peony and a fruiting vine, Chinese, Qianlong period, 1736–96, 6¾in (17cm) wide.
£320–380 / €460–550
$580–690 WW ⚒

Pearlware teapot, probably by Thomas Harley, c1805, 6in (15cm) high.
£320–360 / €460–520
$580–660 TYE ⊞

Creamware coffee pot, probably Swansea, printed with 'The Tea Party', the reverse with a shepherd, slight damage, c1790, 9¾in (25cm) high.
£340–400 / €490–580
$620–720 WW ⚒

Worcester teapot, decorated with Sir Joshua Reynolds pattern, spout restored, c1765, 6¼in (16cm) high. If it were in perfect condition this teapot could achieve twice this amount.
£360–430 / €520–620
$650–780 SWO ⚒

Creamware teapot, painted with an armorial shield, restored, 1770–80, 9½in (24cm) high. Armorial decoration adds interest and value despite the restoration.
£360–430 / €520–620
$650–780 WW

Doccia coffee pot, painted with floral sprays, 1770–80, 9in (23cm) high.
£420–500 / €610–720
$760–910 WW ⚒

Measham ware teapot and stand,
c1870, 9in (23cm) high.
£450–500 / €650–720
$820–910 JBL ⊞

Porcelain teapot, slight restoration, Chinese, 18thC,
5in (12.5cm) high.
£460–550 / €660–790
$840–1,000 S(P) ↗

Measham ware bachelor's teapot, inscribed
'W. Thompson, Hyde Park', c1870, 4in (10cm) high.
£540–600 / €780–870
$980–1,100 JBL ⊞

Creamware teapot, printed with Harlequin,
Columbine and Pierrot, c1765, 7¼in (18.5cm) high.
£500–600 / €720–870
$910–1,100 WW ↗

Staffordshire salt-glazed stoneware teapot,
painted with figures, restored, c1760, 7¼in (18.5cm)
high. It is more unusual to find Staffordshire pieces
decorated with figures, a feature that has enabled this
teapot to keep its value despite the restoration.
£880–1,050 / €1,250–1,500
$1,600–1,900 WW ↗

Staffordshire salt-glazed stoneware teapot,
damaged and restored, c1770, 4½in (11.5cm) high.
£630–700 / €900–1,000
$1,150–1,300 G&G ⊞

Tiles

Tile, decorated with stylized flowerheads, c1900, 6in (15cm) square.
£30–35 / €45–50
$55–65 DAD ⊞

Tile, decorated in the style of Louis F. Day, c1890, 8in (20.5cm) square.
£50–55 / €65–75
$85–100 SaH ⊞

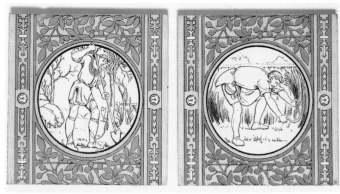

Sherwin & Cotton tile,
by George Cartlidge, depicting William Gladstone, slight damage, impressed factory marks, dated 1898, 9in (23cm) high. This tile would appeal to collectors of political ephemera as well as collectors of tiles.
£80–95 / €120–140
$145–170 WW ⚒

Two Minton tiles, probably by John Moyr Smith, decorated with agricultural scenes, c1890, 9in (23cm) square.
£90–100 / €130–145
$165–180 each OLA ⊞

► **Victorian majolica tile,**
by James Gamble, 12 x 11in (30.5 x 28cm).
£95–110 / €135–160
$170–200 NSal ⚒

Pair of Wedgwood earthenware tiles,
depicting Helena and Mustard from Shakespeare's *A Midsummer Night's Dream*, moulded marks, 1878–85, 8in (20.5cm) square.
£190–220 / €270–310
$350–400 DN ⚒

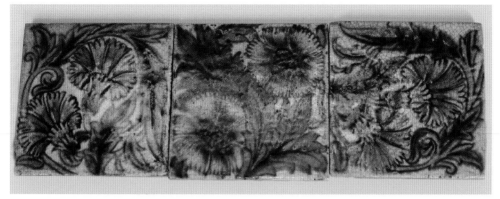

Three William De Morgan tiles, impressed marks, 1882–88, each 6¼in (16cm) square.
£240–280 / €350–410
$440–510 SWO 🔨

◄ **Minton butcher's tile,** late 19thC, 12in (30.5cm) square.
£270–300 / €390–430
$490–540 SMI ⊞

Six Minton tiles, by John Moyr Smith, c1890, 6in (15cm) square.
£540–600 / €780–870
$980–1,100 OLA ⊞

Two William De Morgan tiles, painted with flowers and leaves, impressed marks, c1890, 5¼in (13.5cm) square.
£520–620 / €750–900
$950–1,100 G(L) 🔨

▶ **Pair of tile pictures,** depicting ploughing scenes, Dutch, 19thC, 25 x 30in (63.5 x 76cm).
£650–780 / €940–1,100
$1,200–1,400 NSal 🔨

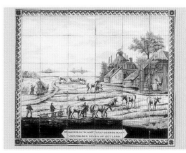

Vases

Pilkington's Royal Lancastrian vase,
marked, early 20thC, 5½in (14cm) high.
£75–90 / €110–130
$135–160 G(B) ⚒

Dresden porcelain vase and cover,
crossed swords mark, restored, German,
19thC, 9in (23cm) high. The extensive
restoration has reduced the value of this vase.
£140–165 / €200–240
$250–300 DN(BR) ⚒

Pouch vase, printed with a
chinoiserie pattern, 1800–15,
5½in (14cm) high.
£80–95 / €115–135
$145–170 DN ⚒

Bottle vase, Chinese, 18thC,
6in (15cm) high.
£95–110 / €135–160
$170–200 GIL ⚒

Find out more in

*Miller's Collecting Chinese & Japanese Antiques
Buyer's Guide*, Miller's Publications, 2004

Pair of Satsuma vases, decorated with figures, c1900,
9½in (24cm) high.
£160–190 / €230–270
$290–340 SWO ⚒

Pair of Paris porcelain vases,
19thC, 13in (33cm) high.
£185–220 / €270–320
$340–400 JAA 🔨

Linthorpe vase, by Henry
Tooth and Christopher Dresser,
restored, c1880, 8in (20.5cm)
high. The Victoria & Albert
Museum, London, recently held
an exhibition of items designed
by Christopher Dresser and as a
result there is currently a lot of
interest in his work. However,
restored items are harder to sell.
£260–290 / €280–420
$470–530 HUN ⊞

▶ Imari vase, late 19thC,
18¼in (46.5cm) high. A pair of
vases in this style could fetch
£1,200 / €1,750 / $2,200.
£320–380 / €460–550
$580–690 SWO 🔨

▶ Coalport vase, with floral
decoration, c1820,
6in (15cm) high.
£200–230 / €290–330
$360–420 TYE ⊞

Royal Worcester ewer, the
handle in the form of a dragon,
slight damage, printed marks,
1884, 11in (28cm) high.
£240–280 / €340–400
$440–510 DN 🔨

The look without the price

Samson Chinese-export-style
vase, late 19thC, 23in (58.5cm) high.
£350–410 / €510–590
$630–750 NOA 🔨

This vase is a reproduction of
18th-century Chinese export
style. An original piece would
fetch over £10,000 /
€14,500 / $18,200.

The look without the price

Pair of Vienna-style vases and covers, one inscribed 'Jupiter, Ariadne', the other 'Opsernole and Venus', finials restored, beehive mark, c1900, 8in (20.5cm) high.
£320–380 / €460–550
$580–690 WL ⚘

Although these vases are not authentic, they are still very attractive and would make good display pieces. If they had actually been made at the Vienna porcelain factory in the 19th century, the price would be nearer £2,500 / €3,650 / $4,550.

Porcelain vase, applied with swags and two handles, possibly Italian, Naples, late 18thC, 4in (10cm) high.
£480–570 / €690–820
$870–1,050 S ⚘

Pair of Staffordshire vases, applied with deer, c1830, 12in (30.5cm) high.
£440–520 / €640–750
$800–950 JAA ⚘

◄ **Imari porcelain vase,** decorated with cranes and flowers, Japanese, Meiji period, 1868–1911, 30¾in (78cm) high, on a hardwood stand.
£450–540 / €650–780
$820–980 RTo ⚘

► **Arita vase,** decorated in relief with a dragon, Japanese, late 19thC, 37in (94cm) high, on a hardwood stand. Japanese items decorated with dragons are more desirable, and this, together with its large size, accounts for the value of this vase.
£520–620 / €750–900
$950–1,100 DN(BR) ⚘

Minton vase, pattern No. 780, c1815, 5in (12.5cm) high. This is a rare Minton shape and it is therefore desirable to collectors.
£480–540 / €690–780 $870–980 JOR ⊞

◀ **Arita porcelain vase,** Japanese, 18thC, 15in (38cm) high.
£480–570 €690–820 $870–1,050
HOLL ⚘

▶ **Mason's Ironstone vase and cover,** moulded with dragons, c1825, 24¾in (63cm) high. Mason's Ironstone pieces would normally be expected to achieve a higher price than this.
£550–660 €800–950 $1,000–1,200
SWO ⚘

The look without the price

Pair of ormolu-mounted Sèvres-style vases, painted with reserves of figures, covers missing, late 19thC, 14½in (37cm) high.
£580–690 / €840–1,000 $1,050–1,250 DN(BR) ⚘

With covers, these vases could have fetched £1,200 / €1,750 / $2,200, and although not direct copies of 18th-century Sèvres pieces, they are very attractive. Original 18th-century Sèvres vases could command a five-figure sum.

Wemyss vase, painted with an Iris, Scottish, c1880, 6½in (16.5cm) high.
£580–650 / €840–940 $1,050–1,200 SDD ⊞

Wemyss vase, painted with dragonflies, impressed marks, Scottish, 1915–30, 5½in (14cm) high.
£580–650 / €840–940 $1,050–1,200 RdeR ⊞

◀ **Royal Crown Derby two-handled vase,** by C. Gresley, painted with a riverside view and a floral bouquet, signed, printed marks, c1929, 4¼in (11cm) high.
£600–720 / €870–1,050 $1,100–1,300 S(O) ⚘

◄ **Minton majolica vase,** modelled by Joseph Holdcroft, in the form of an elephant, c1870, 8in (20.5cm) high.
£690–780 / €1,000–1,150
$1,250–1,400 BRT ⊞

The look without the price

Wemyss Elgin vase, Scottish, c1880, 17½in (44.5cm) high.
£690–780 / €1,000–1,150
$1,250–1,400 SDD ⊞

Red-figure vase, decorated with Greek figures and bands, restored, Italian, 19thC, 18¼in (46.5cm) high.
£800–960 / €1,200–1,400
$1,450–1,750 WW ⚒

This is a replica of a Greek Attic vase, probably c4th century BC. Although unlikely to be in perfect condition, a genuine piece would command a five-figure sum.

Meissen vase, encrusted with flowers, crossed swords mark, German, late 19thC, 17in (43cm) high. The Meissen encrusted flower decoration was often copied by other German as well as English manufacturers in the 19th century. This style of decoration is prone to damage.
£850–1,000 / €1,250–1,450
$1,550–1,800 E ⚒

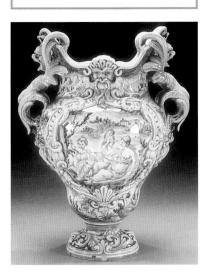

Royal Worcester vase, painted with carnations, c1904, 11in (28cm) high.
£810–900 / €1,150–1,300
$1,500–1,650 JUP ⊞

► **Cantagalli maiolica vase,** with painted and moulded decoration, slight damage, c1900, 21in (53.5cm) high. The Cantagalli firm specialized in good-quality copies of early Italian maiolica and Hispano-Moresque lustre wares.
£960–1,150 / €1,400–1,650
$1,750–2,100 S(O) ⚒

Miscellaneous

Ladle, decorated with Willow pattern, 1830–40, 7in (18cm) long.
£75–85 / €110–125
$140–155 GRe ⊞

Davenport asparagus server, decorated with Bridgeless Willow pattern, c1810, 3in (7.5cm) wide.
£80–90 / €115–130
$145–165 GRe ⊞

Spongeware chamber pot, Scottish, c1840, 4in (10cm) high.
£110–125 / €160–180
$200–230 GAU ⊞

Oil bottle, with transfer-printed decoration, c1840, 5in (12.5cm) high.
£145–165 / €210–240
$260–300 GN ⊞

Pepper pot, transfer-printed with Curling Palm pattern with Royal State Barge, 1805–15, 4½in (11.5cm) high. Although this pot is by an unknown maker, it is decorated with a rare pattern, making it attractive to collectors.
£220–260 / €320–380
$400–470 DN ⚲

Pratt-style pearlware tea caddy, moulded with figures, c1790, 5in (12.5cm) high. The missing cover has reduced the value of this tea caddy.
£160–190 / €230–270
$290–350 Hal ⚲

Royal Worcester silver-mounted scent bottle, Birmingham 1911, 1½in (4cm) high.
£220–260 / €320–380
$400–470 BWL ⚲

Crown Staffordshire inkwell,
decorated with a satyr riding a goat, c1910,
3½in (9cm) high.
£260–290 / €380–420
$470–530 DIA ⊞

Wemyss preserve pot,
painted with oranges,
impressed mark, Scottish,
c1900, 5½in (14cm) high.
£270–300 / €390–440
$490–550 RdeR ⊞

Wemyss preserve pot,
painted with branches of
fruiting oranges, Scottish,
c1910, 5in (12.5cm) high.
£290–330 / €420–480
$530–600 GLB ⊞

Carpet boule, transfer-printed with
flowers, c1830, 4in (10cm) diam.
£290–330 / €420–480
$530–600 GN ⊞

Meissen mirror, decorated
with putti and garlands,
crossed swords mark, 19thC,
13in (33cm) high.
£320–380 / €460–550
$580–690 GAK 🔨

Satsuma *koro* and cover,
with a *shishi* knop, Japanese,
19thC, 22½in (57cm) high.
£320–380 / €460–550
$580–690 GIL 🔨

Famille rose tea caddy,
painted with floral sprays,
Chinese, Qianlong period,
1736–95, 3¾in (9.5cm) high.
£340–380 / €490–570
$620–690 G&G ⊞

▶ **Wemyss
trinket tray,**
painted with roses,
Scottish, c1900,
10in (25.5cm) wide.
£340–390
€490–570
$620–710 GLB ⊞

Wedgwood cheese dome, c1830,
10in (25.5cm) high.
£400–450 / €580–650
$730–820 SCO ⊞

Minton spittoon, c1825, 3in (7.5cm) high.
£450–500 / €650–720
$820–910 GN ⊞

◄ **Delftware
flower brick,**
decorated with
flowers, Irish,
5½in (14cm) wide.
£550–660
€800–960
$1,000–1,200
JAd ➹

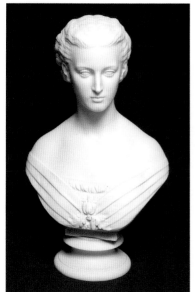

Copeland porcelain bust of a lady, by
Mary Thornycroft, 1863, 15in (38cm) high.
£540–600 / €230–860
$980–1,100 JAK ⊞

Staffordshire pottery egg, inscribed 'Thomas', c1850,
2½in (6.5cm) wide.
£560–630 / €810–910
$1,000–1,150 ReN ⊞

◄ **Famille vert supper set,** comprising 19 dishes, in a wooden
frame, slight damage, Kangxi period, 1662–1722,
16¼in (41.5cm) diam.
£740–880 / €1,050–1,250
$1,350–1,600 WW ➹

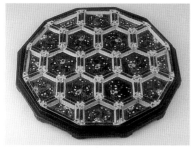

Silver & Plate

The words 'affordable antiques' mean different things to different people and can easily be misinterpreted when discussing a price. As an antiques dealer I often have customers coming to my shop looking to buy an affordable antique to give as a present. This request is followed by my having to spare them embarrassment by gently enquiring what sort of amount they are thinking of spending.

The variety of answers that I have heard over the years have been quite surprising. On one occasion a gentleman, who had been invited out to dinner, said that he wanted a present to take with him. After a brief discussion he declared that a claret jug would best suit his needs and proceeded to purchase a Victorian silver and cut-crystal claret jug, made in London in 1886 by the silversmiths Wakely & Wheeler, for just under £5,000 / €7,300 / $9,100. To say the least I was quite amazed at his generosity, especially as he did not know his hosts. At the other end of the scale I have had other customers declaring that they would be happy to spend up to £25 / €35 / $45, and still I endeavour to fulfil their needs.

These examples just highlight the range of perceptions as to what would be considered an affordable antique. However, Miller's has sensibly tackled the conundrum and produced this useful book which shows that a vast range of good and decorative antiques can be purchased within a reasonable budget. In this current market, prices of antiques from several collecting fields are fluctuating wildly but there is confidence in silver and, as a result, prices are remaining fairly stable.

Silver is a perennially fascinating metal and its beauty has traditionally reflected both the image and the wealth, social status and importance of its owner. Collectors gain huge pleasure when thinking of the amount of time, skill and artistry that the silversmith has put into the item. Even an everyday piece of cutlery can show that loving care, attentive detail and pride have gone into the making.

The more frequently one handles silver items, the easier it will be to recognize and appreciate the subtle superiority of the work of the great silversmiths. However, even superb pieces may have been owned by the inexperienced or unappreciative and been mistreated, thus causing irreversible damage or repair that will affect the value but, at an affordable price, even such pieces can find a loving home.

There are, of course, other pitfalls for the unwary. Just buying on price alone can lead to disappointment – you may discover that your treasure has turned out to be a bit of a lemon in that it is worn, damaged or, worse still, a fake. So, when buying, never be afraid to ask questions of the seller. Even an obvious answer will help you decide whether he or she really knows their subject and how reliable he or she would be in resolving any problems or disputes that may arise. Choose a dealer who is a member of a known organization such as The British Antiques Dealers' Association or the National Art and Antique Dealers' Association of America, and remember to ask for a detailed receipt.

Daniel Bexfield

Baskets, Bowls & Dishes

Victorian sugar bowl, the sifter spoon with pierced decoration, spoon damaged, Sheffield 1900, 4oz. Although the spoon is damaged, this Arts & Crafts-style sugar bowl is an attractive piece at a reasonable price.
£35–40 / €50–60
$65–75 FHF ✎

Silver-plated oak and horn salad bowl, with a ceramic liner and matching servers, 8in (20.5cm) wide. This style of bowl would have been used in a Scottish manorial home. The ceramic liner might possibly be a later replacement.
£70–80 / €100–115
$130–145 GAK ✎

◀ **Silver vesta pot,** by Bernard Muller, London 1895, 2in (5cm) high. This might appeal to collectors of egg-cups but it would originally have been used to hold vestas.
£130–150
€190–220
$240–270 SAT ⊞

Victorian silver sugar basin, by Robert Hennell, with chased foliate decoration, 1847, 8½in (21.5cm) wide.
£130–155 / €185–220
$240–280 Mal(O) ✎

Silver sugar basin, by Robert Hennell, with two handles and floral decoration, London 1800, 8in (20.5cm) wide.
£140–165 / €200–240
$250–300 Mal(O) ✎

Pair of silver bonbon dishes, by William Hutton & Sons, Sheffield 1910, 6in (15cm) wide.
£140–165 / €200–240
$250–300 AMB ✎

▶ **Sheffield plate tureen and cover,** 19thC, 13in (33cm) wide. Sheffield plate, once worn, should not be restored by electroplating as this will decrease its value.
£150–180 / €220–260
$270–330 PF ✎

◀ **Sterling silver rose bowl,** embossed and engraved with foliate motifs, c1890, 5½in (14cm) diam, 22oz.
£220–260
€320–380
$400–480 JAd 🔨

For more examples of
Baskets, Bowls & Dishes see Ceramics (page 64–131)

Silver brandy saucepan, by Samuel Meriton, handle missing, London 1782, 3in (7.5cm) high, 6oz. With its original handle intact this saucepan would double in value. However, it could be restored by having a replacement handle made at very little cost.
£160–190 / €240–280
$290–350 WW 🔨

▶ **Silver-mounted glass butter dish and cover,** by Messrs Barnard, the cover with later melon finial, London 1845, base 7in (18cm) diam. This dish would originally have had a cow finial – in its original condition it could be worth double this amount.
£260–310 / €380–450
$470–560 HYD 🔨

Miller's compares...

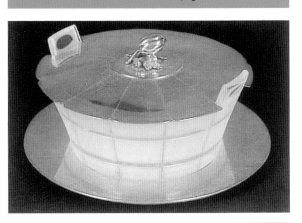

A. Silver basket, by Martin Hall & Co, with repoussé and pierced foliate decoration, Sheffield 1866, 11½in (29cm) diam, 25oz.
£310–370 / €450–540
$560–670 PF 🔨

B. Silver basket, by Martin Hall & Co, with swing handle, with pierced stylized geometric decoration and embossed flowers, Sheffield 1874, 12½in (32cm) wide, 24oz.
£520–620 / €750–900
$950–1,100 PF 🔨

Although both Items A and Item B are by the same maker, Item B is more elaborately decorated, and it is this that accounts for its higher price.

Silver dish, with enamel decoration, damaged, c1900, 6¼in (16cm) diam, 8oz. It is the enamel decoration that gives this dish its value. If the enamel were in perfect condition this dish could achieve £2,500 / €3,600 / $4,550.
£300–340 / €440–500
$550–620 BEX ⊞

Sterling silver bowl, with repoussé decoration, with later glass liner, dated 1893, 10in (25.5cm) diam. This style of bowl is popular in the US. Had this bowl been sold in the UK rather than America it would not have achieved such a high price.
£380–450 / €540–650
$690–820 JDJ ♘

◄ Silver bowl, by Adolf Lillja, Swedish, Stockholm 1848, 9¾in (25cm) diam. There is a good market for Swedish silver in the UK. If this piece had been sold in an English auction house rather than a European one it could have achieved a higher price.
£480–580
€700–840
$870–1,050
BUK(F) ♘

Silver dish ring, by Thomas Bradbury, with pierced decoration, with later glass liner, 1894, 8½in (21.5cm) diam.
£460–550 / €670–800
$840–1,000 G(L) ♘

Silver and glass butter dish, by Reily & Storer, with a cow finial, London 1833, 8in (20.5cm) diam.
£540–600 / €780–870
$980–1,100 SAT ⊞

Silver sugar bowl, by E. Hugo, with two handles, French, 1880, 9in (23cm) wide.
£630–700 / €910–1,000
$1,150–1,300 BEX ⊞

Boxes & Cases

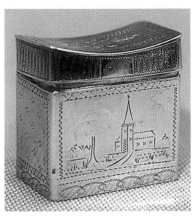

◀ **Silver box,** with floral decoration, Birmingham 1896, 2¾in (7cm) diam.
£50–60 / €75–85 $95–110 FHF ☙

Silver snuff box, Continental, 18thC, 1½in (4cm) high. This snuff box is probably of Dutch origin. Had it been sold in Europe rather than the US, it could have achieved a higher price.
£65–75 / €95–105 $125–145 DuM ☙

Miller's compares...

A. Silver card case, Birmingham 1897, 3¾in (9.5cm) high.
£80–90 / €115–130 $145–170 FHF ☙

B. Silver castle top card case, by James Nasmyth & Co, engraved with the Scott Memorial, Scottish, Edinburgh 1851, 3¾in (9.5cm) long, 2½oz. Castle top card cases are so-called because they are embossed or engraved with a view of a tourist attraction such as a castle or other historic buildings.
£720–860 / €1,050–1,250 $1,300–1,550 WW ☙

Silver snuff box, by Joseph Willmore, with a hinged cover, slight damage, Birmingham 1817, 2½in (6.5cm) long, 10oz. Had this snuff box been in perfect condition it could have sold for £250 / €360 / $450.
£75–85 / €110–125 $135–155 DN ☙

Item A is an attractive card case in good condition. Item B, however, has much more interesting decoration. Pieces decorated with churches and historic buildings command high prices and are very collectable, hence the higher price of Item B.

▶ **Silver card case,** with foliate decoration and monogrammed cartouche, with chain attachment, Birmingham 1904, 4¼in (11cm) wide. This style of card case would have been used by women to carry their calling or dance cards.
£80–90 / €115–130 $145–170 FHF ☙

Silver niello cheroot case, in the form of a suitcase, marked 'HF', Russian, Moscow 1869, 3½in (9cm) long, 4oz. Russian silver is currently selling well. Had this case been in perfect condition it could have sold for £350 / €510 / $640.
£90–100 / €130–145
$165–185 WW ⚒

▶ **Silver powder compact,** with enamel decoration, 19thC, 2½in (6.5cm) diam. Compacts are a good investment as they are again being purchased for use rather than to form part of a collection. When buying it is important to check that the enamel decoration is in perfect condition.
£110–130 / €160–190
$200–240 DuM ⚒

◀ **Silver cigar case,** by James Gloster, shaped for three cigars, with engraved decoration, initialled, Birmingham 1907, 5¼in (13.5cm) long, 3½oz.
£110–130 / €160–190
$200–240 WW ⚒

Silver sovereign case, Birmingham 1903, 1in (2.5cm) diam.
£115–135 / €165–195
$210–250 GRe ⊞

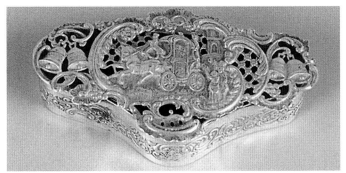

Silver trinket box, the hinged cover chased and engraved with a bridal carriage flanked by wedding bells, London 1905, 5in (12.5cm) wide, 3½oz. As well as trinkets, this pierced box could be used for containing potpourri.
£135–160 / €200–230
$240–290 JAd ⚒

Silver box, in the form of a shoe, decorated in relief with figures and riverscapes, Dutch, late 19thC, 4¾in (12cm) long, 4¼oz. This box would appeal to both collectors of silver and collectors of shoes.
£140–165 / €200–240
$250–300 DN ⚒

Silver snuff box, by Samuel Pemberton, Birmingham 1799, 2½in (6.5cm) diam.
£145–160 / €210–240
$260–290 SAT ⊞

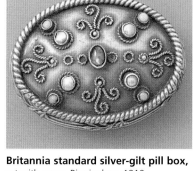

Pair of silver boxes, with chased and repoussé decoration of musicians, marked, London 1808, 2½in (6.5cm) diam. These boxes probably formed part of a dressing table set and would have contained rouge. The decoration is possibly of a later date.
£185–220 / €270–310
$340–400 JDJ ⚒

Britannia standard silver-gilt pill box, set with gems, Birmingham 1910, 2in (5cm) wide.
£190–220 / €270–310
$340–400 G(L) ⚒

Britannia standard

Britannia standard silver is of a higher quality than sterling silver. It was introduced in 1697 to prevent silversmiths using melted-down coinage as a source of metal, and it was stamped with a figure of Britannia.

▶ **Silver snuff box,** the hinged cover chased with foliate scrolls and inset with a jasper panel, London 1746, 2¾in (7cm) wide.
£200–240
€290–350
$360–430 DN ⚒

◀ **Silver tea caddy,** by Charles Stewart Harris, London 1896, 4½in (11.5cm) high. This is an excellent copy of 18thC-style chinoiserie decoration.
£240–280
€340–400
$440–520 G(B) ⚒

Silver vinaigrette, by John Shaw, Birmingham 1818, 1½in (4cm) wide.
£210–240 / €300–340
$380–430 SAT ⊞

Find out more in

Miller's Silver & Plate Buyer's Guide, Miller's Publications, 2002

▶ **Silver snuff box,** maker's mark 'KW', c1900, 2¼in (5.5cm) wide. Chinese export items are currently selling well in both the UK and USA.
£250–300
€360–430
$450–540 DuM ⚒

Silver jewellery box, by William Comyns, embossed with figures, London 1904, 8in (20.5cm) wide, 27½oz.
£290–340 / €420–500
$520–620 DN ✎

▶ **Silver pomander,** in the form of an egg, German, c1700, 1¼in (3cm) high. Pomanders are small silver boxes, often with a pierced lid and sometimes with several internal compartments or a little sponge. They were originally made as neck or wrist ornaments and were filled with sweet-smelling herbs.
£290–330 / €420–480
$530–600 LBr ▦

Miller's compares...

A. Silver-gilt snuff box, by Taylor & Perry, the engine-turned cover with a crest, Birmingham 1833, 3¼in (8.5cm) wide, 3¾oz.
£300–360 / €440–520
$550–660 WW ✎

B. Silver-gilt squeeze-action snuff box, by C.L. Rawlings and W. Summers, with engine-turned decoration, London 1831, 3½in (9cm) wide, 3oz.
£800–900 / €1,150–1,300
$1,450–1,650 BEX ▦

Item A is a standard example of a snuff box whereas Item B has a working squeeze-action mechanism, attractive shape **and is in good condition. All this accounts for the higher value of Item B.**

The look without the price

Silver snuff box, with engraved decoration, maker's mark indistinct, Birmingham 1800, 2in (5cm) wide, ¾oz.
£300–360 / €440–520
$550–660 WW ✎

If the maker's marks on this snuff box were more distinguishable it could have achieved nearer £450 / €650 / $820.

Silver patch box, by Samuel Pemberton, Birmingham 1799,
¾in (2cm) diam.
£330–370 / €480–540
$600–670 BEX ⊞

◄ **Silver card case,**
maker's mark 'I.S.G',
Birmingham 1908,
3in (7.5cm) long.
£340–380
€490–550
$620–690 BEX ⊞

Silver playing card case, with embossed
floral decoration, Chester 1899, 2¾in (7cm)
high. Early Chester silver carries a premium,
as later pieces were assayed in Birmingham.
£340–400 / €490–580
$620–730 CHTR ⚲

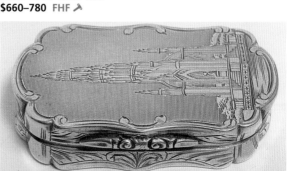

Georgian silver snuff box, relief-decorated with a horse and a
lion, the gilt interior with presentation engraving, maker's mark
'WS', 3¼in (8.5cm) wide. Presentation inscriptions can affect price.
If added at the time of manufacture they can add to value, but the
opposite is true if they were added later. The removal of an
inscription also has a detrimental affect on price – check for this by
holding the piece up to the light to see if there is a dip in the silver,
as this may indicate that an inscription has been erased.
£360–430 / €520–620
$660–780 FHF ⚲

Silver purse, Russian, St Petersburg 1885,
3in (7.5cm) wide. This purse is good quality
and is in good condition, which makes it
desirable and more valuable.
£610–680 / €880–990
$1,100–1,250 SHa ⊞

► **Silver vinaigrette,** engraved with The
Scott Memorial, Edinburgh, Birmingham
1862, 2in (5cm) wide.
£620–690 / €900–1,000
$1,150–1,300 CVA ⊞

Candlesticks & Chambersticks

Silver-plated candelabra,
by Superior Silver Co, c1900,
14½in (37cm) high.
£110–130 / €160–190
$200–240 DuM ⚒

**Pair of Edwardian silver
candlesticks,** by W. I.
Broadway & Co, Birmingham
1901, 8in (20.5cm) high.
£130–155 / €190–220
$240–280 G(L) ⚒

Pair of silver candlesticks,
by The Goldsmiths & Silversmiths
Co, with shell decoration and
detachable nozzles, loaded,
London 1906, 9¾in (25cm) high.
£360–430 / €520–620
$650–780 WW ⚒

Miller's compares...

A. Silver candlestick,
embossed with shell decoration,
with a loaded base, Sheffield
1856, 9in (23cm) high.
£120–140 / €170–200
$220–260 FHF ⚒

B. Silver taperstick, by John
Cafe, London 1755,
5¼in (13.5cm) high, 5oz.
£540–640 / €780–920
$980–1,150 Bea ⚒

Item A is only a single candlestick, probably from a pair, and
has been filled – such items were often made from thin-gauge
silver. Item B is a taperstick, and these were made as single
pieces. It is also by a good maker, is older and has been cast.
These facts account for the higher value of Item B.

Miller's compares...

A. Pair of silver candlesticks,
Sheffield 1898, 7¾in (19.5cm) high.
£140–165 / €200–240
$250–300 G(L) ⚒

**B. Pair of silver Corinthian
column candlesticks,** by Dixon
& Sons, Sheffield 1896,
8in (20.5cm) high.
£720–800 / €1,000–1,200
$1,300–1,450 SHa ⊞

Item A has begun to show signs of damage and this has
reduced its value. Item B, however, is in very good condition
and has a named maker which accounts for its higher price.

Pair of silver candlesticks, by Thomas
Bradbury & Sons, loaded, Sheffield 1902,
9¾in (25cm) high.
£380–450 / €550–650
$690–820 DN ✧

◄ **Pair of Neo-
classical-style
silver candlesticks,**
decorated with
trailing foliage,
loaded, maker's mark
'TH', Birmingham
1898, 12¼in
(31cm) high.
£450–540
€650–780
$820–980 WL ✧

◄ **Pair of Adam-style silver
candlesticks,** by Rupert Favell,
1886, 11¼in (28.5cm) high.
Although Adam-style pieces
are desirable to collectors,
the prevailing fashion is for
plainer designs.
£700–840 / €1,000–1,200
$1,250–1,500 L ✧

► **Pair of silver-plated
three-light candelabra,**
with detachable branches
1850–1900, 22¾in (58cm) high.
£720–860 / €1,050–1,250
$1,300–1,550 S(O) ✧

The look without the price

**Pair of Louis-XVI-style
silver-plated candelabra,**
probably French, 19thC,
15¼in (38.5cm) high.
£790–930 / €1,150–1,350
$1,450–1,700 S(P) ✧

Although these
candlesticks are silver-
plated, they are an
attractive and popular
design. However, had
they been made of
silver they could have
sold for £12,000–14,000
/ €17,400–20,300 /
$21,800–25,400.

Pair of silver candlesticks,
by Emick Romer, London 1760,
12in (30.5cm) high, with two later
Pullman candle lights and shades.
£900–1,050 / €1,300–1,500
$1,650–1,900 DN ✧

Condiments & Cruets

◄ **Silver mustard pot,** by Frederick Augustus Burridge, London 1904, 2in (5cm) high.
£165–185
€240–270
$300–340 GRe ⊞

► **Silver pepper pot,** in the form of a milk churn, Chester 1897, 2in (5cm) high.
£195–220 / €280–320
$350–400 CoHA ⊞

Silver pepper caster, by Samuel Wood, London 1745, 4½in (11.5cm) high, 2oz. This is a very good price and proves that there are still bargains to be had at auction.
£90–100 / €130–145
$170–190 WW ⚒

Silver shaker, Austrian, 19thC, 5½in (14cm) high.
£220–260 / €320–380
$400–470 G(L) ⚒

Silver pepper caster, by Thomas & Jabez Daniell, 1793, 5in (12.5cm) high.
£270–300 / €390–440
$490–550 GRe ⊞

Silver mustard pot, Sheffield 1875, 3in (7.5cm) high.
£360–400 / €520–580
$650–730 GRe ⊞

Sterling silver spice pot, 1906–07, 9½in (24cm) high. This is an attractive copy of a 17thC design.
£380–450 / €550–650
$700–840 DuM ⚒

Salt cellars

Salt is very corrosive, particularly when damp, so many salt cellars are corroded or stained with black spots, which reduces value. It is therefore vital to buy items that are in good condition.

Pair of silver salts, by Willam Evans, London 1894, 2¾in (7cm) diam.
£380–430 / €550–620
$690–780 BEX ⊞

◄ **Set of four silver salts,** by Hamilton & Inches, Edinburgh 1904, 3in (7.5cm) diam, 14oz. The interior of these salts would originally have been gilded to protect from salt corrosion.
£400–480
€580–700
$730–870 L&T ⚒

Pair of silver salts, by Marcus Star, American, New York, c1880, 2½in (6.5cm) diam, 4oz.
£430–480 / €620–700
$780–870 BEX ⊞

◄ **Silver-gilt and glass pepper pot,** in the form of a dog, European, c1910, 3in (7.5cm) high.
£430–480 / €620–700
$780–870 SHa ⊞

► **Silver mustard pot and cover,** by Edward Aldridge, with a glass liner, London 1764, 2¾in (7cm) high, 3oz. This is an unusual mustard pot by a good maker.
£460–550 / €670–800
$840–1,000 WW ⚒

Silver mustard pot and spoon, by Thomas Goodfellow, with a glass liner, London 1899, spoon Dublin 1834, 2½in (6.5cm) high.
£450–500 / €650–730
$820–910 BEX ⊞

Silver Warwick cruet stand, by Thomas Whipham, London 1772, 11in (28cm) diam, 31oz, with four associated cut-glass containers, three containers missing. With the original bottles and casters, this cruet set could have sold for four times this amount.
£550–660 / €800–960
$1,000–1,200 DN ⚘

▶ **Silver spice caster,** by Thomas & Jabez Daniell, with an acorn finial, 1780, 5¾in (14.5cm) high, 3½oz.
£580–650 / €840–940
$1,050–1,200 BEX ⊞

◀ **Silver mustard pot,** by Arvid Castman, with a glass liner, Swedish, Eksjö 1797, 5¼in (13.5cm) high.
£700–840
€1,000–1,200
$1,300–1,550
BUK(F) ⚘

Silver salt, German, c1710, 2¾in (7cm) high, 2½oz.
£790–880 / €1,150–1,300
$1,450–1,600 BEX ⊞

Cups, Mugs & Tankards

Silver christening mug, by Henry Wilkinson & Co, embossed with panels of scrolls and baskets of flowers, with engraved inscription, Sheffield 1859, 3¾in (9.5cm) high, 4¼oz. The later inscription has reduced the value of this item.
£110–130 / €160–190
$200–240 DN ✯

Silver mug, possibly by Samuel Whitford, with embossed decoration and gilt interior, London 1766, 3½in (9cm) high, 5oz.
£150–180 / €210–250
$270–320 WW ✯

Silver three-handled cup, by Ackroyd Rhodes, London 1909, 8in (20.5cm) high, 24oz.
£160–190 €230–270
$290–340 WW ✯

Britannia standard silver cup, by The Goldsmiths & Silversmiths Co, London 1905, 5in (12.5cm) diam, 9oz.
£200–240
€290–340
$360–430 WW ✯

Silver goblet, by Hester Bateman, chased with swags, shells and flowers, with inscription, London 1788, 6¼in (16cm) high. This goblet has later decoration. If it were completely original it could have achieved double or even treble this amount.
£200–240 / €290–350
$360–430 CHTR ✯

► **Silver mug,** by Dorothy Langlands, Newcastle 1813, 5½in (14cm) high, 9½oz.
£250–300 / €360–430
$450–540 WW ✯

Pair of silver goblets, by John Walton, each bearing an inscription relating to the New Jerusalem Temple, Newcastle-upon-Tyne, Newcastle 1830, 7½in (19cm) high, 18½oz. If these goblets had been sold in the Newcastle area, the inscription and local interest could have trebled their value.
£220–260 / €310–370
$400–470 WW ✯

Silver christening mug, by Joseph Angell, London 1826, 4in (10.5cm) high, 4½oz.
£260–310 / €380–450
$470–560 WW ✗

Silver christening mug, by John Evans, London 1838, 4¼in (11cm) high, 4oz.
£450–500 / €650–720
$820–910 BEX ⊞

Silver cup and cover, engraved with Masonic text and symbols, Sheffield 1911, 16½in (42cm) high.
£480–580 / €700–840
$870–1,050 BUK(F) ✗

▶ **Silver armorial tankard,** London 1777, 4½in (11.5cm) high. Although this decoration is later, it has been carried out to a high standard and therefore has not detracted too much from the value.
£280–330
€400–480
$510–600 WilP ✗

Miller's compares...

A. Silver niello beaker, maker's marks 'AK', Russian, Moscow 1850, 3¾in (9.5cm) high.
£340–410 / €500–600
$620–750 BUK(F) ✗

B. Silver-gilt beaker, maker's marks 'VA' and 'FK', damaged, Russian, Moscow 1770, 3¾in (9.5cm) high.
£450–530 / €650–780
$820–960 BUK(F) ✗

Item B is earlier, rarer and more valuable than Item A, which makes it more desirable. However, had Item B been in perfect condition it could have achieved nearly double this price.

◀ **Silver christening mug,** by R. Martin & E. Hall, London 1868, 4¼in (11cm) high, 5½oz.
£580–650
€840–940
$1,050–1,200
BEX ⊞

◀ **Silver goblet,** c1870, 12½in (32cm) high, 7½oz.
£580–650 / €840–940
$1,050–1,200 BEX ⊞

▶ **Silver tankard,** by William Shaw, with later floral decoration and inscription, London 1762, 4½in (11.5cm) high, 29oz. The later inscription has reduced the value of this tankard. Had it been in original condition it could have achieved three times this amount.
£600–720 / €870–1,050
$1,100–1,300 L&T ⚒

Silver two-handled cup, maker's mark 'IH', Channel Islands, Jersey, late 18thC, 2¾in (7cm) high, 2oz. Jersey silver is very hard to find, hence the high price of this cup.
£620–740 / €900–1,050
$1,150–1,350 WW ⚒

Sterling silver cup and saucer, by Tiffany & Co, 1873–91, saucer 5¾in (14.5cm) diam.
£630–700 / €900–1,000
$1,150–1,300 BEX ⊞

Silver mug, by Joshua Jackson, London 1781, 3¼in (8.5cm) high.
£630–700 / €900–1,000
$1,150–1,300 BEX ⊞

Silver beaker, by Johan Zimmerman, partly gilt, Swedish, Stockholm 1796, 9in (23cm) high.
£690–830 / €1,000–1,200
$1,250–1,500 BUK(F) ⚒

Silver goblet, by John Emes, applied with a fruiting vine, the base with an inscription, traces of gilding, London 1805, 7in (18cm) high.
£760–890 / €1,100–1,300
$1,400–1,650 HOK ⚒

Cutlery & Serving Implements

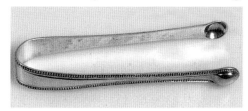

Pair of sugar tongs, maker's mark 'HP', Continental, 19thC, 5½in (14cm) long.
£25–30 / €40–45
$50–60 FHF 🔨

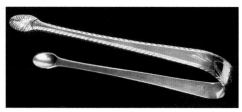

Pair of sugar tongs, by George Smith, London 1782, 5in (12.5cm) long.
£50–60 / €75–85
$100–115 WAC ⊞

◀ **Silver salt spoon,** by Walker & Hall, Birmingham 1897, 2½in (6.5cm) long.
£25–30 / €40–45
$50–55 SAT ⊞

▶ **Silver spoon,** London 1809, 8in (20.5cm) long.
£35–40 / €50–60
$65–75 GGD ⊞

◀ **Silver salt spoon,** by Atkins Bros, Sheffield 1890, 2½in (6.5cm) long.
£35–40 / €50–60
$65–75 SAT ⊞

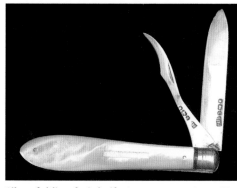

Silver folding fruit knife, by Henry Hemming, with a pip pick and a mother-of-pearl handle, Sheffield 1885, 3in (7.5cm) long.
£70–80 / €100–115
$135–155 CoHA ⊞

Pair of silver serving spoons, by Martin Hall & Co, Sheffield 1872, 5in (12.5cm) long.
£80–95 / €115–135
$145–170 G(L) 🔨

◄ **Pair of silver-plated fish servers,** with engraved decoration, the stag-horn handles with silver collars, Sheffield 1888, 13in (33cm) long.
£80–90 / €115–130
$155–175 GRe ⊞

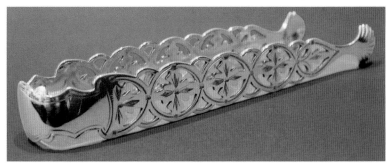

► **Pair of silver sugar tongs,** by H. W, Sheffield 1900, 4½in (11.5cm) long, 1oz.
£110–125
€160–180
$200–220 BEX ⊞

Silver and steel carving knife and fork, Continental, c1890, 11½in (29cm) long.
£120–135 / €175–195
$220–250 BEX ⊞

Set of silver tea spoons, with simulated-bamboo decoration, Sheffield 1909, 5in (12.5cm) long.
£125–140 / €180–200
$220–250 SAT ⊞

Silver Old English pattern caddy spoon, by Mitchell & Son, Scottish, Glasgow 1823, 3½in (9cm) long. Despite showing signs of wear, this caddy spoon has kept its value as it is Scottish silver, which is rare and very sought after.
£130–155 / €190–220
$240–280 G(L) ⚒

► **Silver folding fruit knife,** by J. Y. Cowlishaw, with a mother-of-pearl handle, Sheffield 1862, 5½in (14cm) long, with original case.
£130–150 / €190–220
$240–270 CoHA ⊞

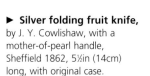

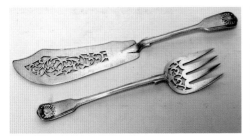

Silver Fiddle and Shell pattern fish server and fork, London 1864. This pattern is sought after by collectors. This is a good price for such silver fish servers.
£150–180 / €220–260
$270–320 CHTR ↗

Silver caddy spoon, by Joseph Wilmore, Birmingham 1814, 2in (5cm) long.
£150–170 / €220–250
$270–310 SAT ⊞

▶ **Silver butter knife,** by Aldwinkle & Slater, 1887, 7in (18cm) long, in fitted case. Original boxes can add almost 50 per cent to the value of an item.
£155–175 / €220–250
$280–320 BEX ⊞

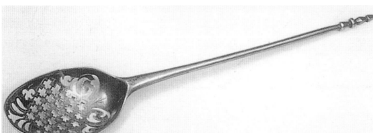

◀ **Silver mote spoon,** by George Hodges, with pierced and engraved decoration, London 1728, 5¼in (13.5cm) long.
£170–200
€250–300
$310–370
Mal(O) ↗

▶ **Sterling silver ladle,** by Tiffany & Co, American, c1909, 11½in (29cm) long, 7oz.
£190–220
€280–330
$340–400 JAA ↗

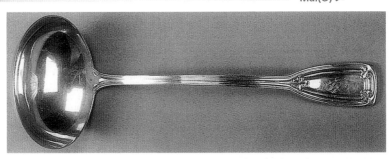

Pair of silver and gilt berry spoons, by William Eley & William Fearn, London 1800, 8in (20.5cm) long. These spoons have later decoration. Prices for them can vary greatly. Berry spoons are very popular in the US.
£180–200 / €260–290
$330–360 SAT ⊞

Pair of silver sugar tongs, by Thomas Allen, Sheffield 1870, 5½in (14cm) long.
£200–230 / €290–330
$360–410 BEX ⊞

▶ **Set of six Old English pattern silver teaspoons,** by James Scott, Dublin c1795, 4½in (11.5cm) long, 3½oz.
£250–300 / €360–430
$460–550 JAd ⚏

◀ **Silver sauce ladle,** probably by Michael Keating, with crested handle and scallop bowl, Irish, Dublin 1789, 13in (33cm) long, 2oz. Irish silver is very sought after and collectable.
£220–260 / €320–380
$400–470 JAd ⚏

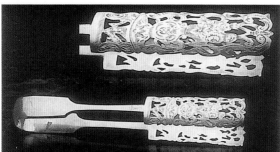

Pair of silver Fiddle pattern asparagus tongs, with pierced and engraved decoration, Irish, Dublin 1864, 4¾in (12cm) long, 4oz.
£280–330 / €400–480
$510–600 JAd ⚏

Set of three Fiddle pattern silver teaspoons, by Henry Gardener, Irish, Dublin, c1820.
£340–410 / €500–600
$620–750 MEA ⚏

Pair of silver Fiddle and Shell asparagus tongs, by William Traies, with pierced blades, crested, London 1835, 8in (20.5cm) long.
£380–450 / €550–650
$690–820 SWO ⚏

Silver bone marrow spoon, possibly by Thomas Mann, London 1716, 9in (23cm) long. This spoon would have been used for scooping marrow. Diners of this period would have taken it with them when eating out.
£360–430 / €520–620
$660–780 SWO ⚏

▶ **Pair of silver serving spoons,** by William Hutton & Sons, the handles decorated with mistletoe, London 1901, 8¾in (22cm) long, in a fitted case.
£380–430 / €550–620
$690–780 BEX ⊞

Silver ladle, by Robert Pilkington, with a wooden handle, London 1740, 14in (35.5cm) long.
£380–430 / €550–620
$690–780 GRe ⊞

▶ **Silver and glass salad servers,** by John Grinsell & Sons, London and Birmingham, 1895, 11in (28cm) long.
£390–440
€570–640
$710–800 BEX ⊞

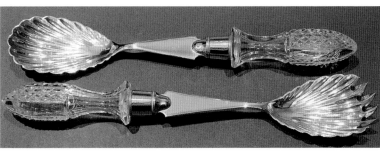

Silver caddy spoon, by William R. Sobey, Exeter 1836, 7in (18cm) long.
£450–500 / €650–720
$820–910 BEX ⊞

Hester Bateman

Hester Bateman married John Bateman in 1732 and they set up a family business of silversmiths. Although she registered her first mark in 1761 after the death of her husband, her mark rarely appears on items made before 1774. From this time onwards she produced a wide range of high-quality silverware, much of which were small domestic items. Her work is usually elegant and attractively engraved.

▶ **Silver cream ladle,** by Hester Bateman, with duty drawback marks for London 1784–85, 4¼in (11cm) long.
£460–550
€660–790
$840–1,000
WilP ⋏

Find out more in

Miller's Silver & Plate Antiques Checklist, Miller's Publications, 2001

▶ **Silver-gilt ladle,** Russian, Moscow 1872, 10in (25.5cm) long.
£850–950 / €1,250–1,400
$1,550–1,750 SHa ⊞

Jugs & Sauce Boats

◀ **Silver hot water jug and cover,** maker's mark 'SR' and 'CR', Sheffield 1876, 8in (20.5cm) high, 16oz. Silver water jugs are currently unfashionable, hence the low price of this example.
£90–105 / €130–150
$165–190 WL ⚒

Georgian-style silver cream jug, with Greek-key border, indistinct London mark, c1800, 3½in (9cm) high.
£90–105 / €130–150
$165–190 GAK ⚒

Silver-mounted glass claret jug, maker's mark 'TW', London 1883, 10¼in (26cm) high.
£105–125 / €150–180
$200–240 WEBB ⚒

◀ **Silver cream jug,** with engraved monogram, London 1800, 4¼in (11cm) high.
£120–140 / €170–200
$220–260 WilP ⚒

▶ **Silver cream jug,** by Nathaniel Appleton & Ann Smith, London 1782, 4in (10cm) high, 1¾oz.
£140–165 / €200–240
$250–300 WW ⚒

Silver cream jug, by William Hall, London 1808, 5in (12.5cm) wide.
£150–170 / €210–240
$270–310 SAT ⊞

Silver cream jug, with an applied rib and engraved initials, Irish, Dublin 1770, 5½in (14cm) high, 5oz.
£250–300 / €360–430
$460–540 JAd ⚒

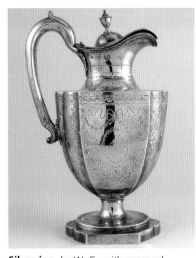

Silver-mounted glass claret jug, with a hinged cover, London 1903, 10¾in (27.5cm) high.
£400–480 / €580–700
$730–870 G(L) 🔨

Silver jug, by W. G., with engraved decoration, crested, with a later Victorian handle, 1825, 11¼in (28.5cm) high.
£500–600 / €730–870
$910–1,100 WW 🔨

Silver-gilt-mounted glass claret jug, London, c1887, 11¾in 30cm) high. This jug has retained its original stopper, and this has added to its value.
£550–660 / €800–960
$1,000–1,200 G(B) 🔨

Silver sauce boat and stand, by Antoine Hience, French, Paris, 1798–1809, 11½in (29cm) wide.
£580–690 / €840–1,000
$1,050–1,250 S(P) 🔨

Silver cream jug, by Ann Robertson, Newcastle, c1800, 4in (10cm) high, 2¾oz.
£580–650 / €840–940
$1,050–1,200 BEX ⊞

◀ **Sterling silver water jug,** by Gorham Manufacturing Co, American, c1880, 9in (23cm) high.
£710–850 / €1,050–1,250
$1,300–1,550 DuM 🔨

Gorham Manufacturing Co

One of America's most prolific manufacturers of silverware, Gorham Manufacturing Co was founded by Jabez Gorham in Providence, Rhode Island in 1818. From c1841 mechanical methods of manufacturing were increasingly used and, in 1868, the firm began marking their products with a trade mark. Gorham's early silver was predominantly influenced by 18th-century French styles and later by Art Nouveau and Art Deco designs.

Salvers & Trays

Miller's compares...

A. Silver salver, on three claw-and-ball feet, Birmingham 1898, 7½in (19cm) diam, 8½oz.
£110–130 / €160–190
$200–240 FHF ⚒

B. Silver waiter, by Richard Rugg, London 1779, 6in (15cm) diam, 8oz.
£790–880 / €1,100–1,250
$1,450–1,600 BEX ▦

Salvers such as Item A are frequently found whereas Item B is rarer, by a good maker, in very good condition and older.

It is these factors that account for the higher price for Item B.

Miller's compares...

A. Silver salver, with engraved armorial, maker's mark indistinct, London 1740, 10½in (26.5cm) wide, 17oz.
£210–250 / €300–360
$380–450 WW ⚒

B. Silver salver, by Charles Hatfield, with engraved armorial, London 1732, 10in (25.5cm) diam, 22oz.
£780–930 / €1,150–1,350
$1,450–1,700 S(O) ⚒

George I-style silver salver, by Charles Boyton, 1894, 11½in (29cm) square, 31¾oz. This square salver is a rare shape and this has probably added 40 per cent to its auction price.
£220–260 / €320–380
$400–470 L ⚒

Item A and Item B are from the same period and are both the same size. Item B, however, is made of heavier silver and is in better condition than Item A, which is why it achieved a higher price.

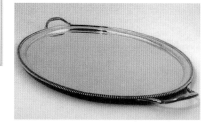

▶ **Old Sheffield plate two-handled tray,** with a tinned base, c1795, 10in (25.5cm) wide.
£320–380 / €460–550
$580–690 WW ⚒

◄ **Edwardian silver salver,** by Edward Barnard & Sons, with crest and motto, 14¼in (36cm) diam, 43oz.
£320–380 / €460–550
$580–690 SWO ⚹

► **Silver salver,** by John Robinson, with hoof feet, London 1749, 10in (25.5cm) diam, 17oz.
£340–400 / €490–580
$620–730 WW ⚹

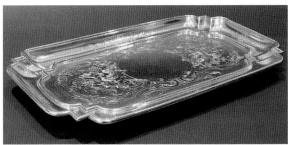

Silver waiter, by Joseph Jackson, on pad feet, Irish, Dublin 1788, 6in (15cm) diam, 7oz.
£360–430 / €520–620
$660–780 JAd ⚹

Silver tray, by Morel & Co, French, c1880, 10¼in (26cm) wide, 12½oz.
£410–470 / €600–680
$750–850 BEX ⊞

Victorian silver-plated tray, with engraved decoration and a reticulated gallery, marked 'KH & Co', 26in (66cm) wide. This tray came from the sale of the Woolworth Collection and this provenance has added value to the piece.
£410–480 / €590–700
$740–880 JDJ ⚹

Silver-plated stand, on three feet, c1875, 18in (45.5cm) diam. This style of multi-purpose item is currently popular in the US where it was sold at auction.
£440–520 / €640–750
$800–960 NOA ⚹

Silver-plated tray, with cast handles and a pierced gallery, with engraved decoration and presentation inscription, c1880, 22¾in (58cm) wide.
£460–550 / €660–790
$840–1,000 WW ⚹

◄ **Silver waiter,** by Robert Piercy, crested, London 1765, 6¾in (17cm) diam, 8oz.
£500–600
€720–870
$910–1,100 TEN ⚹

Tea, Coffee & Chocolate Pots

Sheffield plate coffee pot, c1790, 11in (28cm) high.
£135–160 / €195–230
$250–290 HOK 🔨

Silver bachelor's teapot, by Edward and John Barnard, each side engraved with a vacant cartouche, London 1865, 4¾in (12cm) high, 11oz. A bachelor's teapot is a small pot that brews enough tea for one serving.
£210–250 / €300–360
$380–450 WW 🔨

Silver three-piece tea service, by Walker & Hall, comprising teapot, sugar bowl and cream jug, Sheffield 1922, teapot 11in (28cm) wide.
£250–300 / €360–430
$460–550 TEN 🔨

Silver coffee pot, by Johan Edvard Fagerroos, Finnish, Helsinki 1861, 7in (18cm) high.
£340–400 / €500–600
$620–730 BUK(F) 🔨

Silver five-piece tea and coffee service, by Hamilton & Diesinger, comprising a coffee pot, teapot, covered sugar bowl, creamer and slop bowl, American, 1894, coffee pot 8½in (21.5cm) high, 65.5oz. This is a very reasonable price for such a service.
£320–380 / €460–550
$580–690 LHA 🔨

Find out more in

Miller's Silver & Sheffield Plate Marks Pocket Fact File, Miller's Publications, 2001

▶ **Silver hot water jug,** by Francis Borne Thomas, London 1885, 9in (23cm) high.
£360–400
€520–580
$660–730 SAT ⊞

◀ **Silver teapot,** by William James Barnard, with engraved decoration, London 1881, 8in (20.5cm) high.
£360–400
€520–580
$660–730 SAT ⊞

Silver four-piece tea set, by J. Heath and J. Middleton, with wicker-bound handles, London 1902, 38oz. Silver tea sets are currently unfashionable, possibly due to the cleaning involved, and their prices are low. Now would be a good time to invest in a tea set.
£380–450 / €550–650
$690–820 HYD 🔨

Silver coffee pot, by Asprey & Co, London 1910, 10½in (26.5cm) high, 25¾oz.
£580–650 / €840–940
$1,050–1,200 BEX ⊞

▶ **Silver teapot,** probably by John Mewburn, inscribed to base 'Bequeathed by Capt. Robert Dalrymple of the 3rd Regt of Guards who fell by a musket shot at Talavera de la Reyne on the 28th July 1809 to Capt. Chas. L. White of the same Regt. as a token of esteem and affection and as a memorial of their friendship Oct 26th 1809', London 1808, 11in (28cm) wide, 17oz. The historical interest of this teapot has added to its value. Without the interesting inscription it would only be worth £200–300 / €290–440 / $360–550.
£800–960 / €1,200–1,400
$1,450–1,750 WW 🔨

▶ **Silver coffee pot,** with an ivory handle, later embossed decoration, marks indistinct, possibly London 1727, 8½in (21.5cm) high, 22oz. If this coffee pot were in its original, undecorated condition, it could be worth £4,000–5,000 / €5,800–7,200 / $7,200–9,100.
£500–600
€730–870
$910–1,100 Bea 🔨

Silver teapot, by Philip Rundell, with a gadrooned rim and anthemion and acanthus-decorated spout, the reeded body with an ivory handle and finial, crested, London 1819, 10½in (26.5cm) wide, 27oz. This teapot has many desirable qualities: it was made by a well-known maker; it is of a good weight and popular design, and it has an ivory handle. These factors have made it sought after and therefore valuable.
£660–790 / €960–1,150
$1,200–1,450 Bea 🔨

Toast Racks

Miller's compares...

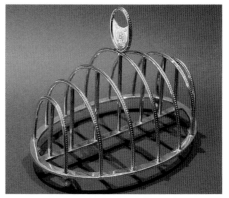

A. Silver toast rack, c1890, 4in (10cm) wide.
£100–115 / €145–165
$180–210 EXC ⊞

B. Silver toast rack, by J. Bradbury & J.
Henderson, London 1878, 6½in (16.5cm) wide.
£610–680 / €880–990
$1,100–1,250 BEX ⊞

Item A is a plain toast rack. Item B is
attributable to a maker, decorated with
bead pattern and is larger and heavier than

item A, all of which make it more desirable
and therefore more valuable.

▶ **Silver toast
rack,** by Richard
Hennell, with a
beaded rim base, on
bracket feet, London
1870, 5in (12.5cm)
wide, 9½oz.
£180–210
€250–300
$330–390 FHF ⚒

Silver toast rack, by G. Harrison, London
1897, 4½in (11cm) wide, 6oz.
£165–185 / €240–270
$300–340 GRe ⊞

▶ **Silver toast rack,** decorated with Indian
figures, Indian, c1890, 6in (15cm) wide.
The unusual decoration has contributed to
the value of this item.
£220–250 / €320–360
$400–450 BLm ⊞

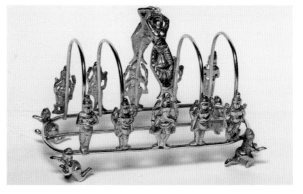

Writing Equipment

Silver pen/pencil, by Sampson Mordan & Co, with a reeded holder, the reversible end for propelling pencil and pen, the screw-off terminal enclosing a lead reservoir, one tip missing from nib, 19thC.
£80–95 / €120–140
$145–175 BBA ⚲

Silver pocket penholder, by Sampson Mordan & Co, decorated with barley, line and dot pattern, with reversible slip pen holder, 1890s, 3¾in (9.5cm) long.
£90–110 / €130–160
$170–200 BBA ⚲

Silver filigree pen, by Carey, filigree losses, stamped marks, American, 1900–10, 3in (7.5cm) long. This damage would be difficult to repair. In original condition this pen could have made two or three times this price.
£90–105 / €130–150
$165 –200 BBA ⚲

Silver sealing wax holder, the cover with a spring catch and engraved with a seal, the base with an engraved monogram and coronet, probably Continental, c1830, 3in (7.5cm) long.
£90–105
€130–165
$165–190 BBA ⚲

Silver-mounted crystal inkwell, c1880, 4½in (11.5cm) wide.
£95–110 / €140–160
$175–200 DuM ⚲

Silver inkstand, by The Goldsmiths & Silversmiths Co, the two inkwells with covers and glass liners, and two pen recesses, London 1901, 8¾in (22cm) wide, 20½oz.
£200–240 / €290–350
$370–440 DMC ⚲

Silver inkstand, by Henry Wilkinson & Co, fitted with two silver-mounted ink bottles and a box with a taperstick cover, inscribed, snuffer missing, Sheffield 1862, 10½in (26.5cm) wide, 17oz. Complete, and with two keen bidders, this inkstand could easily have made double this amount.
£300–360 / €440–520
$550–660 WW ⚘

Silver and cut-glass inkstand, with two silver-mounted cut-glass inkwells, some losses and replacements, maker's mark 'TBS', c1775, 10¾in (27.5cm) wide. If this inkstand had been complete it could have achieved more than twice this price.
£280–330 / €410–480
$510–600 JDJ ⚘

Miller's compares...

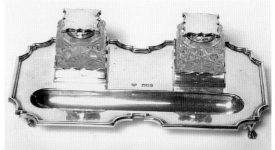

A. Silver inkstand, by Messrs Barnard, with two silver-mounted cut-glass ink bottles, inscribed, London 1896, 11in (28cm) wide, 25oz.
£300–360 / €440–520
$550–660 WW ⚘

B. Silver inkstand, by The Goldsmiths & Silversmiths Co, with a pen recess and two cut-glass silver-mounted ink bottles, London 1904, 11in (28cm) wide.
£540–600 / €780–870
$980–1,100 SAT ⊞

Current fashions are leaning towards plainer designs and this could be the reason that

Item A, with its more elaborate decoration has not commanded as high a price as Item B.

Silver and agate pencil, c1857, 11½in (29cm) long.
£310–350 / €450–510
$560–640 BEX ⊞

▶ **Silver, gold and glass travelling inkwell,** by Thomas Dicks, London 1838, 2¼in (5.5cm) diam.
£540–600 / €780–870
$980–1,100 BEX ⊞

Miscellaneous

Pair of silver decanter labels, by Yapp & Woodward, in the form of vine leaves, pierced 'Port' and 'Sherry', Birmingham 1853, 2½in (6.5cm) wide.
£70–80 / €100–115
$125–145 CS ⊞

▶ **Silver pin cone,** by W. Thornhill & Co, with a hinged cover, the body embossed with birds and flowers, with chatelaine attachment, 2in (5cm) high. This item is by a well-known maker and was a good buy at auction.
£90–105
€130–155
$160–190 FHF ⋗

Miller's compares...

A. Silver sugar caster, by Mappin & Webb, with a pierced cover, London 1908, 6¼in (16cm) high, 3½oz.
£125–150
€180–210
$230–270 WEBB ⋗

B. Britannia standard silver sugar caster, crested and initialled, maker's mark indistinct, London 1720, 5¾in (14.5cm) high, 5¾oz.
£440–520 / €640–750
$800–950 Bea ⋗

Item A is a later copy of Item B, and the age difference between the two accounts for its lower price. In original condition and with legible maker's marks, Item B would have achieved twice as much as this at auction.

◀ **Pair of silver spirit labels,** by Phipps & Robinson, inscribed 'Brandy' and 'Rum', London 1813, 1in (2.5cm) wide.
£100–120
€145–175
$180–210 G(L) ⋗

Silver rattle, with an ivory teething bar and ring and six silver bells, Birmingham 1871, 8in (20.5cm) long. This rattle has replacement bells. Had these been original, it would have achieved double this price.
£120–140 / €170–200
$210–250 FHF ⋗

◀ **Silver napkin ring,** by David and George Edward, decorated with signs of the Zodiac, Glasgow 1905, 1¼in (3cm) diam.
£130–145
€190–210
$230–260 BEX ⊞

Silver and ivory paper knife, Birmingham 1890, 14in (35.5cm) long.
£170–190 / €250–280
$310–350 SAT ⊞

Silver sugar caster, by William Bagnall, date letter indistinct, London, c1740, 6in (15cm), 6oz. In original condition, with the hallmarks clearly legible, this caster could have achieved over twice this price.
£160–190 / €240–280
$290–350 WW ⚘

Silver pin cushion, in the form of a gentleman's shoe, Birmingham 1910, 5in (12.5cm) wide. Silver pin cushions are popular, and this would appeal to both collectors of pin cushions and collectors of shoes.
£170–190 / €250–280
$310–350 FHF ⊞

Silver bottle stopper, in the form of a monkey, c1880, 3¼in (8.5cm) high.
£200–230 / €290–330
$360–400 BEX ⊞

Silver scent bottle container, with a hinged top and side, Birmingham 1905, 2in (5cm) high. These items were made to hold a glass scent bottle. They are very collectable.
£220–250 / €320–360
$400–450 SAT ⊞

Sheffield plate wine cooler, with two handles, drop-in liner and detachable gadrooned rim, each side engraved with a coat-of-arms, c1820, 9in (23cm) high. Today, wine coolers are often used for cooling Champagne. This item was a good buy at auction.
£240–280 / €350–410
$440–500 WW ⚘

Silver sugar caster, Birmingham 1911, 7in (18cm) high.
£200–230 / €290–330
$360–400 EXC ⊞

◀ **Silver egg cruet,** the stand with pierced decoration and lion-mask ring handles, with five spoons, London 1860, egg cup 2¾in (7cm) high. These spoons do not appear to be original. Not all egg cruets were made with matching spoons.
£300–360 / €440–520
$530–640 CHTR ⚘

Silver wine funnel, with a beaded border, associated spout, London, probably 1820, 5in (12.5cm) high.
£340–400 / €490–580
$620–730 G(L) 🔨

Silver and tortoiseshell pique photograph frame, Birmingham 1913, 7in (18cm) high.
£350–420 / €510–610
$640–760 G(L) 🔨

Silver-plated hot water urn, on reeded lion-paw supports with leaf and shell decoration, with reeded and foliate scroll handles, the detachable lid with a scroll handle, late 19thC, 17¼in (44cm) high.
£380–450 / €550–650
$690–820 TEN 🔨

Chinese export silver hand mirror, by Hung Chong, Chinese, c1890, 9¾in (25cm) long.
£580–650 / €840–940
$1,050–1,200 BEX ⊞

Silver candle snuffer, by John and Frank Pairpoint, in the form of a harlequin, London 1899, 4½in (11.5cm) long, 1½oz.
£390–440 / €570–640
$710–800 BEX ⊞

To find out more about antique silver see the full range of
Miller's books at
www.millers.uk.com

Silver table mirror, by William Comyns, the pierced frame decorated with putti, scrolls and foliage, on a velvet mount, 1901, 24¾in (63cm) high. William Comyns was a respected silversmith whose output included many good dressing table pieces.
£600–720 / €870–1,050
$1,100–1,300 L 🔨

◀ **Pair of Britannia standard silver casters,** by John Chartier, 1723, 5¼in (13.5cm) high.
£620–740 / €900–1,050
$1,150–1,350 SWO 🔨

Glass

As we all know, tastes change over the years. This gradual evolution has profound implications for collectors of all types as the value of their favourite pieces will rise or fall according to demand. As any general dealer or visitor to antique shops and fairs will readily confirm, the price of certain objects or styles have risen dramatically over recent years while others have fallen away.

In glass terms, the great winners over recent decades have been 18th-century drinking glasses. Collectors who bought certain pieces ahead of the market are now laughing all the way to the bank. These pieces include heavy baluster goblets dating from 1710 to 1730, twist-stem wine glasses decorated in enamels by the Beilby family, c1760 and wine glasses decorated with gold by James Giles during the 1760s and '70s. A recent survey has shown that the prices commanded by such pieces have risen by as much as 42 times in as many years.

However, for every winner there is usually a loser. The great losers over the same period have been cut-glass and decanters. Time was when both of these were highly sought after and commanded high prices. It is relatively easy to see why cut-glass has fallen from popularity as it is too fiddly or busy for modern taste. However, it is harder to explain why the value of decanters has retreated.

With the consumption of wines having risen inexorably over recent decades, both in Europe and North America, it seems strange in the extreme that the practice of decanting has broadly fallen into disuse. Wine connoisseurs are unanimous in agreeing that virtually all wines benefit significantly from being decanted. This is due to several reasons, but primarily because it allows wines to breathe, or 'de-oxidise'. As Paddy McGill, buyer for wine merchants Jeroboams, explained: 'I decant almost anything. In my view, everything from house reds to top clarets and whites all benefit. A wine needs time to breathe, stretch and flex its muscles after being confined in a bottle.' As another Master of Wine put it, 'You don't have to be a pedant to decant wine, just sensible.'

Historically, bottles were simply viewed as a convenient means of packaging – the means by which relatively small quantities of wine could be delivered to the cellar, not to the table. Even as late as the 1950s, a host who placed a wine bottle on a dining table would have been considered ill-mannered. Yet the practice has become common, with the result that decanters are now plentiful and usually very cheap.

Decanters come in all shapes, forms and sizes. They can be entirely plain or profusely cut, engraved, etched, enamelled, gilded or otherwise decorated. They range from tiny versions capable of holding a single glassful to a monster, made by Stevens & Williams in 1896, that held 26 bottles of wine, but proved so heavy when full that it could not be lifted, let alone poured from.

Fortunately most decanters are far more practical and, aside from particularly rare or early examples, are available from most antique shops and fairs from as little as £10 / €15 / $19. How many other forms of antiques offer such practicality and lend so much style to a table for such a small outlay?

Andy McConnell

Baskets, Bowls & Dishes

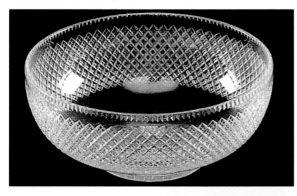

◀ **Cut-glass bowl,** c1900,
10¼in (26cm) diam.
£95–110 / €140–160
$175–200 DN ⚹

Locate the source

The source of each illustration in
Miller's can be found by checking
the code letters below each
caption with the Key to
Illustrations, pages 286–290.

**Georgian glass tea caddy
bowl,** 4in (10cm) high.
£105–120 / €150–175
$200–230 KET ⊞

Cut-glass bowl, with Van
Dyke rim, early 19thC,
10in (25.5cm) diam. Van Dyke
rims take their names from the
shape of the scalloped lace
collars worn by the subjects of
the portraits painted by Anglo-
Dutch painter Sir Anthony Van
Dyke (1549 and 1641).
£220–260 / €320–380
$400–470 TEN ⚹

The look without the price

**Two cut-glass and white-
metal-mounted bowls and
covers,** 5¾in (14.5cm) high.
£200–240 / €290–350
$370–440 TEN ⚹

English cut glass evolved
through a series of distinctive
stages which enable examples
to be dated accurately.
These unusual, silver-mounted
covered bowls are cut in a
pattern known as 'hollow
diamonds', popular between
1750 and 1765. Further, their
mounts are in solid silver but
are unmarked because the
hallmarking laws did not
require small fittings to be
stamped before c1800.
This knowledge enables those
in the know to recognize
what they are looking at.

Daum glass salt, painted in enamel with a windmill beside a
lake, gilded rim, French, 1895, 2in (5cm) diam.
£250–280 / €360–410
$460–510 MiW ⊞

▶ **Cut-glass punch bowl and stand,** with hobstar decoration, c1900, 14in (35.5cm) diam. The predominant motif in this cut design is the 'pinwheel', a pattern that resembles a repeating zig-zag created on a Spirograph machine. Dating from 1899, the pinwheel is the only all-American cut-glass motif as all other motifs in the rich-cutting repertoire had been developed elsewhere before being adopted by US glass cutters. It is distinguished by a series of tapering v-grooves or vanes radiating around a central circular motif, often a hobstar, as in the case of this bowl and stand.
£300–360 / €440–520
$550–660 JAA ✎

Pair of glass jars, covers and stands,
late 18thC, 10¼in (26cm) diam.
£280–330 / €410–480
$510–600 BUK ✎

Glass bowl, Irish, 8¼in (21cm) high.
£340–410 / €500–600
$620–750 HOK ✎

▶ **Osler Cut-glass bowl,** Birmingham, on an ormolu stand, stamped mark, c1860, 8½in (21.5cm) wide.
£420–500
€600–720
$760–910 TEN ✎

F. & C. Osler

The name of F. & C. Osler, founded in Birmingham in 1807, has become inextricably linked with its monumental glass fountain that stood beneath the central atrium of the Crystal Palace during the Great Exhibition in 1851. The company also made a wide range of glassware, some of it set in gilded brass, or ormolu mounts. Its finest work included some of the largest chandeliers of the Victorian age and a range of spectacular cut-glass furniture, much of it made for Indian maharajas.

Cut-glass bowl and cover, slight damage, 18thC, 10½in (26.5cm) high.
£760–850 / €360–410
$460–510 G&G ⊞

Bottles & Decanters

◄ **Cut-glass decanter,**
with hobstar decoration and
stopper, American, c1900,
11in (28cm) high.
£40–45 / €55–65
$70–80 JAA ⚲

► **Cut-glass decanter,**
decorated in Russian pattern,
with stopper, American, late
19thC, 12½in (32cm) high.
£95–115 / €140–165
$175–210 JAA ⚲

Russian pattern

The Russian pattern
was one of the most
popular in the 'rich-
cutting' repertoire.
At the time of Grover
Cleveland's presidency
at the White House in
1885, he acquired a
600-piece 'Russian'
service, and the design
was widely adopted by
European makers. Its
original designer is
unknown as its
previous attribution to
Phillip McDonald, a
cutter at T. G. Hawkes
of Corning, is now
known to be incorrect.
The pattern is based
on a diagonal axis with
multi-mitred central
diamonds. English and
American makers
produced both deep
and shallow versions,
the latter being known
as 'cheap Russian'.

The look without the price

Pair of glass decanters,
with stoppers, Irish, c1820,
9in (23cm) high.
£175–210 / €250–300
$320–380 NSal ⚲

This pair of large English decanters, dating around 1800,
is fitted with their original stoppers and will each comfortably
hold a bottle of wine. It would have taken a craftsman a
day to create each one with their cut decoration of
diamonds, prisms and fans, and would have been very
expensive at the time, probably equivalent to a labourer's
wages for two or three weeks. Despite wine consumption
reaching new heights and the fact that decanting improves
the taste of most wines, decanters remain strangely
unpopular and thus this pair are remarkably good value.

► **Richardsons glass decanter,** cut with swags, with spire stopper and
star-cut base, 1845, 14¼in (36cm) high. Founded in Wordsley, near Stourbridge
in 1829, Richardsons was Britain's longest family-owned glassworks until it was
finally taken over by Thomas Webb almost exactly a century later. During its
early period, Richardsons gradually emerged as one of Britain's leading
glassmakers, producing a wide range of superior table glass, generally cut
and often tinted in various shades of green.
£220–260 / €320–380
$400–470 LTA ⚲

The look without the price

Glass decanter, cut with a scene depicting men on a village green beneath a crest, stopper possibly associated, 19thC, 9¾in (25cm) high.
£220–260 / €320–380
$400–470 TEN ⚏

While the shape of this decanter is unremarkable, the scene engraved onto its body is nothing less than extraordinary. A standard cylinder shape, with a cut mushroom stopper, it appears to be English, dating around 1830. However, no Englishman living at that date was capable of executing such a masterpiece of engraving. The scene, resembling a grand painting, portrays a gathering of men being addressed by a speaker standing on high ground. It was sold without any further information, but the engraved crest provides a clue that its new owner could use to research into the background of this mysterious and remarkable piece of history. If the scene were proved to be of a famous historical event, a price of over £1,000 / €1,450 / $1,800 could be easily achievable

▶ **Glass bladder-shaped bottle,** c1700, 7½in (19cm) high.
£260–310
€380–450
$470–560 TMA ⚏

◀ **Brass-bound mahogany decanter set,** comprising six glass bottles with stoppers, late 19thC, 8½in (21.5cm) wide.
£260–310
€380–450
$470–560 SK ⚏

▶ **Glass decanter,** the neck applied with three rings, with stopper and coaster, c1820, 10¾in (27.5cm) high. From 1835–45 British glassmakers followed the Continental example with a steep rise in their output of coloured glassware, evidenced by a rash of different greens, yellow/ambers and reds. However, this aquamarine-tinted Prussian-shaped decanter is rare and earlier, probably dating 1800–20. The matching coaster is also very rare, which makes this decanter a very reasonable price.
£300–360 / €440–520
$550–660 DN ⚏

Pair of decanters, for Rum and Hollands, 1800–25, 9in (23cm) high.
£300–360 / €440–520
$550–660 DN ⚏

Pair of cut-glass decanters, with strawberry-cut decoration, with stoppers, Anglo-Irish, c1810, 10in (25.5cm) high.
£380–450 / €550–650
$690–820 NOA ⚹

Sets/pairs

Unless otherwise stated, any description which refers to 'a set' or 'a pair' includes a guide price for the entire set or the pair, even though the illustration may show only a single item.

Oak and brass tantalus, by Drew & Son, with three glass decanters and stoppers above two covered compartments, with silver labels, 12in (30.5cm) high. It is always difficult to find replacement bottles if decanter sets are incomplete. This is a reasonable price for a set that is complete and in good condition.
£340–400 €490–580
$620–730 JBe ⚹

Elizabeth Graydon-Stannus

Elizabeth Graydon-Stannus was a London dealer who published three books on the subject of Irish glass in the 1920s and '30s. Graydon-Stannus managed to deceive her customers into believing her view of the superiority of Irish glass. It was not until the collection of one of her customers was sold in 1936 for just seven per cent of his original investment of £13,000 / €18,800 / $23,600, that her antics were exposed. Some of the glass that Mrs Graydon-Stannus had proposed as being Irish was in fact made in Liège in Belgium, probably between 1790 and 1850.

Pair of glass decanters, decorated with flowering vines, with stoppers, c1790, 9¾in (25cm) high.
£440–520 / €640–750
$800–950 CGC ⚹

Irish Glass

Some fine glassware was produced in Ireland between 1785 and 1820. The pieces illustrated in this section include some of the idiosyncratic shapes and forms of decoration that were exclusive to Irish glassworks. The easiest Irish glass to identify is a group of moulded taper- and Prussian-shaped decanters that bear their makers' names branded into their bases: 'The Cork Glass Co' and 'Waterford'.

Glass decanter, engraved with stars, with associated stopper, Irish, probably Cork, c1810, 10¼in (26cm) high. The maker's marks applied to some Irish glassware between 1780 and 1820 can be faint to the point of invisibility but their presence can double the value of the pieces they were applied to.
£580–690 / €840–1,000
$1,050–1,250 DN ⚲

Set of three Bristol blue glass decanters, with painted labels, on a later silver-plated stand, c1830, 11in (28cm) high.
£530–590 / €770–860
$960–1,100 GRe ⊞

Pair of glass decanters, engraved with swags and anchors, with stoppers, slight damage, c1800, 11½in (29cm) high.
£680–810 / €990–1,150
$1,250–1,450 SWO ⚲

Glass ship's decanter, with stopper, c1780, 9½in (24cm) high.
£680–810 / €990–1,150
$1,250–1,450 TEN ⚲

▶ **Cork Glass Co decanter,** engraved with Vesica pattern, associated stopper, marked, Irish, 10¾in (27.5cm) high.
£720–860 / €1,050–1,250
$1,300–1,550 S(O) ⚲

Drinking Glasses

◀ **Pair of wine glasses,** c1800, 5in (12.5cm) high.
£25–30 / €40–45
$50–55 HTE ⊞

18th-century coloured glass

Virtually all the glassware produced in 18th-century Britain was colourless until the late 1700s. Green glass was relatively easy to make, created by the simple addition of some iron oxide, such as that derived from a rusty horseshoe. The problem arose when attempting to create consistent colours, which required a more scientific approach. Blue and amethyst became popular from the mid-1760s, but commercial forms of red, amber and yellow were not developed until the 19th century.

◀ **Wine glass,** c1850, 5in (12.5cm) high.
£60–70 / €85–100
$115–135 JHa ⊞

Wine glass, c1820,
5in (12.5cm) high.
£50–60 / €75–85
$100–115 JHa ⊞

▶ **Bohemian glass goblet,**
with opaque white overlay of petals, c1860, 7in (18cm) high. This style of decoration is now widely viewed as old fashioned and demand has fallen. This glass goblet fetched only half the upper auction estimate.
£80–90 / €115–130
$155–175 DN ✎

Bohemian glass beaker, c1840, 4¼in (10.5cm) high. Beakers such as this were produced in every conceivable decorative form, applied with cutting, engraving, enamelling, gilding and in every colour. This variety makes them extremely collectable, and examples by the leading decorators such as the Mohn family or Anton Kothgasser can fetch very high prices.
£95–110 / €140–160
$170–200 DORO ✎

◄ **Glass goblet,** with acid-etched decoration, c1860, 7in (18cm) high.
£95–110 / €135–160
$170–200 JHa ⊞

Pair of cordial glasses, with engraved decoration, on a diamond-cut stem, c1780, 4¾in (12cm) high.
£100–120 / €145–170
$180–210 LFA ⚒

Ale glass, on a facet-cut stem, c1780, 7¼in (18.5cm) high. This glass may have had the foot trimmed. It is important to check such details as restoration can be seriously detrimental to value. The rule of thumb for 18thC glasses is that the foot should be larger than the rim of the bowl.
£100–120 / €145–170
$200–230 DN ⚒

Glass goblet, c1860, 7in (18cm) high.
£105–120 / €150–170
$200–230 JHa ⊞

Ale glass, engraved with hops and barley, on a mercury-twist stem, c1770, 7½in (19cm) high.
£180–210 / €260–300
$330–380 WW ⚒

Miller's compares...

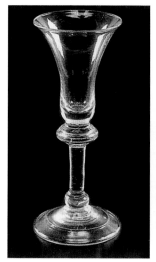

A. Gin glass, the bell bowl on an annular knop, c1740, 6in (15cm) high. This auction price shows that mid-18thC glasses do not necessarily cost a fortune.
£220–260 / €320–380
$400–470 DN ⚡

B. Wine glass, the trumpet bowl with tear inclusion, on an inverted-baluster stem with a cushion knop, c1720, 7in (18cm) high.
£650–780 / €940–1,150
$1,200–1,400 DN ⚡

Wine glass, the trumpet bowl on a multi-spiral air-twist stem, c1750, 6¾in (17cm) high.
£220–260 / €320–380
$400–470 LFA ⚡

English 18th-century drinking glasses have proved one of the most hotly contested collecting fields over the past 40 years. The average price has risen steeply since 1970, driven by one factor – rarity, and the earlier pieces tend to be rarer. Item B, a light baluster, is a rarer glass than Item A, the heavier gin glass, which is why Item B is the more expensive piece.

◄ **Wine glass,** with part-moulded bowl, on a double-series opaque-twist stem, c1770, 5¾in (14.5cm) high.
£220–260 / €320–380
$400–470 WW ⚡

Find out more in

Miller's Glass Antiques Checklist, Miller's Publications, 2001

► **Cordial glass,** with an ogee bowl on an opaque-corkscrew twist stem, 1760–70, 6¼in (16cm) high.
£230–270 / €330–390
$420–490 WW ⚡

◄ **Pair of Bohemian glass mugs and covers,** overlaid and engraved with wildlife and fruiting vines, with pewter mounts, c1850, 6in (15cm) high.
£280–330
€410–480
$510–600 G(L)

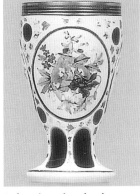

Bohemian glass beaker, by Wilhelm Hoffman, c1850, 5in (12.5cm) high.
£270–320 / €400–480
$490–580 DORO

◄ **Set of six Victorian glass rummers,** with fluted bowls, 5in (12.5cm) high.
£300–360 / €440–520
$550–660 G(L)

Wine glass, the bell bowl on a double-series opaque-twist stem, c1765, 7in (18cm) high.
£310–350 / €450–510
$560–640 JHa

◄ **Wine glass,** the ribbed ogee bowl on a double-series opaque-twist stem, c1765, 6in (15cm) high.
£310–350 / €450–510
$560–640 JHa

Wine glass, the bell bowl on a double-series triple-knopped stem, slight damage, c1770, 6½in (16.5cm) high. The tiny chips on the foot of this glass have reduced the value by around £150 / €220 / $270.
£300–360 / €440–520
$550–660 DN

Bohemian glass tumbler, decorated with a hunting scene and a monogram, c1840, 4in (10cm) high.
£320–380 / €460–550
$580–690 DORO ➢

Bohemian glass beaker, with overlaid decoration and a gilded rim, c1845, 4¾in (12cm) high.
£340–410 / €500–600
$620–740 DORO ➢

Wine glass, the trumpet bowl on a multi-air-twist stem, slight damage, c1750, 6¾in (17cm) high.
£380–450 / €550–650
$690–820 DN ➢

Wine glass, the funnel bowl engraved with a fruiting vine, on a multi-spiral knopped stem, c1750, 6in (15cm) high.
£380–450 / €550–650
$690–820 DN ➢

Wine glass, the trumpet bowl on a double-series opaque-twist stem, c1765, 7in (18cm) high.
£400–450 / €580–650
$730–820 JHa ⊞

Wine glass, the bucket bowl on a multi-spiral stem, c1750, 6½in (16.5cm) high.
£400–480 / €580–700
$730–870 DN ➢

Wine glass, the bell bowl on a double-knopped stem with tear inclusion, c1740, 6in (15.5cm) high.
£420–500 / €610–730 $760–910 DN ✗

Glass goblet, the ogee bowl decorated with a fruiting vine and bird, on a double-series twist stem, c1770, 7¾in (19.5cm) high.
£480–570 / €700–830 $870–1,050 DN ✗

Wine glass, the bell bowl engraved with floral decoration, on a multi-spiral air-twist stem, mid-18thC, 6¼in (16cm) high. Engraving can add £100 / €150 / $180 to a piece.
£500–600 / €730–870 $910–1,100 DN ✗

Miller's compares...

A. Set of three Kosta glass wine goblets, Swedish, 1750–1800, 6¾in (17cm) high.
£460–550 / €670–800 $840–1,000 BUK ✗

B. Pair of glass goblets, possibly by John Frederick Amelung, New Bremen Glassworks, the ogee bowls each with inscription, American, c1790, 6½in (16.5cm) high.
£960–1,150 / €1,400–1,650 $1,750–2,100 S(O) ✗

The glasses in Item A are engraved with a royal cipher and are by a named maker. However, those in Item B are tentatively attributed to the American New Bremen Glassworks of the German émigré, John Frederick Amelung of Maryland. They are

also engraved with a toast, wishing success to the *St Agnetta*, presumably a trading ship, and its commander. Attributable examples of 18th-century American glass are much rarer than European equivalents and this is why Item B achieved a higher price than Item A.

Glass goblet, the funnel bowl on a pedestal stem, c1750, 6in (15cm) high.
£520–620 / €750–900
$950–1,100 DN 🔨

Emile Gallé glass, with enamel decoration, 1890, 5½in (14cm) high. This shape is a stylized version of a German römer, one of the most distinctive shapes of wine glasses.
£540–600 / €780–870
$980–1,100 MiW ⊞

Wine glass, the bell bowl on a triple-knopped opaque-twist stem, c1765, 6½in (16.5cm) high.
£540–600 / €780–870
$980–1,100 JHa ⊞

Set of six Champagne glasses, 19thC, 7in (18cm) high. Champagne flutes are more popular than coupes of a similar age and are worth twice as much.
£550–660 / €800–960
$1,000–1,200 BUK(F) 🔨

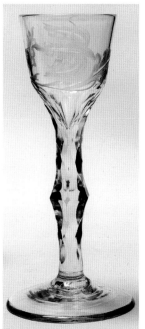

▶ **Two glass goblets and covers,** the funnel bowls engraved with bouquets of flowers and garlands, on faceted stems, Dutch or German, c1750, 9¼in (23.5cm) high. Fine quality engraving of this type was also widely adopted in mid- to late Victorian England.
£660–790 / €960–1,150
$1,200–1,400 S(Am) 🔨

Wine glass, engraved with an opening bud and a jay bird, c1765, 6in (15cm) high.
£620–690 / €900–1,000
$1,100–1,250 JHa ⊞

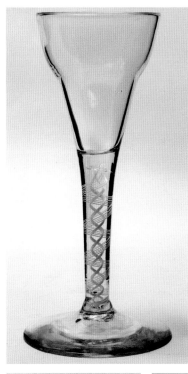

Glass beaker, with enamel floral decoration, c1840, 6in (15cm) high.
**£760–890 / €1,100–1,300
$1,400–1,600** DORO ⚲

◀ **Wine glass,** the trumpet bowl on a double-series opaque-twist stem, c1760, 7in (18cm) high.
**£670–750 / €970–1,100
$1,200–1,350** JHa ⊞

Wine glass, the bell bowl engraved with a flower and a moth, on a multi-spiral knopped stem with bead inclusions, c1750, 6½in (16.5cm) high.
**£780–930 / €1,150–1,350
$1,450–1,700** DN ⚲

Baccarat glass

Baccarat was one of the few glassworks to survive the economic fall-out from France's 1830 and 1848 revolutions and the Franco-Prussian War. The Russian aristocracy was an unlikely but significant contributor to the company's late-19th-century success. Following the Tzar's example, Russian nobles embraced the extravagant custom of smashing their glassware after each meal, to deny lesser beings the honour of using it, thereby inadvertently providing employment for some 800 of Baccarat's 2,000-strong workforce.

Wine glass, the bell bowl engraved with a rose and a bud, on a multi-knopped double-series air-twist stem, c1770.
**£900–1,050 / €1,300–1,550
$1,650–1,900** DN ⚲

Baccarat ruby-stained glass goblet, the double-ogee bowl engraved with a shield, horses and stags, French, c1850, 6in (15cm) high.
**£900–1,100 / €1,300–1,600
$1,650–2,000** S(O) ⚲

Jugs

Glass jug, decorated with Thumbprint pattern, American, c1870, 8in (20.5cm) high. Once popular items, demand for these late-Victorian decorative pieces has fallen in recent years. A fact that is reflected in the price achieved by this jug.
£30–35 / €45–50
$55–65 DuM ✎

Glass cider jug, French, Normandy, c1800, 7in (18cm) high.
£135–150 / €195–220
$240–270 G&G ▦

▶ **Cut-glass claret decanter,** with stopper, c1812, 9¾in (25cm) high. The area where handles are joined to Georgian claret decanters are notoriously prone to damage. Always check before buying as cracked examples are virtually worthless but out-number perfect examples by about 30 to 1.
£150–180 / €220–260
$270–320 SWO ✎

The look without the price

Silver-plate-mounted glass claret jug, c1900, 9½in (24cm) high.
£120–140
€175–200
$220–250
TMA ✎

Demand for silver-mounted claret jugs has soared in recent years, with prices for rare examples exceeding £20,000 / €29,000 / $36,400 while the price of equivalents with plated mounts has fallen. The glass component of this example is of fine quality, expertly decorated with intaglio-engraved chrysthemums, probably by one of the leading Stourbridge glassmakers, such as Thomas Webb or Stevens & Williams. If it had a solid silver mount it could fetch as much as £1,000 / €1,450 / $1,800.

Nailsea-style glass jug, with applied handle, 1800–25, 5½in (14cm) high.
£150–180 / €220–260
$270–320 DN ✎

Miller's compares...

Silver-mounted claret jug,
Birmingham, 1908,
10¾in (27.5cm) high.
£280–330 / €410–480
$510–600 DN(BR) ✯

A. Silver-mounted glass claret jug, with embossed decoration, maker's mark 'POSFN', German, late 19thC, 11¾in (30cm) high. Although this is good-quality glass, it is Continental silver. The same jug made with British hallmarked silver would have achieved £100 / €145 / $180 more.
£200–240 / €290–350
$360–440 DN(BR) ✯

B. Silver-mounted cut-glass claret jug, by Charles Boyton, inscribed and embossed with a Bacchanalian mask within vines, London 1886, 11½in (29cm) high. The silver mount has enabled this claret jug to achieve a high price.
£700–840 / €1,000–1,200
$1,250–1,550 G(B) ✯

Both the mounts on these claret jugs are decorated in the historical revival style that proved so popular accross Europe towards the end of the 1800s. Item A features asymmetrical rococo scrolls, stylistically dating from the 1750s, whereas the more expensive example bears Renaissance-style masks of Bacchus, the god of wine, framed by a fruiting vine. The disparity in their prices is probably explained by the fact that Item A was made in Germany, where silverware can be difficult to attribute to specific makers and the silver standard is 80 per cent. Item B, however, is British and is both attributable to a maker and formed in silver of 92.5 per cent purity, as required under British hallmarking laws. This accounts for its higher price.

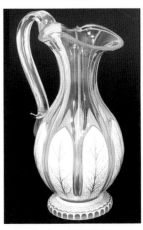

Pair of Victorian glass ewers, overlaid with opaque leaves and gilded veins, one handle repaired, 10¾in (27.5cm) high.
£400–480 / €580–700
$730–870 G(L) ✯

◀ **Silver-mounted cut-glass claret jug,** London 1892, 8¾in (22cm) high.
£450–540 / €650–780
$820–980 HOK ✯

▶ **WMF pewter-mounted cut-glass claret jug,** with etched decoration, German, c1906, 12in (30.5cm) high. The value of this claret jug lies in the mount made by WMF, which is a very collectable factory, even though a high proportion of the output was in base metals rather than silver. Attraction also lies in the good design.
£490–550 / €710–800
$890–1,000 NAW ⊞

Paperweights

Scrambled millefiori glass paperweight, possibly St Louis, set with twisted ribbons, cables and a silhouette cane, French, mid-19thC, 3¼in (8.5cm) diam.
£250–300 €360–430
$450–540 RTo ✤

Clichy glass miniature paperweight, set with five roses, c1850, 2in (5cm) diam.
£400–440 / €580–640
$720–800 DLP ⊞

Baccarat scrambled glass paperweight, French, 1845–60, 2½in (6.5cm) diam.
£270–300 / €390–440
$490–540 SWB ⊞

◀ **Baccarat glass miniature paperweight,** set with an anemone, c1850, 2in (5cm) diam.
£400–440 / €580–640
$720–800 DLP ⊞

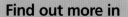

Find out more in

Miller's Paperweights of the 19th & 20th centuries: A Collector's Guide, Miller's Publications, 2000

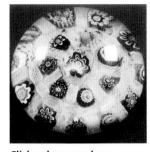

Clichy glass paperweight, set with concentric garlands, surface damage, mid-19thC, 2in (5cm) high.
£480–570 / €690–820
$870–1,050 WW ⚒

Clichy chequer glass paperweight, set with millefiori canes on a ground of latticinio tubing, surface scratches, mid-19thC, 2½in (6.5cm) diam.
£580–690 / €840–1,000
$1,050–1,250 DN ⚒

Clichy scrambled glass paperweight, French, 1845–60, 3in (7.5cm) diam.
£620–690 / €900–1,000
$1,100–1,250 SWB ⊞

Clichy glass paperweight, set with concentric canes, surface damage, French, mid-19thC, 2in (5cm) high.
£650–780 / €940–1,100
$1,200–1,400 WW ⚒

▶ **St Louis glass paperweight,** set with mixed fruit, French, 1845–60, 3in (7.5cm) diam. St Louis are well-known for their fruit and vegetable paperweights.
£850–950 / €1,250–1,400
$1,550–1,750 SWB ⊞

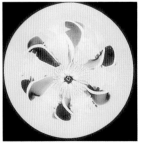

St Louis crown glass paperweight, with latticinio threads, French, c1850, 2½in (6.5cm) diam.
£900–1,050 / €1,300–1,500
$1,650–1,900 S ⚒

Some paperweight terms

- **Chequer:** a paperweight pattern resembling a chequer-board; also large canes separated by strips of latticinio
- **Concentric:** the centre of the weight is a single cane encircled by larger circles of canes
- **Crown:** where latticinio and coloured ribbons radiate out from a centre point at the top of the weight
- **Latticinio:** lengths of white opaque twist glass, sometimes called filigree, muslin or lace
- **Millefiori:** literally translates as 'a thousand flowers'; also means a group of canes
- **Scattered millefiori:** millefiori patterns, particularly on muslin. The canes are usually spaced rather than scattered
- **Upset muslin:** strips of latticinio used as a ground

Scent Bottles

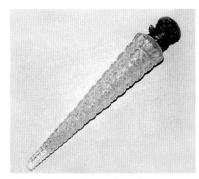

Silver-mounted scent bottle, c1880,
6½in (16.5cm) long.
£80–95 / €115–135
$150–180 DUM ⚲

Scent bottles

Glass bottles for containing exotic essences and perfumed oils have been made since the days of the Egyptian pharaohs and are a long established area of collecting. Their sizes and decorative variations are almost boundless and, being fairly small, they are easy to transport and display. Rare coloured examples painted in gold and enamels by the 18th-century London decorator James Giles (1717–80) are highly sought after and can command five-figure sums. However, Victorian pieces are fairly common, with prices ranging upwards of £20 / €30 / $35. The presence of silver mounts, the marks of leading makers and unusual novelty shapes boost values considerably.

Miller's compares...

A. Silver-mounted glass scent bottle, with embossed decoration, late 19thC, 5in (12.5cm) long.
£90–105 / €130–150
$170–200 FHF ⚲

B. Cut-glass scent bottle, with 19thC mount, Dutch, 18thC, 3¼in (8.5cm) high.
£480–570 / €700–830
$870–1,050 WW ⚲

Scent bottles are among the most sought-after categories of antiques, and these two pieces are typical of the available variety. Both are of fine quality but Item B fetched five times more than Item A. Item A is a fairly common example but Item B is far rarer, being around 150 years earlier. Item B also possesses two unusual features consisting of

a silver cover beneath the cap that enabled the contents to be sprinkled onto a handkerchief, and a central cavity still containing a tiny, removable silver box that was probably used to contain cosmetic patches, a popular 18th-century fashion accessory. These factors combine to make it a more desirable and therefore more expensive piece.

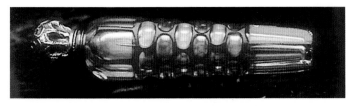

◄ **Victorian glass scent bottle,** with embossed white-metal hinged cover, 4½in (11.5cm) long.
£110–130 / €160–190
$200–240 JAd ⚲

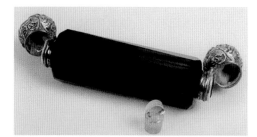

◀ **Silver-mounted double-ended glass scent bottle,** with embossed decoration, 19thC, 6in (15cm) long.
£140–165
€200–240
$250–300 FHF ⚲

Silver-mounted cut-glass scent bottle, the mount pierced and embossed with putti and birds, the cover with a mask, maker's mark rubbed, Birmingham 1904, 5½in (14cm) high. The value of this piece lies in its ornate Rococo-revival silver mount.
£150–180 / €220–260
$270–330 DN ⚲

Brilliant-cut glass scent bottle, with a sterling silver stopper, American, c1890.
£165–195 / €240–280
$300–360 DuM ⚲

Silver-mounted glass scent bottle, by Horton Allday, set with paste stones, Birmingham 1901, 1½in (4cm) long.
£140–155 / €200–220
$250–280 BEX ⊞

Brilliant cutting

Brilliant cutting is a form of glass decoration that was pioneered in America from 1876. It is characterized by deep, crisp and extremely complex motifs, tightly grouped to create an effect of great luxury. The fashion for brilliant cutting spread quickly to Europe, with versions soon being made in England, France, Sweden and Bohemia, where it is still produced today. Pieces made after 1900 often involved the use of figured blanks. This consisted of the basic shape and decoration being pressed and the resulting pre-formed pieces being brought in by cutting shops and the final pattern wheel-finished. Prior to that date, all cut glass was created exclusively by hand.

Silver-mounted cut-glass scent bottle, by Frederic Purnell, London 1876, 4in (10cm) high.
£165–185 / €240–270
$300–340 BEX ⊞

◀ **Pair of silver-mounted cut-glass scent bottles,** Birmingham 1902, 5in (12.5cm) high.
£180–210
€260–300
$320–380 FHF ⚲

Silver-mounted glass scent bottle,
by William Hutton & Sons, London 1898,
4¾in (12cm) high.
£210–250 / €300–360
$380–450 DN ⚒

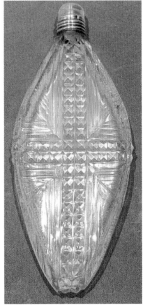

**◄ Silver-mounted glass
scent bottle,** by William
Comyns, the embossed mounts
and hinged cover depicting a
flower seller, London 1899,
4¾in (12cm) high.
£250–300 / €360–430
$460–550 DN ⚒

**◄ Silver-mounted cut-glass
scent bottle,** c1800,
4½in (11.5cm) long.
£220–250 / €320–360
$400–460 BEX ⊞

Cut-glass scent bottle, with
silver filigree overlay, by William
Comyns, London 1906,
5½in (14cm) high.
£260–310 / €380–450
$470–560 WilP ⚒

Set of three gilt-metal-mounted glass scent bottles,
each cover with a watercolour depicting a Parisian scene, in a bone-
mounted and gilt-brass case, slight damage, late 19thC,
6in (15cm) wide.
£280–330 / €410–480
$510–600 RTo ⚒

◄ Rock crystal snuff bottle, carved with a bird, the reverse
with pine and bamboo, 19thC, 2½in (6.5cm) high.
£300–360 / €440–520
$550–660 SWO ⚒

Vases

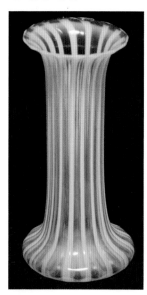

Whitefriars Vaseline glass vase, marked 'Powell', 1900, 6in (15cm) high.
£105–120 / €150–175
$200–230 MiW ⊞

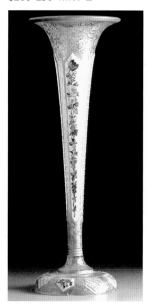

Bohemian glass vase, with floral decoration, c1860, 11½in (29.5cm) high. There is fading demand for this style of ornate glass.
£150–180 / €220–260
$270–320 WW ✣

Vaseline glass

Vaseline glass is a confusing term that describes a variety of effects. For instance, American collectors use it to describe a particular colour of yellow-green glass made by adding two per cent uranium dioxide to the formula. The resulting glass always turns bright green when viewed in ultra-violet light and, if it does not, then Americans do not regard it as true Vaseline glass. On the other hand, in Britain and Australia virtually any glass containing a light green, blue or white opalescence is termed 'Vaseline'.

Mary Gregory glass

It has long been known that Mary Gregory, who worked as a decorator at the Boston & Sandwich Glassworks, Massachusetts, between 1886 and 1888, never created glassware of the type that now bears her name. Yet the term continues to be used in the absence of any alternative. Coloured glassware of this type, usually decorated with romantic or pastoral scenes in opaque-white enamels, continues to be produced today and it can be difficult to discern late-Victorian pieces from recent examples.

Vaseline glass vase, 1900, 5in (12.5cm) high.
£105–120 / €150–175
$200–230 MiW ⊞

◄ **Pair of cranberry glass vases,** one painted with a spaniel and puppies, the other with a swan and a fox, 9¾in (25cm) high.
£110–130 / €160–190
$200–240 PFK ✣

Bohemian cranberry glass vase, with an applied porcelain plaque hand-painted with a portrait of a lady, 19thC, 10½in (26.5cm) high.
£180–210 / €260–300
$330–380 PF ✣

Vaseline glass vase, c1900,
4in (10cm) high.
£250–280 / €360–410
$460–510 MiW ⊞

**Bohemian amber-flashed
glass vase,** with eight panels
wheel-cut with animals, damaged,
19thC, 9¼in (23.5cm) high.
£200–240 / €290–350
$360–440 CHTR ⚒

Pair of Vaseline glass vases,
c1900, 8in (20.5cm) high.
£250–280 / €360–410
$460–510 MiW ⊞

▶ **Pair of Mary
Gregory glass
vases,** c1880,
13in (33cm) high.
£350–420
€510–610
$640–760 DuM ⚒

Vaseline glass vase, by John Walsh
Walsh, 1900, 4½in (11.5cm) high.
£270–300 / €390–440
$490–550 MiW ⊞

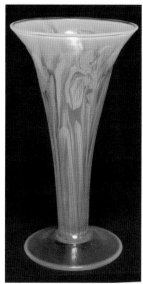

Glass vase, c1900, 8in (20.5cm) high.
£380–420 / €550–610
$690–760 SHa ⊞

Vaseline glass vase, Austrian,
1900, 12in (30.5cm) high.
£360–400 / €520–580
$660–730 MiW ⊞

Vaseline glass vase, Austrian,
1900, 10in (25.5cm) high.
£360–400 / €520–580
$660–730 MiW ⊞

Loetz glass vase, applied with tear-drop motifs, Austrian, c1900, 8in (20.5cm) high.
£500–600 / €730–870
$910–1,100 S(O) ✎

For more examples of
Vases see Ceramics (page 64–131)

Emile Gallé cameo glass vase, French, c1900, 3in (7.5cm) high.
£540–600 / €780–870
$980–1,100 MiW ⊞

▶ **Moser bottle vase,** with enamelled decoration, and gilt handles, Bohemian, c1890, 9in (23cm) high.
£840–1,000
€1,200–1,450
$1,550–1,800 S ✎

Moser

Moser, based at Karlovy Vary, Bohemia, was one of the greatest glassworks in the inter-war years between 1918 and 1939. Even during the late-19th century, its output, directed by Leo Moser, achieved a superior quality and was expensive when originally retailed.

The look without the price

Gallé is a magic name for glass collectors. The greatest Art Nouveau glassmaker, Emile Gallé was born in Nancy, France in 1846. Widely educated and trained, Gallé was fascinated by nature, the bizarre and practical chemistry. Gallé's output can be divided into two categories, his personal pieces and a factory output that subsidized the former. This particular pair of vases, created with acids, fall into the factory category, hence the price of £860 / €1,250 / $1,600 as examples of his superior work fetch five-, six- or even seven-figure sums.

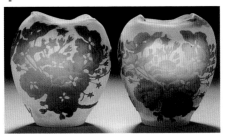

Pair of Emile Gallé cameo glass vases, etched with clematis, marked, French, c1900, 5½in (14cm) high.
£860–1,050 / €1,250–1,500
$1,600–1,900 S(O) ✎

Miscellaneous

◄ **Glass spirit measure,** c1860, 4½in (11.5cm) high. Spirit measures are widely collected and examples with lead seals stamped 'Richardson's Patent' are particularly sought after, c1860.
£50–60 / €75–85
$100–115 GAU ⊞

► **Glass jar and cover,** French, 19thC, 13in (33cm) high.
£180–200
€260–290
$330–370 KET ⊞

► **Two Bohemian glass spirit flasks,** c1760, larger 8¾in (22cm) high.
£310–370
€450–540
$560–670
DORO ⚷

Glass tazza, c1740, 8in (20.5cm) diam. Tazzas of this type were made in England between 1730 and 1780. They were used as table centrepieces, comprising three or four pieces of differing diameters, each seated on top of the other to create what were known as 'trees' or 'pyramids'. When placed on the table, each layer was decked out with colourful sweets or glasses containing exotic fruits, jellies or syllabub desserts and often bearing a sweetmeat glass at the top containing a pineapple.
£350–420 / €510–610
$640–760 DN ⚷

◄ **Silver-mounted glass cruet set,** by Henry Wilkinson, London/Birmingham, 1873.
£400–450
€580–650
$730–820 BEX ⊞

► **Glass liqueur set,** comprising four decanters and 13 glasses, three glasses missing, in a tortoiseshell and brass-inlaid boulle-style box, French, c1870, 14¼in (36cm) wide.
£840–1,000 / €1,200–1,450
$1,550–1,800 S(O) ⚷

Clocks, Watches & Barometers

This year's edition of *Miller's Buying Affordable Antiques Price Guide* yet again gives a good selection of clocks and barometers that can be found readily in auction rooms and antiques shops.

The continuing trend for minimalism prevails, thus leaving good opportunites for the young enthusiast or impoverished collector alike to buy examples at prices below those that were being asked five years ago. As this trend progresses so do the gaps between the good, bad and indifferent. Auction rooms are reporting extremely good prices for the finest examples, which is what every collector is aiming for, but the examples illustrated in this guide are a good place to start.

A good bench mark for the clocks market is the standard carriage timepiece, which has barely moved in price for the last five years. It is still very easy to purchase a good example for around £50–70 / €75–100 / $90–130. However, one should start to look beyond this range and typically try to find a striking example with added features such as a repeat or alarm movement; these can still be purchased at around £200–300 / €290–440 / $370–550. Look out for any blemishes like cracked dials or panels as these will really reduce the value of the clock and these types of repair and restoration can be quite costly. The range of examples shown here demonstrates what extremely good value can be had for relatively low sums.

One area that has shown improvement in popularity and price is the simple fusee wall clock. Perhaps this is because it fits in easily with modern design vogues, or maybe people are finally realizing that even though these clocks were made in prolific numbers, extreme care and craftsmanship were used in their construction.

As with furniture, the busy French style and more ornate designs are finding less favour with the auction rooms at the moment so now is a good time to look for the best examples if you like this style of clock. They may or may not come back into fashion but if you buy what you like you will always have the pleasure of living with the antique.

Barometers continue to sell with modest prices for the mundane examples. Do not touch anything in this category that requires extensive restoration as the cost will easily outstrip the capital value. Flat-back stick barometers still represent good value for money but bowfronted examples by good makers continue to command prices that exceed the parameters of this book.

Pocket watches and wristwatches are still widely collected. As ever, it pays to buy the best examples you can find while being cautious of fakes, especially in the wristwatch world. If you buy from a reputable dealer they will often have repaired and restored the watch to working condition before selling it and they will often agree to take the watch back for regular cleaning and repair.

Jeremy Sparks

Bracket Clocks

Gilt-brass cased bracket clock, with an urn surmount, 19thC, 9in (23cm) high. Clocks such as this, which is of classic French style, are currently out of fashion. Prices have been stable for five years or so and this piece represents really good value.
**£180–210 / €250–300
$320–380 WilP** 🔨

Walnut bracket clock, the Continental movement striking on two gongs, the case with a raised gallery, late 19thC, 11¾in (30cm) high.
**£280–330 / €410–480
$510–600 WilP** 🔨

▶ **Victorian Regency-style mahogany dome-top bracket clock,** the enamelled dial inscribed 'Finnigans Ltd', the Continental movement chiming on a gong, with brass carrying handles and fretwork panels to the sides, 16in (40.5cm) high. This is a handsome, classical-looking clock at a reasonable price.
**£190–220
€270–320
$350–400 GIL** 🔨

◀ **Edwardian mahogany pagoda-top bracket clock,** the break arch dial with a strike/silent indicator and a silvered plaque inscribed 'Webster Qn Victoria St London', with an eight-day double fusee movement chiming on a gong, the base carved with a frieze of stylized leaves, 16¼in (41.5cm) high.
**£250–300 / €360–430
$460–550 RTo** 🔨

▶ **Edwardian carved walnut bracket clock,** with a Junghans movement and Westminster chime, together with a matching carved walnut bracket, 12½in (32cm) wide.
**£320–380
€460–550
$580–690 WilP** 🔨

The look without the price

Gilt-metal-mounted kingwood bracket clock, with an enamelled dial, the eight-day movement striking the hour and half-hour on a gong, the case inlaid with flowers and foliage, French, 19thC, 27in (68.5cm) high.
£380–450 / €550–650
$690–820 M 🔨

This clock is a classic French design with attractive marquetry decoration. Had the gilt-metal mounts been made of ormolu, this clock would have been considerably more valuable.

Mahogany lancet bracket clock, with an enamel dial, the Vincenti brass drum-shaped twin-train movement with an anchor escapement striking on a gong, the case decorated with line inlay, with brass handles, French, late 19thC, 11½in (29cm) high. Lancet-case clocks are always popular and this clock has the benefit of the quality feature of brass ogee bracket feet.
£450–540 / €650–780
$820–980 DN(BR) 🔨

◀ **Bracket clock,** by Gosselin, Paris, French, 18thC, 12in (30.5cm) high. This clock shows traditional French characteristics in its enamelled porcelain numeral markers, although the case is more understated than usual. It is an attractive piece.
£750–900 / €1,100–1,300
$1,350–1,600 JNic 🔨

Victorian mahogany lancet bracket clock, the brass face with a silver chapter ring, the eight-day movement striking on four gongs, the case with satinwood banding, 13in (33cm) high.
£480–570 / €700–830
$870–1,050 PF 🔨

Find out more in

Miller's Clocks & Barometers Buyer's Guide, Miller's Publications, 2001

▶ **Regency mahogany bracket clock,** the movement and dial associated, with inlaid decoration, 14½in (37cm) high. Over the years, as clocks fell into disrepair, component parts would be used to make up complete working pieces.
£840–1,000
€1,200–1,450
$1,500–1,800
S(O) 🔨

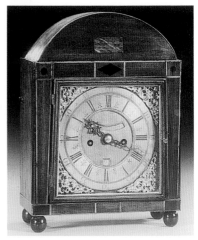

Carriage Clocks

◀ **Gilt-brass carriage clock,** French, 19thC, with a tooled leather travelling case.
£90–105
€130–150
$165–190 WilP ✗

Miniature brass carriage clock, with blind-fret decoration, 19thC, 4in (10cm) high. Miniature pieces tend to be proportionally more valuable than their larger counterparts. While this clock is not of high quality, it is still good value. Always check the condition of enamel dials as any damage can be difficult and expensive to repair.
£120–140 / €170–200
$210–250 WilP ✗

▶ **Engraved brass carriage clock,** with an enamel dial, compensated balance and lever escapement striking on a gong, French, late 19thC, 6in (15cm) high. Although this clock has a repeating mechanism striking the hour and half-hour, the dull finish has held its value down, possibly by 50 per cent.
£160–190
€240–280
$290–350 G(L) ✗

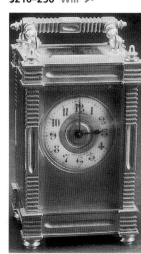

◀ **Brass carriage clock,** by Tiffany & Co, with a striking movement, c1900, with a leather carrying case. This clock was probably made in France. A good retailer's name always adds to the value of a piece.
£260–310
€380–450
$470–560 L&E ✗

Gilt-bronze carriage clock, with a porcelain chapter ring, French, c1890, 5½in (14cm) high. The design of this clock may not appeal to all tastes, but the gilt-bronze case has raised its value.
£270–320 / €390–460
$490–580 JAA ✗

The look without the price

Brass carriage clock, with an enamel dial, lever escapement and striking movement, late 19thC, 7in (18cm) high.
£340–400 / €490–580
$620–730 BWL 🔨

This clock has good, bold design which gives the impression of being of good quality.

▶ **Brass gorge-cased carriage clock,** with an enamel dial, repeat button and eight-day twin-train striking mechanism, stamped No. 22369, French, late 19thC, 5in (12.5cm) high. The repeat mechanism and case design have added value to this clock.
£400–480
€580–700
$730–870 DMC 🔨

Carriage Clocks

Carriage clocks originated in France from the complicated *pendule de voyage*, literally 'travel clock', made by Abraham Louis Breguet (1747–1823). Paul Garnier (1801–69) then simplified the design, making it possible to produce these clocks more cheaply. The range of cases varied widely, although there were certain standard case shapes, of which the obis, corniche and gorge were the most common. Many French carriage clocks were exported to England at the time of manufacture. England did have its own carriage clock makers, but they produced far fewer clocks for a more select market. Their clocks tended to be larger, heavier and more expensive and made use of a fusee and chain.

Brass carriage clock, with an eight-day movement, c1890, 4in (10cm) high. Oval clocks always command a high value. When buying any clock it is wise to take the cost of insurance premiums into consideration, especially small examples such as this which may be more likely to attract thieves.
£510–570 / €740–830
$930–1,050 SAT ⊞

▶ **Louis XVI-style tortoiseshell-veneered and ormolu-mounted arch-top carriage clock,** by Tiffany & Co, the enamel dial decorated with floral swags and surrounded by a paste bezel, the two-train chiming movement by Vincenti & Cie, on fluted feet, c1900, 9¾in (25cm) high. This clock represents the excesses of French design but is not without style and panache. The Tiffany name has also added value to the piece.
£510–600 / €740–870
$940–1,100 SK(B) 🔨

◄ **Brass carriage clock,** the enamel dial with an alarm subsidiary dial, the ratched tooth platform escapement striking and repeating on a gong, the case with a handle and corner finials, fretted borders and corner columns, French, c1900, 6in (15cm) high. While the intricate decoration of this clock may not appeal to all tastes, it has the added attractions of an alarm and a repeating movement which will have increased the value of the piece.
£640–750
€940–1,100
$1,150–1,350
S(Am) ⚘

Brass carriage clock, French, 19thC, 6½in (16.5cm) high. The bold design and enamel dials have added value to this clock.
£650–780 / €960–1,150
$1,200–1,400 JNic ⚘

Brass carriage clock, by Henri Jacot, with later platform escapement, French, c1890, 7in (18cm) high. This clock is by a good maker, but the fact that it has a replacement escapement has reduced its value.
£690–770 / €1,000–1,100
$1,250–1,400 ⊞ CPC

Brass carriage clock, by Duverdry & Bloquel, with silver-plated pillars, c1900, 5⅝in (14.5cm) high. Many carriage clocks had silver decoration and this often improves the price achieved.
£840–940 / €1,200–1,350
$1,500–1,700 CPC ⊞

Brass baroque-style carriage clock, with a foliate-engraved silvered dial, the eight-day two-train movement with a platform lever escapement striking the hour and half-hour on a gong, with button repeat, the backplate numbered 11978, maker's stamp for Margaine, French, late 19thC, 6¾in (17cm) high. Although rather fussy in design this clock is by a good maker and these factors have added value to the piece.
£880–1,050 / €1,250–1,500
$1,600–1,900 DN ⚘

Longcase Clocks

Brass *Comtoise* clock, with enamel dial and fitted verge movement, French, late 18thC, 9½in (24cm) wide.
£250–300 / €360–430
$460–550 CHTR ⚒

▶ **Oak and mahogany longcase clock,** by Geo. C. Heater, Wantage, with a painted dial and 30-hour movement with anchor escapement striking on a bell, repairs to case, 19thC, 77¼in (196cm) high. The 30-hour mechanism has reduced the value of this clock.
£400–480 / €580–700
$730–870 DN ⚒

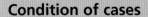

Condition of cases

All clocks should have their original finish and decorative features intact. Some restoration is acceptable if carried out sympathetically but cases in need of extensive reconstruction and repair are best avoided. Humidity and temperature changes cause veneers to lift and doors to warp. Mouldings may loosen as the original glue dries out and bubbles caused by excessive heat and humidity can appear under the lacquer on lacquered cases. No clock should be kept in direct sunlight as this causes the finish to bleach. Always check for missing finials, broken glass, damaged mouldings and scratches or damage to polish

Oak longcase clock, the engraved brass dial with a date aperture, the associated eight-day movement striking on a bell, the case with mahogany banding, later moulding to base, 18thC, 90in (228.5cm) high. This marriage of a movement and a case is often found in longcase clocks. When purchasing a longcase clock, check that there is no gap between the dial and the hood door. If there is a gap, investigate carefully before buying the piece.
£420–500 / €610–730
$760–910 WW ⚒

◀ **George III oak longcase clock,** by Thomas Wood, Painswick, with a silvered chapter ring, the hood with gilt-capped columns, 73in (185.5cm) high.
£520–620 / €750–900
$1,000–1,150 HYD ⚒

◄ **Mahogany line-inlaid longcase clock,** with a painted dial and date aperture, the spandrels painted with figures representing the four continents, the arch with a scene entitled 'Robert Burns at the Plough', the eight-day twin-train four-pillar movement with an anchor escapement and rack striking on a bell, 19thC, 84in (213.5cm) high. This clock has a well-painted and interesting dial which would appeal to collectors.
£520–620
€750–900
$950–1,100
DN ✦

Inlaid mahogany longcase clock, the painted dial with subsidiary seconds and a moonphase, the movement with anchor escapement and rack striking on a bell, slight damage, c1820, 90½in (230cm) high. The value of this clock has been lowered because of the condition of the case. Restoration would be advisable, as once completed this clock could be worth twice this price.
£570–680 / €830–990
$1,050–1,250 S(Am) ✦

◄ **Victorian oak longcase clock,** by Gatward, Huntingdon, with a painted dial, the twin-train movement with anchor escapement striking on a bell, 80¼in (204cm) high. The painted dial contributes to the attraction of this clock, but the badly restored plinth has detracted from the value and further restoration is required.
£600–720 / €870–1,050
$1,100–1,300 SWO ✦

The look without the price

George III oak and mahogany-banded longcase clock, the painted enamel dial with subsidiary seconds and date aperture, the arch with a moonphase, the twin-train movement with anchor escapement striking on a bell and 'Walker Hughes, Birmingham' false plate, 86¾in (220.5cm) high.
£680–810 / €990–1,150
$1,250–1,450
DN(BR) ✦

A moonphase feature always adds value to a longcase clock. Prices for longcase clocks have remained stable for the last five years, and this example represents really good value.

Mantel Clocks

► **Victorian marble *en suite* mantel clock,** surmounted by three domes above a gilt-metal dial, clock 17in (43cm) wide. The price of this clock is low, possibly because of damage to the marble. Always check the condition of stoneware and avoid damaged pieces.
£85–95 / €120–135
$155–175 JAd ↗

Victorian marble mantel clock, with a silvered dial, 19¼in (49cm) high. This traditional-style small mantel clock conforms more easily to modern-day living compared to larger examples and this will have added value to this piece.
£115–135 / €170–200
$200–240 JAd ↗

The look without the price

Spelter and alabaster mantel clock, with a figural surmount, French, 19thC, 11in (28cm) high.
£60–70 / €85–100
$110–125 PF ↗

This is an attractive spelter clock. Had the surmount been made of bronze the value of this clock could have doubled or trebled.

Edwardian mahogany mantel clock, with an eight-day movement striking on a gong, the case with a pendulum bob window, 12½in (32cm) high. The wooden case of this clock appears to have split and this may account for its low value.
£130–155 / €185–220
$240–280 DA ↗

► **Late Victorian gilt-brass domed mantel clock,** with a glazed dial, the eight-day movement striking on a gong, the case with an eagle surmount and cast foliate and mask decoration, 15¾in (40cm) high. This clock, with its attractive dial set against gilt metal, is as much a decorative statement as it is a timepiece.
£160–190 / €240–280
$290–350 RTo ↗

◄ **Edwardian mahogany and boxwood-strung mantel clock,** with a silvered dial and German Westminster chime movement, 15¾in (40cm) high. This is an attractive and affordable clock in a quality case.
£190–220 / €280–330
$340–400 L&E ⚒

Empire-revival-style gilt-metal mantel clock, with an enamel dial, the eight-day movement striking on a gong, with a gridiron pendulum, the bowed case surmounted by an eagle finial and flaming urns, French, c1880, 19in (48.5cm) high. This clock is of typical Continental design and has a mercury-style gridiron pendulum. Genuine mercury pendulums are a sign of a good-quality clock, but beware because *faux* mecury pendulums were sometimes used.
£190–220 / €280–330
$340–400 Hal ⚒

Gilt-metal-mounted oak mantel clock, the dial with a silvered chapter ring, with an eight-day quarter-striking movement, the case surmounted with five brass finials, the sides with metal grilles, German, late 19thC, 11in (28cm) wide. The oak case of this clock will have kept the value down. With a mahogany case the price would have increased by 50 per cent.
£300–360 / €440–520
$550–660 PF ⚒

Victorian carved mahogany mantel timepiece, with a painted dial and single fusee movement, 12¾in (32.5cm) high. Timepieces are clocks that do not have a striking mechanism; they are always less expensive than clocks that strike or chime.
£280–330 / €410–480
$510–600 WW ⚒

Mantel Clocks

Mantel clocks were made in France in large numbers from 1780 to 1880 and in a wide range of highly decorative cases with figural decoration. Those made in the 1830s to 1850s are usually a little more subtle and of better quality. As with the garnitures of that period, the movements are of a fairly standard type and not therefore of great importance. Mantel clocks are abundant and widely available, being second in popularity to the carriage clock, but quality and condition do vary. Most European countries have produced mantel clocks in large numbers since the mid-19th century.

Late Victorian gilded spelter and alabaster timepiece, the enamel dial flanked to one side by a figure of an artist, with an eight-day movement, on an ebonized stand, 18in (45.5cm) high. This clock is typical of the period – figures and rococo-style motifs played a large part in the decoration of clocks in the late 19thC.
£300–360 / €440–520
$550–660 DA ⚒

Gilt-bronze mantel clock,
with an eight-day movement,
the case with acorn finials and
glass front and side panels,
French, c1890, 10in (25.5cm)
high. Gilt-bronze is a sign of
good quality, and this
timepiece is attractive which
makes it desirable and therefore
more valuable.
£370–420 / €540–610
$670–760 K&D ⊞

**Late Victorian oak arch-top mantel
clock,** by Heitzman & Son, Cardiff, with
a silvered dial and eight-day movement
striking on a gong, the case with carved
decoration and five brass finials, on brass
ball feet, 15½in (39.5cm) high. This is a
classic clock design – 18thC style with
19thC features.
£400–480 / €580–700
$730–870 PF ✧

**Brass four-glass mantel
clock,** by Japy Frères, with
an enamel dial, the twin-train
movement with a mercury
compensated pendulum, French,
late 19thC, 12in (30.5cm) high.
This clock is a well-made piece
and represents good value.
£400–480 / €580–700
$730–870 DMC ✧

**Wood and metal mantel
clock,** with a silvered dial
and striking movement, the
case decorated with gilt and
stucco, some losses, c1830,
21in (53.5cm) high.
£480–570 / €700–830
$870–1,050 DORO ✧

Brass rococo-style mantel clock, with a
silvered dial, the movement signed 'Lewis &
Son, Paris' striking on a bell, late 19thC,
8¼in (21cm) high.
£440–520 / €640–750
$800–950 CHTR ✧

◄ **Gilt-bronze mantel
timepiece,** the enamel dial
with subsidiary seconds, the case
in the form of a fluted column
surmounted by figures of a boy
carrying a girl on his back, on a
marble base, 19thC, 11¾in (30cm)
high. Figural clocks depicting
children are appealing and
therefore command a premium.
£460–550 / €670–800
$840–1,000 Bea ✧

Chateau clock, No. 2649, the enamel dial decorated with floral swags, the backplate stamped 'Maple & Co, Paris', the case with turrets and spires, French, late 19thC, 16in (40.5cm) high. This is a French version of a Gothic clock. It is unusual and attractive and made for a good retailer; and these factors add value.
£490–580 / €710–840
$890–1,050 BWL

Ormolu mantel clock, with a silvered dial, the eight-day movement with an outside countwheel striking on a bell, inscribed 'Guyerdet Ainé Paris 4813 127', the case decorated with scrolling leafage and shells, surmounted with a seated Turkish lady, French, early 19thC, 10¾in (27.5cm) high. This clock was possibly made for the Turkish market, but Turkish images were often used as decoration in England in the 18th and 19thC.
£500–600 / €730–870
$910–1,100 WW

Ormolu and Sèvres porcelain clock, by Le Roy & Fils, Paris, No. 7438, French, 19thC, 15in (38cm) high. This clock is by Le Roy & Fils, a well-known maker whose output was prolific, and it is also in a good-quality case. These two qualities make it a desirable piece for collectors.
£500–600 / €730–870
$910–1,100 JNic

Rosewood and marquetry-inlaid mantel clock, with a silvered dial and eight-day striking movement, the outside countwheel stamped 'Osmont ainé à Paris', French, late 19thC, 9¼in (23.5cm) high. Good marquetry inlay is always desirable and adds to the value of a clock.
£550–660 / €800–960
$1,000–1,200 WW

Mahogany and brass-inlaid mantel clock, with a painted dial and eight-day striking movement, the pierced side panels with ring handles, early 19thC, 17¾in (45cm) high.
£580–690 / €840–1,000
$1,050–1,250 LFA

Bird's-eye maple mantel timepiece, by Viners & Co, London, with an engine-turned gilt-brass dial and a single-train movement, 19thC, 6¾in (17cm) high. The use of an exotic wood has made this an attractive and particularly collectable piece.
£600–720 / €870–1,050
$1,100–1,300 DMC

Siena marble and bronze mantel clock garniture, the dial with an enamel chapter ring enclosing a relief centre, the movement with anchor escapement and countwheel striking on a bell and silk suspended pendulum, the case surmounted by a pelican feeding its young, flanked by an old soldier holding an infant, together with two marble and bronze *coupes*, French, c1830, clock 18½in (47cm) high. To some tastes this impressive garniture may be overwhelmed by the decoration and this may have held the price down.
£650–780 / €940–1,100
$1,200–1,400 S(Am) 🔨

Rosewood inlaid portico mantel clock, with a painted dial, the twin-barrel movement with an outside countwheel striking on a bell, the gridiron pendulum with a foliate-cast bob, the columns with engine-turned capitals, the backplate stamped '46431 5701', c1880, 18in (45.5cm) high. This pleasing, simple style of clock is always popular.
£650–780 / €940–1,100
$1,200–1,400 TEN 🔨

Porcelain mantel clock, with a silver dial, the eight-day movement with a rear countwheel striking on a bell and silk thread suspension, in a two-piece porcelain base, bell missing, French, c1880, 12in (30.5cm) high. When purchasing porcelain clocks always check the case for damage or repair.
£670–800 / €970–1,150
$1,200–1,450 LHA 🔨

Brass and *champlevé* mantel clock, surmounted by a cherub, with urn finials at each corner and two caryatid supports, on a stepped base, French, 19thC, 18½in (47cm) high. The use of enamel on clocks was widespread throughout the 19thC in France; it complements ormolu and gilt-metal extremely well.
£700–840 / €1,000–1,200
$1,250–1,500 L&T 🔨

Gilt-bronze and marble mantel clock, by Henri Marc, Paris, with an enamel dial, the case with marble inset panels and applied trophies of arms, surmounted by a figure of a Saracen, French, late 19thC, 20in (51cm) wide. This highly decorative clock may not be to all tastes.
£700–840 / €1,000–1,200
$1,250–1,500 PF 🔨

Louis XVI marble and ormolu mantel clock, by François, Paris, with a striking brass eight-day movement, in a pillared marble case with an urn finial and an ormolu knop, on a base with ormolu decoration, French, 14in (35.5cm) high. Although silk suspended pendulums were widely used, they always add value.
£780–930 / €1,150–1,350
$1,400–1,650 TRM(C) 🔨

Wall Clocks

A mahogany-veneered wall clock, by Gilbert, American, c1900, 26in (66cm) high. This is an attractive wall clock with a mass-produced movement.
£95–110 / €140–160 $175–200 JAA ⚲

Carved oak cuckoo wall clock, with a twin-train movement striking on a gong, the case decorated with a carved bird surmount, 19thC, 18½in (47cm) high. There are now many collectors of cuckoo clocks. The finer and more prolific the carving, the higher the value. Always check that the bellows that work the cuckoo are not split before purchasing.
£130–155 / €185–220 $240–280 G(L) ⚲

◄ **Victorian mahogany drop-dial wall clock,** by K. B. Iker, Birmingham, with a painted dial and striking fusee movement, the case inlaid with rosewood.
£290–340 / €420–490 $530–620 L&E ⚲

Victorian mahogany wall timepiece, by Bennett, London, with a painted dial and single fusee mechanism, 12in (30.5cm) diam. The small size of this clock has affected its value as, generally speaking, the larger the clock the higher the price.
£280–330 / €410–480 $510–600 Mal(O) ⚲

Victorian oak wall timepiece, with a painted dial and single fusee movement, in a leaf-carved case, 18¼in (46.5cm) diam.
£320–380 / €460–550 $580–690 WW ⚲

► **Ebonized vineyard wall clock,** by Chalon, Pontarlier, with a reverse-painted glass dial within a mother-of-pearl stars and scrolls surround, the eight-day movement striking on a coiled rod, French, 19thC, 23¾in (60.5cm) high. This is a traditional French design of clock with highly decorative ornamentation to the glass.
£340–400 / €490–580 $620–730 CGC ⚲

► **Mahogany wall clock,** decorated with brass inlay, early 19thC, 9in (23cm) diam. This unusual and attractive wall clock is of small proportions, making it suitable for most houses today.
£360–400 / €520–580 $660–730 DEB ▦

Victorian mahogany drop-dial wall clock, by Boyce, Dereham, with a painted dial, the case carved with leaves and berries, 27in (68.5cm) high. This clock has extremely fine carving which makes it desirable and therefore more valuable.
£400–480 / €580–700 $730–870 SWO

Drop-dial wall clock, with a painted dial, the case inlaid with brass leaf scrolls, altered, early 19thC, 24in (61cm) high. Pitting to a dial can be a problem and requires restoration, the cost of which should be taken into consideration before purchase.
£420–500 / €610–730 $760–910 LFA

Mahogany pedestal wall clock, with an enamel dial and twin fusee movement striking on a gong, the base with applied foliage scroll decoration, 19thC, 22½in (57cm) high.
£480–570 / €700–830 $870–1,050 WW

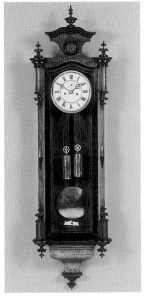

Regency rosewood and brass-inlaid wall clock, with a single fusee movement, 17¼in (44cm) diam. The attractive combination of brass and rosewood is always a desirable feature in a clock.
£480–570 / €700–830 $870–1,050 SWO

Locate the source

The source of each illustration in Miller's can be found by checking the code letters below each caption with the Key to Illustrations, pages 286–290.

Brass and iron *Comtoise* wall clock, the enamelled dial signed 'Navand', the iron and brass-posted movement with an inverted verge escapement and trip repeating rack striking on a bell, the pierced cresting with three eagles, signed 'Ferdinand Pagny A Poligny' and 'Jean Chasa De Ponsa', French, c1800, 15½in (39.5cm) high. The earlier movement, together with a verge escapement, makes this a sought-after piece.
£650–780 / €960–1,150 $1,200–1,400 S(Am)

Walnut-veneered and ebonized Vienna wall clock, the enamel dial with subsidiary seconds, the twin weight-driven movement striking on a gong, backplate numbered '68105', the case with a shaped pediment and turned finials, c1890, 49¼in (125cm) high.
£750–900 / €1,100–1,300 $1,350–1,600 TEN

Miscellaneous

Brass braille clock, early 19thC, 2¼in (6cm) diam. Any unusual clock creates interest and such pieces are rarely on the market.
£190–220 / €280–330
$340–400 SWO ✎

▶ **Bronzed metal and marble Empire-style clock case,** modelled with a seated Greek philosopher, damaged, 19thC, 26in (66cm) high. Purchasers should beware of the term 'bronzed' which means that it is probably not real bronze. A new movement could be obtained to fit this case.
£280–330 / €410–480
$510–600 DN ✎

Silver timepiece, in the form of a heart, the dial set in an embossed case, c1900, 4in (35.5cm) high. Small silver pieces are currently popular.
£500–550 / €730–810
$900–1,000 BELL ⌗

Marble table clock, with visible escapement and a mercury pendulum, French, 19thC, 15in (38cm) wide. This style of clock may be too heavy for modern tastes, but a visible escapement is always a good feature.
£200–240 / €290–350
$360–430 G(L) ✎

▶ **Metal sculptural mystery timepiece,** by Guilmet, with an enamel dial, the eight-day movement with a fixed winding, with a tic-tac escapement, stamped 'GLT1855', the drum case on a gridiron pendulum held by a figure of a classical lady, on an ebonized base, French, c1875, 21¼in (54cm) high. Mystery clocks are very collectable and there is always a ready demand, which makes them more valuable than most other mantel clocks.
£730–870 / €1,050–1,250
$1,350–1,600 S(Am) ✎

French-style gilt and embossed 'Gabriel' clock, by the Gilbert Clock Co, the case with porcelain inserts, American, c1900, 14½in (37cm) high.
£250–300 / €370–440
$460–550 JAA ✎

Pocket Watches

◄ Gold-filled pocket watch, by Regina, with an open face, c1900.
£30–35 / €45–50
$60–70 DUM ✐

◄ Late Victorian silver pocket watch, the enamel dial with subsidiary seconds dial, the case with engine-turned decoration, Birmingham 1884. The unusual dial configuration makes this watch a collectable example.
£45–50 / €65–75
$80–90 HOLL ✐

Silver pocket watch, the silver dial turned with gold flowers, with swing-out movement, maker's mark 'F.W.', slight damage, London 1787, with key.
£95–110 / €140–160
$175–200 JDJ ✐

18ct gold pocket watch, the dial engraved with a coastal scene, the movement signed 'W. H. Jackson, London', maker's mark 'JB', the movement and case numbered '25088', London 1848, 1½in (4cm) wide, with winder. This is a well-crafted piece at a reasonable price.
£120–140 / €170–200
$210–250 PFK ✐

18ct gold open-faced fob watch, by A. W. Butt, Chester, with three-quarter plate keyless lever movement and a four-piece hinged case, Birmingham 1894.
£130–155 / €185–220
$240–280 DN ✐

◄ 18ct gold pocket watch, the dial engraved with foliate scrollwork and with a subsidiary seconds dial, the movement with a diamond endstone, the back chased and engraved with flowers, movement signed 'George Thomson, Glasgow', case signed 'London 1870', with a morocco case. This is a pleasing example of a pocket watch; the original travelling case has increased its value.
£170–200 / €250–290
$310–360 PFK ✐

Lady's yellow metal fob watch, with an enamel chapter ring, the case with engraved decoration, Continental, 19thC. Enamel dials should be checked for damage as they are costly to repair.
£150–180 / €220–260
$270–320 WilP ✐

Gold-plated pocket watch, by Paillard Watch Co, Chicago, the hunting case movement with a Chalmers patent regulator, dial replaced, American, 1882, 2in (5cm) diam. The unusual configuration of this watch with a side-winding movement makes it a collectable item.
£170–200 / €250–290
$310–360 JDJ ✐

14ct gold pocket watch, by Elgin, No. SN 11308528, with a decorated dial, slight damage, American, 1904, 1½in (4cm) diam.
£180–210 / €250–300
$320–380 JDJ ✗

Illinois pocket watch, by Sangamo Special, No. SN 2728272, replaced dial marked 'C.R. Smith & Son', case replaced and worn, American, 1887, 1½in (4cm) diam.
£180–210 / €250–300
$320–380 JDJ ✗

Pocket watch, by Elgin, probably gold, No. SN 3508426, with a porcelain dial, the case decorated with a stag, the reverse with a shield, slight damage, American, 1888, 2in (5cm) diam. Condition is all-important with watches – always avoid split and dented cases.
£185–220 / €270–320
$340–400 JDJ ✗

18ct gold pocket watch, by Thomas Russell & Sons, the enamel dial with a sweep second hand, Chester 1875, with case. This watch has a good, clean face with delicate hands. The sweep seconds hand was the next stage of development from the subsidiary seconds dial.
£220–260 / €320–380
$400–470 L&E ✗

Gold fob watch, with an enamel dial and bar cylinder movement, the three-piece hinged case in the form of a stylized flower head decorated with half-pearls, the bi-coloured chased gold back with an applied wirework scroll, dial cover and some pearls missing, late 19thC. This watch has a commercial Swiss movement in an ornate and very decorative case which has made it sought after and therefore valuable.
£240–280 / €350–410
$430–510 DN ✗

Riverside pocket watch, by Waltham, No. SN 6557542, the decorated dial with hair line cracks, American, 1896, 1½in (4cm) diam. These pocket watches are in demand in the US. Many were made, but they all had slightly different characteristics.
£260–310 / €380–450
$470–560 JDJ ✗

◀ **18ct gold pocket watch,** by Elgin, No. SN 440652, with a porcelain dial, damaged and repaired, American, 1876. The condition of this watch is reflected in the price.
£300–360 / €450–520
$540–650 JDJ ✗

14ct gold hunter pocket watch, by Elgin, No. SN 3102007, with a decorated dial, the engraved case with an inscription on the inner cover, American, 1888, 1½in (4cm) diam. Export wares all have slightly different characteristics. The large trade to the Continent and China produced this pleasing watch.
£300–360 / €440–520
$570–660 JDJ ✷

▶ **Bunn Special pocket watch,** No. SN 2295585, with a double-sunk Illinois Railroad dial, with an engraved case, American, 1886, 2in (5cm) diam.
£340–400 / €490–580
$630–730 JDJ ✷

Gold open-faced watch, with a later silvered dial, gilt cylinder movement, the back with engine-turned decoration, signed 'Breguet', with a curb-link chain and steel key, c1830, 1¾in (4.5cm) diam. This watch may have been amalgamated from associated pieces or be a direct copy of a Breguet watch. All Breguet pieces were numbered.
£320–380 / €460–550
$580–690 S(Am) ✷

Pinchbeck pair-cased repoussé pocket watch, by Moore, London, with a verge escapement and single fusee movement, c1750. It is good to find a watch with its original verge escapement and this example should form part of a collection.
£340–400 / €490–580
$620–730 DN(BR) ✷

Silver verge pocket watch, the enamel regulator dial enclosed by engraved bezel, with a full plate gilt fusee movement, in a consular case, signed 'Leroy a Galladron', French, c1790, 2in (5cm) diam. This is a good example of a large French pocket watch and, considering its early date, it is for sale at a very affordable price.
£360–400 / €520–580
$660–730 PT ⊞

18ct gold hunting-cased watch, retailed by Baume, the enamel dial with subsidiary seconds, the case decorated with engine turning, signed 'Examined Baume London', c1900, 1¾in (4.5cm) diam, with Baume presentation box. 'Hunting-cased' means that the whole watch is enclosed by the case to protect it when used on the hunting field. The cases of 'Half-hunter' watches have an inspection dial in the centre so that they may be read while closed.
£360–430 / €530–620
$650–780 S(Am) ✷

14ct gold hunter pocket watch, by Waltham, No. 1,833,622, the dial with subsidiary seconds, in an engraved and monogrammed case, American, 1881–82. American and Continental gold is marked with the number of carats and a 'k' – look for this when buying. English gold should have a full hallmark.
£360–430 / €520–620
$660–780 JDJ ⚲

Silver pair-cased open-faced pocket watch, with a painted dial, the fusee movement by Thos. Clare, Bedford, Birmingham 1808. Painted dials are an attractive feature and add value to pocket watches.
£380–450 / €550–650
$690–820 WilP ⚲

Multi-colour gold open-faced pocket watch, by Lépine, Paris, with an enamel dial and gilt verge movement, the consular case and bezel set with paste, dial associated, French, c1775, 1½in (4cm) diam. The associated dial on this pocket watch will have reduced its value.
£400–480 / €580–700
$730–870 S(Am) ⚲

Silver open-faced lever pocket watch, the enamel dial with centre seconds, maker's mark 'DL', hallmarked London 1876, Swiss, 19thC, 2¼in (5.5cm) diam.
£430–480 / €620–700
$780–870 PT ⊞

Silver open-faced lever pocket watch, by L. Balerna, Halifax, the silver dial with applied gold numerals and subsidiary seconds, the fusee movement with Harrison's maintaining power, Massey-type III lever escapement and a gilt dust cover, signed, maker's mark 'JH', 19thC, 2in (5cm) diam. This pocket watch has a sophisticated movement and would make a good collector's piece.
£450–500 / €650–730
$820–910 PT ⊞

◄ **Silver pair-cased calendar verge watch,** by Charles Cabrier, London, the panelled silver dial with pierced fretwork of birds at the centre, with signed square pillar movement, the case decorated in relief with a classical scene depicting the capture of Helen of Troy within foliate and scroll borders, signed 'D. Cochin', 18thC, 2in (5cm) diam.
£480–570 / €700–830
$870–1,050 F&C ⚲

◀ **Silver open-faced pocket watch,** by Bovet, Fleurier, the enamel dial with centre seconds and a gilt Chinese signature, with keywind gilt bar movement, case marked '900', Swiss, c1840, 2¼in (5.5cm) diam, with a short silver chain and a gilt key. This watch was made for the Chinese market.
£500–550
€720–800
$900–1,000 PT ⊞

Silver verge pocket watch, by Jefferys & Ham, London, with an enamel dial, the verge movement with a Bosley regulator, the case with an engine-turned back, London 1814, 2in (5cm) diam. This watch is in good condition – an important factor with pocket watches as they are complicated to mend and it can be difficult to find a repairer.
£570–630 / €830–920
$1,000–1,150 FOF ⊞

▶ **Silver pair-cased calender verge pocket watch,** the convex enamel dial with a calendar chapter, maker's mark 'LC' over 'F', Swiss, c1790, 2½in (6.5cm) diam.
£610–680 / €880–990
$1,100–1,250 PT ⊞

18ct gold open-faced pocket watch, by Ganthony, Cheapside, London, No. 5172, the enamel dial decorated with forget-me-nots and leaves, with a three-quarter plate fusee lever movement, the three-piece hinged case with floral-engraved borders and bow, London 1836. This is an attractive pocket watch with a decorated enamelled dial. Always check carefully for damage to enamel before purchase.
£650–780 / €960–1,150
$1,200–1,400 DN ⚲

Gold, enamel and paste-set verge pocket watch, by Barbienne le Jeune, Paris, No. 1084, with an enamel dial and paste-set hands, polychrome enamel bezels and central panel, dial and movement signed, French, c1800, 1¼in (3.5cm) diam. This highly decorative piece would originally have had an outer case for protection.
£720–860 / €1,050–1,250
$1,300–1,550 S ⚲

◀ **Late Victorian 18ct gold hunter pocket watch,** by Victor Kullberg, No. 6916, the enamel dial with two subsidiary dials, the case monogrammed in red, white and blue enamel, with original fitted case.
£800–960 / €1,200–1,400
$1,450–1,750 L&T ⚲

Wristwatches

9ct gold wristwatch, with a silvered dial, London 1927. Always check before purchase that wristwatches have not been overwound, as the cost of repair can exceed the purchase price.
£30–35 / €45–50
$55–65 DN(HAM) ✗

Rolex 9ct gold wristwatch, No. 32946, with a silver dial, the three-piece hinged case with an enamelled chapter ring, slight damage, London 1922. Although this watch is by a good maker, beware of wristwatches that are in need of repair.
£130–155 / €185–220
$240–280 DN ✗

▶ **Rolex Precision 9ct gold wristwatch,** No. 24309, the silvered dial with gilt baton numerals, with a two-piece case, case, dial and movement signed, c1964, bracelet associated.
£200–240
€290–350
$360–430 DN ✗

9ct gold Tudor wristwatch, with a brushed silvered dial, in a Rolex two-piece case, No. 24170, in need of attention, Edinburgh 1964, on a later 9ct gold bracelet, Birmingham 1977.
£260–310 / €380–450
$470–560 DN ✗

Juvenia 18ct gold wristwatch, No. 162844, the silvered dial with subsidiary seconds, case, dial and movement signed, stamped '.750', import marks for Glasgow 1952, with an associated bracelet. The marks on both the case and bracelet should be checked carefully as prices will fluctuate according to the weight of the gold.
£340–400 / €490–580
$620–730 DN ✗

Ebel stainless steel chronograph wristwatch, the silvered dial with an inner spiral scale and outer pulsations scale, subsidiary dials for seconds and minutes, water-resistant case, dial signed, c1960, 1½in (4cm) diam. There is a growing trend towards wristwatches with functions. The more functions the watch has the more desirable it becomes.
£720–860 / €1,050–1,250
$1,300–1,550 S ✗

◀ **Piaget 18ct gold bracelet watch,** with a gilt-textured dial, adjusted to five positions and temperature, the integral textured link bracelet with Piaget locking clasp, case, dial and movement signed, 1970, 1¼in (3cm) diam, with presentation box. This classically elegant style of watch is always sought after.
£960–1,150 / €1,400–1,650
$1,700–2,000 S ✗

Barometers

◄ **Hardwood stick barometer,** by Stettinger & Wondrich, with a silvered scale, c1840, 37¾in (96cm) high. This typical 19thC Continental stick barometer was very good value at auction.
£220–260 / €320–380
$400–470 DORO 🔨

► **Line-inlaid mahogany wheel barometer,** by Rimavesi Bros, Bournemouth, with a silvered scale, with hygrometer, thermometer, convex mirror and spirit level, the case surmounted with an urn finial and swan-neck pediment, c1850, 38in (96cm) high.
£240–280
€350–410
$430–510 DN 🔨

George III-style wheel barometer, with a compass dial, thermometer, convex mirror and silvered barometer dial, the case painted to resemble brass inlay, c1875, 37½in (95.5cm) high.
£220–260 / €320–380
$400–470 SK 🔨

◄ **Victorian rosewood wheel barometer,** the silvered dial inscribed 'Cappo, Belfast', with a hygrometer, mercury thermometer and convex mirror, 37in (94cm) high.
£260–310 / €380–450
$470–560 JAd 🔨

Brass marine barometer, by R. Cameron, with supplementary thermometer, c1880, 5in (12.5cm) diam. Barometers and thermometers were standard in all homes in the late 19thC, especially those where the owner's livelihood was dependent upon the weather.
£270–300 / €390–440
$490–550 RTW ⊞

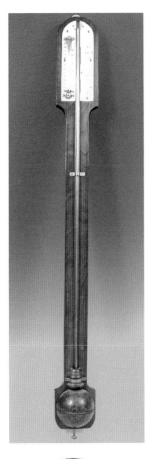

◄ **Mahogany stick barometer,** with ivory registers and a turned cistern cover, 19thC, 35½in (90cm) high.
£320–380 / €460–550
$580–690 SWO ⚒

► **Oak stick barometer,** by J. H. Steward, London, with ivory scales and twin verniers for '10am today' and '10am yesterday', the case with a flat turned cistern cover, late 19thC, 37in (94cm) high. Oak barometers are usually cheaper than mahogany examples.
£400–480
€580–700
$730–870 TMA ⚒

Mahogany wheel barometer, with silvered dials for thermometer, barometer and level, the case with satinwood stringing, swan-neck pediment damaged, 19thC, 37½in (95.5cm) high.
£340–400 / €490–580
$620–730 PF ⚒

◄ **Victorian rosewood wheel barometer,** with a thermometer, the case inlaid with mother-of-pearl, 9¾in (25cm) diam. Mother-of-pearl was used extensively in the 19thC, especially with rosewood, and provided an attractive effect.
£400–480 / €580–700
$730–870 Oli ⚒

Victorian rosewood wheel barometer, by Chiesa Keizer & Co, Liverpool, with a silvered dial, thermometer and a bone adjuster, 40¼in (102cm) high.
£420–500
€610–730
$760–910 WW ⚒

► **Rosewood and mother-of-pearl wheel barometer,** by D. Luvate, Preston, with a signed silvered dial, hygrometer, thermometer and spirit level, 1823–34, 45in (114.5cm) high. This is a highly decorative piece and was a good buy at auction.
£500–600 / €730–870
$910–1,100 TEN ⚒

Wheel Barometers

A wheel barometer, also known as a banjo barometer, has a round register plate and siphon tube, in which the mercury movement is measured by a weight attached to a pulley whose wheel turns the pointer on the dial.

Oak Admiral Fitzroy barometer, with dual scales and slide adjusters, the paper backboard with weather predictions and a storm tube, c1890, 37in (94cm) high. This is a good example of a barometer where indications of ensuing weather conditions were annotated.
£530–590 / €770–920
$960–1,150 K&D ⊞

Ebonized wheel barometer, by Jose Zarribeitia Cuba, with a thermometer, the barometer face indicating low pressure records between 1837 and 1888, c1895, 22in (56cm) high. This barometer has a curled tube which is an unusual feature.
£540–600 / 780–870
$980–1,100 RTW ⊞

Mahogany mercurial wheel barometer, by G. Kalabergo, Banbury, with a silvered dial, the case inlaid with two shell panels and stringing, early 19thC, 38in (96.5cm) high. Inlaid decoration and patera such as shells and flower heads usually adds value to the piece.
£600–720
€870–1,050
$1,100–1,300
HOLL ⚒

▶ George III inlaid mahogany mercury-filled stick barometer, the timber plate inscribed 'Malacrida, Dublin', the case with hinged doors above a trunk with a tube over a turned cistern cover, 38in (96.5cm) high. This is an elegant and highly collectable piece.
£550–660 / €800–960
$1,000–1,200 JAd ⚒

◀ George III mahogany stick barometer, by J. Lione, London, with an engraved brass scale and thermometer, the case with a herringbone veneer, 38½in (98cm) high.
£650–780 / €940–1,100
$1,200–1,400 PF ⚒

Brass combination pocket barometer and compass, by Joseph Davis & Co, London, c1880, each 2in (5cm) diam, in a leather case.
**£740–830 / €1,050–1,200
$1,350–1,500** FOF ⊞

Silver pocket barometer, compass and thermometer, by James Henry Steward of London, the thermometer with an ivory tablet, the barometer case hallmarked London 1882, 2in (5cm) diam, in a shagreen case. Original cases are always desirable, and in this example it is made of shagreen. This factor, combined with the barometer being made by a renowned maker, has made this piece more desirable and therefore more valuable.
**£850–950 / €1,250–1,400
$1,550–1,750** FOF ⊞

Mahogany and line-inlaid stick barometer, by G. Valanterio, Doncaster, the brass register with recording adjust and Fahrenheit thermometer, 19thC, 38½in (98cm) high. This is a classical Georgian stick barometer. The tube needs replacing or refilling, and this has kept the value down. In original condition this example could have been worth twice this price.
**£650–780
€960–1,150
$1,200–1,400**
DN ⚒

Georgian mahogany and line-inlaid stick barometer, the dial and vernier inscribed 'Teste, Salisbury', 37in (94cm) high.
**£720–860 / €1,050–1,250
$1,300–1,550** MCA ⚒

▶ **Rosewood marine stick barometer,** by Moralee, North Shields, the concealed tube with angled ivory plates and vernier, with an inset mercury thermometer and a brass cistern cover, c1860, 37in (94cm) high. Marine barometers tend to command high prices, and this example is of good quality. These barometers were weighted so that when on board ship they would stay in a vertical position.
**£900–1,050 / €1,300–1,550
$1,650–1,950** S ⚒

Marine Barometers

A marine barometer is a stick barometer fitted with gimbals and a constricted tube to minimize oscillations in the mercury.

Other Antiques

When the cold winds of evermore selective buying are lashing the market place there is nothing wrong with concentrating on your chosen niche collecting area, preferably one that you gives you great pleasure. You may not be entirely immune to the problems outside but at least you will have the satisfaction of really loving your chosen speciality.

Of course, it would take an unqualified enthusiast in the field of architectural items to become passionate about the ceramic lavatory pan c1890 shown on page 233, but at £850–950 / €1,250–1,400 / $1,550–1,750 it is a good deal cheaper than one of the famous Thomas Crapper examples and is very collectable. The brass club fender on the same page at £960–1,150 / €1,400–1,650 / $1,750–2,100 is also an attractive proposition which has held its value while many copper and brass items have become very difficult to sell.

Tunbridge ware continues to have its dedicated followers although prices have steadied. Always try to collect the most decorative high-quality items and avoid those with damage; although Tunbridge ware can be restored to great effect it is a highly-skilled undertaking. Also, do not be put off by small examples. These are often much sought after since, due to their size, many have been lost or accidentally discarded over the years.

The evocative pull of toys still lures many new collectors and the Simon & Halbig doll on page 244, with its original wig and pretty features, would be a good value starter for any beginner. Chess sets are always sought after as long as they are complete and undamaged, and there are plenty of nice quality 19th-century examples out there but watch out for repairs and replacement pieces.

As mentioned earlier, some metalware has tumbled in price in the last few years as many people seem to have decided that they have better things to do with their time than spend their weekends closeted with the Brasso and granny's warming pan. However, unusual and stylish pieces like the Margaret Gilmour wall sconce and the Liberty vase, both on page 261, are obvious exceptions to this trend and are very collectable.

Rugs and carpets is still one of the most rewarding areas in which to buy. Not only can you acquire a wonderful unique item but you can actually use it on a daily basis. Could you find a better bargain than the two bag faces illustrated on page 262. At £130–150 / €190–220 / $230–270 they have to be a great way to add colour and class to your home.

Scientific instruments seem to attract an ever-growing band of highly skilled collectors who pursue their chosen subject with admirable tenacity. This is not really a field for the novice but once the necessary knowledge has been amassed it can be extremely rewarding in every respect.

Wooden antiques offers you a wide range of items, from the 19th-century rodent dispenser on page 278 to the wonderfully over-the-top Italian silvered and carved beech grotto stool on page 281.

Add to this the established disciplines of antiquities and sculpture and you have a wealth of specialities to keep you occupied through any chilly spell that you might encounter on the supply and demand curve.

Leslie Gillham

Antiquities

Silver earring pendant, in the form of an axe, Danubian Celtic, 1stC AD, 1in (2.5cm) long.
£30–35 / €45–50
$55–65 ANG ⊞

Bronze armlet, Thracian Celtic, 2nd–1stC BC, 3in (7.5cm) diam.
£40–45 / €60–70
$75–85 ANG ⊞

Fakes

Fakes of antiquities are rare and they are normally found alongside the higher-priced pieces. However, there are altered items on the market that consist of damaged pieces that have been restored, either using modern materials or with similar ancient materials taken from other pieces. Some of these restored pieces are honest attempts at improvement, others are dishonest attempts to present something as a better piece than it really is. So do your homework before purchasing from a reputable dealer and ask for a detailed receipt .

Pottery drinking cup, Roman, 2nd–3rdC AD, 3¼in (8.5cm) high.
£45–50 / €65–75
$85–95 HEL ⊞

Metal buckle, decorated with stylized dolphins, East Anglian, 5thC AD, 1¼in (3cm) wide.
£85–95 / €125–140
$165–185 ANG ⊞

Bronze brooch, East Anglian, 2nd–3rdC AD, 1¼in (3cm) diam.
£55–65 / €80–95
$105–125 ANG ⊞

Bronze buckle, decorated with dolphins, Roman, 4thC AD, 3in (7.5cm) diam.
£105–120 / €150–170
$190–220 MIL ⊞

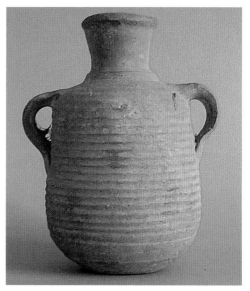

Pottery amphora, Roman Palestine, 1stC AD, 8in (20.5cm) high.
£135–150 / €195–220
$240–270 MIL ⊞

► **Bronze stud,** in the form of a cherub's head, Roman, 1stC AD, 1in (2.5cm) wide.
£140–155
€200–220
$250–280 MIL ⊞

Specialist terms

The following pottery was designed to store and preserve liquids and foodstuffs:

- Pithos: usually very large and oval in shape; intended to be half buried and hold liquids, grains or other provisions
- Amphora: usually oval with a wide mouth and two vertical handles. It was used for storage or for export of wine or oil
- Hydria: used for carrying water; also had other domestic uses
- Krater: used in the household for mixing wine and water

Pottery jug, with painted decoration, Cypriot, 11th–8thC BC, 6in (15cm) high.
£155–175 / €220–250
$280–320 ANG ⊞

Pottery amphora, with moulded and painted decoration, Cypriot, 1650–1050 BC, 4¾in (12cm) high.
£160–180 / €220–260
$290–330 HEL ⊞

Bronze mount, depicting the four seasons, Anglo Saxon, 9th–11thC AD, 1¼in (3cm) diam.
£175–195 / €250–280
$320–360 ANG ⊞

Wall tile, depicting a stag being brought down by a wolf, Roman, north African, 4thC AD, 8in (20.5cm) wide.
£230–260 / €330–370
$420–470 MIL ⊞

Silver bracelet, Greek, 5th–4thC BC, 3in (7.5cm) diam.
£240–280 / €340–390
$440–490 HEL ⊞

Red-Figure painting

An important Red-Figure industry evolved in the Greek colonies of southern Italy and Sicily in the 6th century BC, which was separate from native manufacturers. Unlike Black-Figure vase painting, which portrayed the figure in black against the red background of the clay, Red-Figure painting reversed that technique, and left figures and patterns unglazed on the red clay of the vase, with painted details and the background in glossy black. This made it easier to draw the human figure, which, whether dressed or nude, is depicted in realistic detail.

Red-Figure pottery dish, Greek South Italy, Apulia, 4thC BC, 5¼in (13.5cm) diam.
£240–280 / €350–400
$440–500 ANG ⊞

Mochica terracotta stirrup flask, in the form of a sleeping warrior, stirrup loop missing, Peruvian, c450 AD, 7in (18cm) high. Mochica is a Native American civilization on the coast of north Peru.
£240–280 / €340–390
$440–490 A&O ⊞

Redware wine flagon, north African, early 4thC AD, 7in (18cm) high. Household items are very popular with collectors.
£270–300 / €380–420
$490–550 MIL ⊞

Terracotta figure of a goddess, possibly Demeter, slight damage, Greek, c500 BC, 7½in (19cm) high. This figure is a common subject and there are many on the market.
£350–390 / €490–550
$640–710 A&O ⊞

Authenticity

When buying antiquities, always ask about provenance, keep all the documentation and be aware of export and import regulations – some items will require a passport and this should be available at the time of purchase. It is advisable to buy from dealers who are members of a trade association such as the British Antiquities Dealers Association (BADA), the National Art & Dealers' Association of America and the International Association of Dealers in Ancient Art (IADAA), as this ensures protection of your purchase. For a list of members visit www.the-ADA.org. Alternatively, buy from auction houses, as they will be able to provide the necessary documentation.

▶ **Pair of gold earrings,** with bead drops, Roman, 1stC AD, 1¼in (3cm) high.
£420–470
€600–670
$760–860 MIL ⊞

Glass jug, Roman, 3rd–4thC AD, 4in (10cm) high.
£430–480 / €610–680
$780–870 MIL ⊞

Ceramic shabti figure,
decorated with heiroglyphs,
380–300 BC, 5in (12.5cm) high.
Shabti figures were believed to
provide a workforce for use in
the afterlife. Some burials
contained several hundred
figures, sometimes equipped
with tools for working the fields
and often inscribed with
personal details or spells.
Typically 'Overseer' shabtis were
also included to keep the
magical workforce in check.
£440–490 / €620–700
$800–890 MIL ⊞

◄ **Pottery figure of Silenus
with Dionysus in his arms,**
Greek, 4thC BC,
4½in (11.5cm) high.
£540–600 / €770–850
$980–1,100 HEL ⊞

Glass balsamarium, with four
handles, Roman, 4thC AD, 4in
(10cm) high. The earliest examples
of glass date back from the mid-
15thC BC in the Near East, where
the centres of production
remained for over 2,000 years.
£580–650 / €820–920
$1,050–1,200 MIL ⊞

Glass sprinkler flask, Roman, 3rdC AD,
4½in (11.5cm) high.
£580–650 / €820–920
$1,050–1,200 MIL ⊞

Silver figure of Aphrodite,
Hellenistic, 2nd–1stC BC,
17in (43cm) high.
£670–750 / €950–1,050
$1,200–1,350 ANG ⊞

Axe hammer, haft replaced,
Roman, c300 AD,
41½in (105.5cm) long.
£810–900 / €1,150–1,300
$1,450–1,650 TLA ⊞

Architectural

◄ **Brass padlock,** with keys, c1910, 3¼in (8.5cm) high. These are very collectable. It is essential to buy a padlock with its keys, without which it would be worth only half this amount.
**£25–30 / €40–45
$50–55** WiB ⊞

▶ **Late Victorian brick insert,** in the form of a flower, 13in (33cm) square. This item would be classed as garden architecture which is currently very popular.
**£50–60 / €75–85
$100–115** DEB ⊞

Cast-iron door knocker, c1880, 6in (15cm) high. With door furniture it is vital that there are no parts missing. This door knocker is a very reasonable price as it is complete and has very decorative casting.
**£45–50 / €65–75
$85–95** JUN ⊞

Iron latch and night latch, the lock plate with applied chased rococo panel and initials, with escutcheon latch and three keys, 18thC, German, 7in (18cm) high. These items are a complete set and could have sold for twice this amount.
**£55–65 / €80–95
$105–125** NSal ⚒

Late Victorian glazed stone plinth, 12in (30.5cm) wide.
**£55–65 / €80–95
$105–125** DEB ⊞

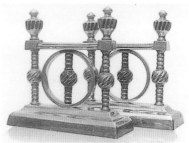

◄ **Brass finger plate,** c1895, 10¼in (26cm) high. Finger plates are decorative pieces that protect the door from dirty hands and scratches. They were also made in ceramic or glass and normally come in pairs. They should be purchased with a specific door in mind. If the door has a wide panel then the finger plate should fit accordingly.
£60–70 / €85–100
$115–135 Penn ⊞

Pair of late Victorian brass fire dogs, 8½in (21.5cm) wide. This set is very decorative and could have sold for twice the price.
£65–75 / €95–105
$125–145 GTH ⚒

Cast-iron boot scraper, late 19thC, 15in (38cm) wide.
£75–85 / €110–125
$145–165 DEB ⊞

Dogon wooden granary door panel, African, Mali, c1890, 27in (68.5cm) high. This detailed piece would appeal to specialist collectors of both African and wooden items.
£95–110 / €135–160
$175–210 DuM ⚒

Cast-iron hitching post, in the form of a horse, c1890, 9in (23cm) high. This item would appeal to both the UK and US markets but it would be worth more if it was made from bronze.
£95–110 / €135–160
$175–210 DuM ⚒

Pair of cast-iron fire dogs, in the form of owls, with glass eyes, 19thC, 15in (38cm) high. Owls are a popular collecting area, making these interesting fire dogs a reasonable purchase at auction. They could have achieved twice this price.
£95–110 / €135–160
$175–210 Mit ⚒

Pair of stained glass windows, c1910, 44½in (113cm) wide. The more colourful the stained glass, the more desirable the piece. However, unusual shapes such as this do limit potential buyers, and these windows sold for a very reasonable price.
£110–130 / €160–190
$200–240 DuM ⚲

Stone gate post finial, c1850, 19in (48.5cm) high. This is a reasonable price for one item: a pair would be more practical and therefore command more than double the price of a single finial.
£110–125 / €160–180
$200–230 DEB ⊞

◀ **Cast-brass footman,** 19thC, 15¾in (40cm) wide.
£120–145 / €175–210
$220–260 PFK ⚲

Miller's compares...

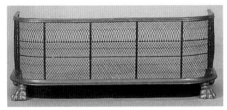

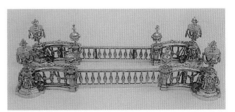

A. Victorian brass and wirework fender, 36½in (92.5cm) wide. It is advisable to check for damage to the mesh on wirework fenders as this will reduce the value.
£120–140 / €175–210
$220–260 WW ⚲

B. Pair of brass extending fenders, French, 19thC, 54in (137cm) extended.
£300–360 / €430–520
$540–650 DD ⚲

Item A is a standard size fender in good condition. However, Item B is larger and more decorative and is also a pair, which makes it more desirable and accounts for the higher auction price.

► **Oak furniture mount,** carved with an angel's face, early 18thC, 19in (48.5cm) high. This mount would have been used to decorate a sideboard or a coffer. It was common practice to reuse these decorative mounts when the body of the item to which they were attached became damaged or riddled with worm. These items are more desirable in pairs.
£150–180 / €220–260
$270–320 TMA 🔨

Miller's compares...

A. Composition stone statue of a lady, on a plinth, late 19thC, 64in (162.5cm) high.
£130–145 / €190–210
$230–260 DEB ⊞

B. Stone statue of a lady, on a plinth, Welsh, late 19thC, 51in (129.5cm) high.
£500–550 / €720–800
$910–1,000 DEB ⊞

Item A appears to have been cast from a mould as it has shallow detail. Item B, on the other hand, has much more detail and would have required a high level of craftsmanship to produce, which is why it is a higher price than Item A.

Late Victorian stone statue, 21in (53.5cm) high. The price of this garden ornament takes into account the subject matter, which is not to everyone's taste.
£160–180 / €230–260
$290–330 DEB ⊞

◄ **Pair of Victorian stained glass windows,** depicting sparrows, slight damage, 16 x 22¼in (40.5 x 56.5cm). Repairs to these windows would be relatively straightforward.
£165–195 / €240–290
$300–360 PFK ⚲

Pair of turned ivory clamps, French, c1800, 5in (12.5cm) long. These clamps may have been used for sewing purposes.
£180–200 / €260–290
$320–360 RdeR ⊞

Metal washstand, French, late 19thC, 49in (124.5cm) high. The worn state of this washstand would appeal to some purchasers, although others may wish to restore by sandblasting and repainting.
£270–300 / €390–440
$490–550 Lfo ⊞

Pair of Victorian terracotta gatepost finials, 19in (48.5cm) high.
£270–300 / €390–440
$490–550 DEB ⊞

► **Nickel-plated door lock,** French, c19thC, 9in (23cm) wide, with key. The decorative beading and the matching key have added value to this lock.
£280–310 / €410–460
$510–570 DRU ⊞

Terracotta garden lantern, c1880, 24in (61cm) high.
£290–330 / €420–480
$530–600 Lfo ⊞

► **Pair of Georgian stone chimney pots,** 34in (86.5cm) high. Original chimney pots can command high prices. These would be very sought after by a purchaser wishing to restore a Georgian property.
£310–350 / €450–510
$560–640 DEB ⊞

Painted pine garden chair, c1860. Certain items, such as this chair, retain their charm if left in their original unrestored condition.
£310–350 / €450–510
$560–640 Lfo ⊞

Pair of late Victorian oak newel posts, carved in the form of lions, 9¾in (24.5cm) high.
£340–400 / €490–580
$620–750 L&E ⚒

Miller's compares...

A. Pair of garden urns,
19thC, 17¾in (45cm) high.
£340–400 / €490–580
$620–750 WiLP 🔨

B. Coalbrookdale cast-iron urn, on a plinth, stamped, No. 16, c1870, 40in (101.5cm) high.
£960–1,150
€1,400–1,650
$1,750–2,100 S(S) 🔨

Item A is a very desirable pair of urns and the natural patina has been left untouched. Item B is a dated and numbered piece by Coalbrookdale and as such carries a premium. It would probably have fetched more at auction if it had not been repainted, but it is a good-quality superior piece with decorative appeal and this has made it the more desirable and valuable of the two items.

Child's wrought-iron double sleigh, with wooden seats, c1900, 49in (124.5cm) wide. This item might appeal to collectors of dolls.
£360–400 / €520–580
$660–730 MLL ⊞

Swift enamel and copper display gas water heater, c1900, 36in (91.5cm) high, with original instructions. This is a purely decorative item that would appeal to collectors of Victoriana. Today's health and safety regulations would prohibit its use.
£400–450 / €580–650
$730–820 DRU ⊞

Pair of Victorian terracotta gate post finials,
19in (48.5cm) high.
£400–450 / €580–650
$730–820 DEB ⊞

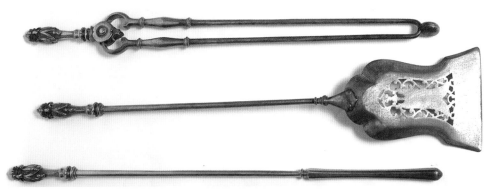

Set of steel fire irons, mid-19thC, 30in (76cm) long. Complete sets of fire irons always command the best price. They should have original patina and it is advisable to ensure that they match the style of the fireplace where they will be used.
£430–480 / €620–700
$780–870 KEY ⊞

Cast-iron garden seat, by Andrew McLaren & Co, stamped 'No. 32', diamond mark, late 19thC, 60in (152.5cm) wide. The diamond mark makes it possible to identify the exact date of manufacture.
£480–570 / €700–830
$870–1,050 S(S) ⚒

Brass coal scuttle, with embossed decoration and a swing handle, on three feet, 1880–90, 20in (51cm) high.
£430–480 / €620–700
$780–870 RPh ⊞

Salt-glazed earthenware model of a lion, inscribed 'Totley, Sheffield, Chadwick Baker & Co', 19thC, 21½in (54.5cm) wide.
£500–600 / €730–870
$910–1,100 AH ⚒

◀ **Painted wood fire surround,** with a cast-iron grate, damaged, early 19thC, 60¾in (154.5cm) wide. The design of this grate would make it difficult to repair, so it is important to take into consideration the cost of repair and restoration when buying.
£480–570 / €700–830
$870–1,050 SWO ⚒

Pair of cast-iron grate ends, c1830, 15in (38cm) wide.
Quality of casting and original patina are important factors when
purchasing cast-iron wares.
£540–600 / €780–870
$980–1,100 SWN ⊞

Brass coal bucket and cover, 1910,
22in (56cm) high.
£540–600 / €780–870
$980–1,100 GGD ⊞

William IV-style rance marble fire surround, late 19thC,
45½in (115.5cm) wide. This unusual fire surround would have made
more had it been sold by an English auction house rather than an
American one, as demand for this style is currently higher in the UK.
£630–740 / €910–1,100
$1,150–1,350 NOA ✄

Pair of wrought-iron fire dogs, French,
c1770, 27in (68.5cm) high. The resting bar
appears to be missing in this set. This design
is still manufactured today.
£700–780 / €1,000–1,150
$1,250–1,400 SEA ⊞

◄ **Cast-iron hob grate,** c1780,
34in (86.5cm) wide. The back of this grate
appears to be damaged. It would be worth the
cost of repair as it has attractive decoration.
£760–850 / €1,100–1,250
$1,400–1,550 OLA ⊞

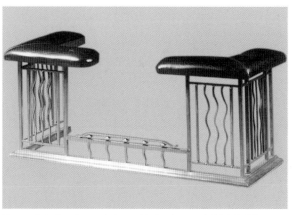

◀ **Cast-iron stick stand,** c1880, 30in (76cm) high. Purchasers should be aware that this is a popular design and there are many copies currently on the market.
£850–950
€1,250–1,400
$1,550–1,750
WAA ⊞

Ceramic lavatory pan, No. 491, 1890, 16in (40.5cm) high. Decorated lavatory pans are very sought after and can command high prices.
£850–950 / €1,250–1,400
$1,550–1,750 OLA ⊞

Pair of wrought-iron and brass fire dogs, French, c1770, 32in (81.5cm) high.
£880–980 / €1,300–1,450
$1,600–1,800 SEA ⊞

Brass club fender, upholstered in leather, early 20thC, 61in (155cm) wide. Club fenders were made to specific sizes so it is important to have the measurements with you when buying.
£960–1,150 / €1,400–1,650
$1,750–2,100 S(O) ↗

Marble wall bench, 19thC, 81in (205.5cm) wide. When buying an item of this size and weight, bear in mind the cost of delivery if you do not have suitable transport.
£960–1,150 / €1,400–1,650
$1,750–2,100 S(S) ↗

Locate the source

The source of each illustration in Miller's can be found by checking the code letters below each caption with the Key to Illustrations, pages 286–290.

Arms & Armour

Copy of a German Hirschfanger, the deer-hoof hand quillons with three deer on the guard, the antler handle with a silver pommel, the leather sheath with a German silver tip and throat, damaged, the 17in (43cm) blade made from an American sword blade marked and dated 1863. This type of side arm was very prolific in the 18thC, especially in the Black Forest, and although many are on the market, this example was sold at a very reasonable price.
£60–70 / €85–100
$115–135 JDJ

Composite rapier, the blade stamped and inscribed, the ricasso with bladesmith's mark, the iron hilt with a wire-bound grip, Italian, early 17thC, 35¼in (89.5cm) long. This sword was a good price at auction. It could have fetched up to twice this price.
£240–280 / €350–410
$430–510 S(O)

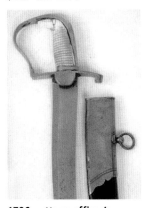

1796 pattern officer's cavalry sabre, with brass guard and bone grip, the steel blade inscribed 'W. Parker, London', with a brass-mounted leather scabbard, damaged, 1796, blade 33in (84cm) long. This sabre was a good buy at auction. It could have achieved up to £350 / €510 / $640.
£280–330 / €410–480
$510–600 DN

1878 pattern officer's home service cloth helmet, with the 1881 pattern QVC helmet plate, slight damage. There are many different helmet plates for enthusiasts to collect. This helmet was a good purchase at auction and could have fetched up to £500 / €730 / $910.
£300–360 / €440–520
$550–660 DNW

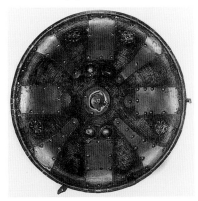

Chieftain's hide shield, decorated with overlay, lined with leather, Ethiopian, slight damage, c1865, 24in (61cm) diam.
£310–370 / €450–540
$560–670 WAL

◀ **Pair of cannon-barrelled percussion boxlock pistols,** by Turvey, London, converted from flintlock, the walnut butts inlaid with silver wire scrolls with silver mask butt caps, damaged, c1775, barrels 2½in (6.5cm) long. Pocket pistols were carried by travellers for protection. A pair such as this would be a good way to start a collection.
£360–430 / €520–620
$660–780 WAL

Woodman's axe, 17thC,
28in (71cm) long.
£500–550 / €730–800
$900–1,000 TLA ⊞

▶ **Leather Raupenhelm,**
with brass mounts and raised
fur comb, Bavarian, c1850,
10in (25.5cm) high.
£540–600 / €780–870
$980–1,100 MDL ⊞

Infantry officer's sword, the
pierced strapwork hilt with a
wire-wrapped sharkskin grip,
with leather-covered scabbard,
1897, etched blade 32½in
(82.5cm) long. There are a large
number of swords on the market,
with prices to suit most budgets.
£520–580 / €750–840
$950–1,050 FAC ⊞

◀ **Cavalry
trooper's sabre,**
the iron hilt with a
leather grip, the blade
with an etched panel
with gold overlay at
the forte and further
etched decoration,
c1810, blade 32½in
(82.5cm) long.
£580–650
€840–940
$1,050–1,200
FAC ⊞

16 bore big game rifle, by Garratt, London, signed
in gold, stamped 'Fullerd', breech, muzzle, tang and lock
with engraved decoration, figured walnut half stock with
a chequered grip, silver fore-end cap and escutcheon,
horn-tipped wooden ramrod, back-sight missing,
slight damage, 1829–34, barrel 31¼in (79.5cm) long.
£600–720 / €870–1,050
$1,100–1,300 S(O) ⚒

Pair of 16 bore officer's flintlock holster pistols, by Henry Richards, the walnut full stocks with chequered butts, engraved trigger guards with pineapple finials and horn-tipped wooden ramrods, flat-topped round twist barrels engraved 'London', c1815, 14in (35.5cm) overall.
£680–810 / €970–1,150
$1,200–1,400 WAL ⚒

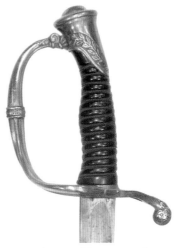

Flintlock target rifle, reconverted from percussion, with an engraved lock, figured walnut full stock, engraved trigger guard, steel ramrod, slight damage and repair, c1800, 37½in (95.5cm) long.
£720–860 / €1,050–1,250
$1,300–1,550 S(O) ⚒

Non-regulation officer's sword, the brass hilt decorated in high relief, with a single side bar and wire-wrapped horn grip, slight damage, French, 1821, blade 29¾in (75.5cm) long. Although there are many US and Continental edged weapons on the UK market and there is strong demand for such items which keeps prices buoyant.
£700–780 / €1,000–1,150
$1,250–1,400 FAC ⊞

Northamptonshire Regimental helmet, the QVC plate with original gilt, c1880.
£720–860 / €1,050–1,250
$1,300–1,550 DNW ⚒

Silvered smallsword, with a brass hilt, lobed pommel, double-shell guard and wire-wrapped hilt, c1760, blade 31¾in (80.5cm) long. Smallswords were a common, everyday item in the 18thC and were blackened for use at funerals.
£760–910 / €1,100–1,300
$1,400–1,650 FAC ⊞

Part suit of 17thC-style armour, engraved with eagles, stylized flowers and rampant lion breastplate, 65½in (166.5cm) high. A genuine suit of armour would cost in excess of £20,000 / €29,000 / $36,000. However, there are some very good-quality Victorian examples on the market manufactured for display purposes only.
£780–930 / €1,150–1,350
$1,450–1,700 L&E ⚒

Pair of double-barrelled percussion sporting pistols, by Guillaume, Berfleur, with walnut stocks, carved foliate scroll decoration and checkered butts, the butt caps engraved with sporting scenes, inlaid with silver wire, with engraved and cut-steel trigger guards, and silver-tipped ramrods, c1840, 13in (33cm) long. Combination/multi-barrelled weapons can be very expensive and these sold at a reasonable price at auction. They could be expected to achieve upwards of £1,000 / €1,450 / $1,800.
**£800–960 / €1,200–1,400
$1,450–1,750** F&C ⚒

Naval artillery sword, the brass hilt incorporating a lion's head pommel with a cast-brass ring, the faceted grip with a stippled 'dog bone'-form cross guard, French, 1771–90, blade 22in (56cm) long.
**£790–880 / €1,150–1,300
$1,450–1,600** FAC ⊞

Flintlock holster pistol, with a signed, tapering barrel, with figured walnut stock carved in relief, with gilt-brass chased mounts, the spurred butt cap decorated with strapwork and grotesques, with a warrior cap, the trigger-guard with an acanthus finial, later ramrod, Belgian, Liège, 1740–50, 19in (48.5cm) long. Many holster pistols found today have had the barrels shortened; this example is in its original state which increases its value.
**£840–1,000 / €1,200–1,450
$1,550–1,800** S(O) ⚒

British cavalry dragoon pistol, by Barnett, with British ordnance marks, c1810, 15½in (39.5cm) long.
**£850–950 / €1,250–1,400
$1,550–1,750** TLA ⊞

▶ **Matchlock musket,**
Indian, 19thC, barrel 50½in (128.5cm) long.
**£960–1,150 / €1,400–1,650
$1,750–2,000** S(O) ⚒

◀ **Miquelet-lock musket,** Turkish, 18thC, barrel 32¼in (82cm) long. Miquelet is the term applied to Spanish and Turkish muskets found with a lock that is on the outside of the gun.
**£960–1,150 / €1,400–1,650
$1,750–2,000** S(O) ⚒

Boxes

Pitch pine box, with ebony, walnut and mahogany inlay, c1890, 10in (25.5cm) wide. Pitch pine has a nice straight grain without knots which makes it desirable to some collectors.
£30–35 / €45–50
$55–65 SAT ⊞

Mauchline ware box, decorated with a view of Windermere, Cumbria, 1900, 5in (12.5cm) wide.
£45–50 / €65–75
$85–95 MB ⊞

Miller's compares...

A. Tunbridge ware box, c1880, 3in (7.5cm) wide.
£55–65 / €80–95
$105–125 HTE ⊞

B. Victorian Tunbridge ware and rosewood box, 8in (20.5cm) wide.
£260–310 / €380–450
$470–560 G(B) ⚒

Item A is less decorative than Item B, which has more detail, sliced veneer and banded borders. It is these attributes that enabled Item B to achieve a higher price at auction.

◀ **Tunbridge ware rosewood box,** 1840, 2in (5cm) diam. This box was turned from solid rosewood and was possibly originally part of a sewing kit.
£60–70 / €85–100
$115–135 MB ⊞

◀ **Mahogany box,** c1880, 8in (20.5cm) wide. This box originally housed a silver chalice from St John's Convent in Windsor, Berkshire.
£70–80
€100–115
$135–155 MB ⊞

Mahogany and marquetry box, c1860, 11in (28cm) wide.
£70–80 / €100–115
$135–155 AL ⊞

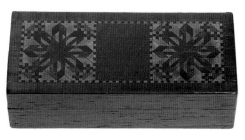

Tunbridge ware rosewood box, 1840, 4in (10cm) wide.
£75–85 / €110–125
$145–165 MB ⊞

Pine box, with a drawer, German, c1870, 22in (56cm) wide. This box would previously have been the plinth for a safe.
£85–95 / €125–140
$165–185 HRQ ⊞

Walnut box, with parquetry banding, c19thC, 10in (25.5cm) wide.
£105–120 / €150–170
$200–230 MB ⊞

Sycamore box, with walnut moulding, c1850, 10in (25.5cm) wide. This attractive box is made of sycamore, which is unusual, and it has good-quality brass fittings.
£105–120 / €150–175
$200–230 SAT ⊞

▶ **Victorian coromandel and gilt-metal-mounted jewellery box,** the hinged cover above two doors enclosing drawers, 7½in (19cm) high. The slight damage to the front panel of this box has reduced its value.
£110–130 / €160–190
$200–240 G(L) 🔨

Ivory box and cover, carved with chrysanthemums and foliage, Japanese, Meiji Period, 1868–1911, 3¼ (8.5cm) diam. This good-quality box was an excellent buy at auction. It could have sold for £200 / €290 / $360.
£130–155 / €190–220
$240–280 WW ➶

Late Victorian silver-mounted oak cigarette box, inscribed 'Made from the wood of Nelson's *Victory*', 7½in (19cm) wide. If the provenance of this box could be proved it could command an impressive premium, especially with the recent celebration of the 200th Anniversary of the Battle of Trafalgar. The silver mounts also add to its value. This box would be an ideal item with which to start a collection.
£150–175 / €220–250
$270–320 BWL ➶

◄ **Late Victorian walnut inlaid money box,** the front decorated with two sailing boats, 6¼in (16cm) wide.
£170–200 / €250–300
$310–370 SWO ➶

Ebonized casket, with ormolu mounts and malachite panels, possibly French or German, 19thC, 10in (25.5cm) wide. The ornate decoration on this box may not suit all tastes, but it was a good buy at auction.
£170–200 / €250–290
$310–360 BWL ➶

◄ **Victorian bird's-eye maple stationery box,** inset with rosewood, the hinged top and fall-front enclosing a well stand, a bone pen rack and two spring-loaded drawers, with Isle of Man mark, 15in (38cm) wide. The ability to trace exact origin adds to value and, with boxes, an unusual interior also increases worth. Complete with its original inkwells this box could have achieved double this price at auction.
£150–180 / €220–260
$270–320 G(L) ➶

Lacquered cigar box,
depicting a carriage racing
through the snow, Russian,
c1860, 4in (10cm) high.
£175–195 / €250–280
$320–360 F&F ⊞

Walnut tea caddy, with brass mounts,
enclosing two covered compartments,
late 19thC, 17½in (44.5cm) wide.
£210–250 / €300–360
$380–450 BWL ⚒

◀ **Walnut candle box,** c1780, 15½in
(39.5cm) high. Kitchenware items are sought
after and this candle box has a good colour
and patina, which accounts for its price.
£270–300 / €390–440
$490–550 F&F ⊞

Papier-mâché snuff box,
painted with a *houri*, c1830,
4in (10in) high. A *houri* is a
beautiful maiden, said by some
Muslims to dwell in paradise for
the enjoyment of the faithful.
£250–280 / €360–410
$460–510 RdeR ⊞

◀ **Lacquered
box,** depicting a
troika in the snow,
Russian, c1885,
6¼in (16cm) wide.
£270–300
€390–440
$490–550 F&F ⊞

The look without the price

Tiffany-style bronze and glass box,
American, c1900, 7in (18cm) wide.
£310–350 / €450–510
$560–640 NAW ⊞

This dressing-table box is good quality.
However, had it been made by Tiffany
rather than just being in Tiffany-style it
would be worth £1,500–2,000 / €2,200–
2,900 / $2,750–3,650.

Horn snuff box, inscribed 'Hy Price 1797', Welsh, 3in (7.5cm) wide. The clear date and provenance has added to the value of this snuff box.
£310–350 / €450–510
$560–640 SEA ⊞

Lacquered box, Russian, c1900, 7in (18cm) wide.
£340–380 / €490–550
$620–690 WAA ⊞

Mother-of-pearl and abalone tea caddy, the hinged cover enclosing an ivory-lined interior with covered compartments, c1850, 6¾in (17cm) wide. Elaborate tea caddies of this type are currently out of fashion and are prone to damage. This example sold for a reasonable price and would make an acceptable addition to a collection.
£340–400 / €490–580
$620–730 WW ⚒

George III ivory and tortoiseshell tea caddy,
with mother-of-pearl inset roundels, the silver escutcheon and cartouche engraved with a crest, damaged, interior cover and lining missing, 5¼in (13.5cm) wide. The damage has reduced the value of this tea caddy. Restoration would be expensive and it would be hard to find a craftsman with the skills to carry it out to a high standard. However, in good condition it could sell for £1,500–2,000 / €2,200–2,900 / $2,750–3,650.
£380–450 / €550–650
$690–820 DN ⚒

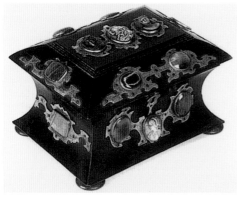

Ebony box, with engraved gilt-metal mounts, agate ovals and four carved stone and lava female cameos, enclosing a silk-lined interior, possibly Continental, late 19thC, 9in (23cm) wide.
£400–480 / €580–700
$720–870 DN ⚒

Burr-yew-wood tea caddy, c1790, 7¼in (18.5cm) wide.
£440–490 / €640–710
$800–890 F&F ⊞

Rosewood box, with mother-of-pearl escutcheon and engraved labels, c1835, 8½in (21.5cm) wide.
£450–500 / €650–730
$820–910 JTS ⊞

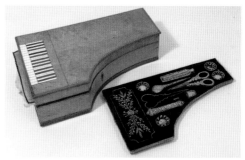

Bird's-eye maple work box, in the form of a piano, with ivory and ebony inlaid keys, the hinged top enclosing silver sewing accessories and a musical box playing two airs, retailer's label, feet missing, Swiss or French, mid-19thC, 11½in (29cm) wide. This work box is an unusual shape and this would attract buyers. The presence of a clear retailer's label has also added value.
£460–550 / €670–800
$840–1,000 G(L) ⚹

Mother-of-pearl and abalone tea caddy, the hinged cover decorated in relief with a landscape, with a later glass interior, Continental, 19thC, 6in (15cm) wide. The later interior of this tea caddy has lowered the auction price.
£460–550 / €670–800
$840–1,000 WW ⚹

Oak bible box, dated 1691, 25in (63.5cm) wide.
£550–660 / €800–960
$1,000–1,200 DN(HAM) ⚹

Burr-yew-wood tea caddy, with two compartments and glass bowl, c1810, 12in (30.5cm) wide.
£540–600 / €780–870
$980–1,100 F&F ⊞

◄ Tunbridge ware stationery box, with bird's-eye maple veneer, c1870, 8in (20.5cm) wide.
£620–700 / €900–1,000
$1,100–1,250 AMH ⊞

Dolls, Teddy Bears & Toys

◀ **Victorian lithograph-mounted wooden jigsaw,** entitled 'Children in the Wood', with original box, 7½in (19cm) wide. This jigsaw was a good buy at auction as the colour lithograph and original box make it very desirable to collectors. It could have reached twice this price.
£120–140
€175–200
$220–250 G(L) ↗

Steiner bisque-headed doll, with sleeping eyes, composition limbs and original costume, German, 19thC, 11¾in (30cm) high.
£100–120 / €145–175
$180–220 L&E ↗

▶ **Victorian pull-along horse and cart,** by A. W. Gamage Ltd, London, with retailer's label, one wheel missing to horse, 12in (30.5cm) high.
£170–200 / €250–290
$310–360 MAL ↗

◀ **Simon & Halbig bisque-headed doll,** No. 1079, with glass eyes, German, c1895, 28in (71cm) high. This is a good example of a high-quality doll. She has the original wig, pierced ears, an attractive expression and is of a good size. This was a good value buy at auction.
£190–220
€280–320
$350–400 JBe ↗

▶ **Pine toy wagon,** c1910, 18in (45.5cm) long. The advertisement on the side of this wagon and the sacks of flour have added value to this toy.
£180–200
€260–290
$330–370 JUN ⊞

Cast-iron Tammany mechanical money box, American, c1900, 6in (15cm) high. This is a common design of a cast-iron money box of this period. It is rare to find a mechanical money box in mint condition as they were used mainly by children. Purchasers should be wary as there are many copies of this money box on the market.
£220–250 / €320–360
$400–460 JUN ⊞

Wilkins Toy Co cast-iron horse-drawn dray, reins replaced, American, c1880, 11½in (29cm) long. Toys in this aged, worn condition should not be restored as this detracts from their value.
£350–420 / €510–610
$640–760 JAA ⚒

Carved wood horse, with jointed head and legs, c1910, 18in (45.5cm) long. This is an unusual toy that may originally have been a puppet.
£270–300 / €390–440
$490–550 JUN ⊞

▶ **Wax and composition Mad Alice doll,** c1860, 22in (56cm) high. Crazing and cracking of these older wax over composition dolls is acceptable. Mad Alice Smith lived in York. She was hanged in 1825 at York Castle for poisoning her husband – a perceived crime of insanity.
£360–400 €520–580
$660–730 GLEN ⊞

Find out more in

Miller's Teddy Bears:
A Complete Collector's Guide,
Miller's Publications, 2001

Papier-mâché dog, with a flock-covered body, glass eyes, articulated neck and jaw and pull-chain barking mechanism, French, late 19thC, 17in (43cm) long. Collectors will pay more for a toy in original condition than for one that has been restored.
£360–430 / €520–620
$660–780 G(L) ⚒

Steiff plush teddy bear, with boot-button eyes, hump, jointed limbs and original button in the left ear, German, c1910, 10in (25.5cm) high.
£360–430 / €520–620
$660–780 G(L) ⚒

Porcelain-headed doll, with glass eyes and a kid leather body, 19thC, 13in (33cm) high. A maker's name attributed to this doll would have increased its value.
£400–480 / €580–700
$730–870 DMC ⚒

Boxwood and rosewood chess set, c1860, king 4in (10cm) high.
£400–450 / €580–650
$730–820 TMi ⊞

Carved pine fairground horse's head, c1900, 19in (48.5cm) high.
£450–500 / €650–730
$820–910 JUN ⊞

Mason & Parker steel and wood runabout, the bonnet stencilled 'Monterey', with an iron flywheel, chain and sprocket turning the rear axle, American, c1904, 10in (25.5cm) long.
£450–540 / €650–780
$820–980 Bert ⚒

▶ **Wooden dolls' house,** with hinged front and rear, with a selection of contemporary and later furnishings, on cabriole front legs and turned rear legs, early 20thC, 32in (81.5cm) wide. Dolls' houses are very collectable in the UK and America, and this example is in good condition and on an attractive stand.
£500–600
€730–870
$910–1,100
NSal ⚒

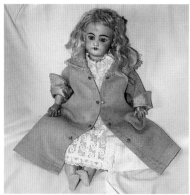

Simon & Halbig bisque-headed doll, No. 1079, with original wig, on a composition shoulder plate, with a cloth body and composition lower limbs, German, 1890s, 19¾in (50cm) high.
£500–550 / €720–800
$900–1,000 BaN ⊞

◀ **Jaques ebony and boxwood Staunton chess set,** the mahogany box with a Jaques paper label, c1890, king 3½in (9cm) high.
£540–600
€780–870
$980–1,100 TMi ⊞

Carved wood rocking horse, with painted decoration, 19thC, 63in (160cm) wide. This rocking horse is in need of professional restoration. The cost of this should be taken into consideration when purchasing either at auction or from a dealer.
£540–640 / €780–930
$980–1,150 WW ⚒

Lund-style Ivory and stained ivory chess set, some damage, with an associated board, 19thC. This is a good quality chess set that achieved twice the estimated price at auction.
£560–670 / €810–970
$1,000–1,200 SWO ⚒

Ivory and stained ivory chess set, c1820, king 4in (10cm) high.
£580–650 / €840–940
$1,050–1,200 TMi ⊞

Late Victorian oak games compendium, by F. H. Ayres, with a hinged cover, fitted interior and drawer for games pieces for chess, draughts, backgammon, dominoes, race game, table croquet, whist, cribbage and bezique, with a cloth-bound guide, 17¾in (45cm) wide.
£600–720 / €870–1,050
$1,100–1,300 SWO ⚒

Kämmer & Reinhardt bisque-headed doll, with sleeping eyes and composition body, German, c1910, 29¼in (74.5cm) high. This is a large doll at a reasonable price. A named doll in an uncharacteristic size will be rare and therefore command a premium.
£800–900 / €1,150–1,300
$1,450–1,650 BaN ⊞

Kitchenware

Miller's compares...

A. Sycamore bread board, carved with flowers, 1910, 11½in (29cm) diam.
£15–20 / €22–29
$29–38 JWK ⊞

B. Sycamore bread board, inscribed 'The Earth is the Lords and the Fullness Thereof', c1900, 11½in (29cm) diam.
£220–250 / €320–360
$400–460 B&R ⊞

Items A and B are both made of sycamore and are the same size. Item A has simpler decoration whereas Item B has been finely carved with flowers and an inscription, which makes it more unusual and more desirable to collectors, hence the higher price.

The look without the price

Ceramic butter dish, cover missing, 1910, 7in (18cm) wide.
£20–25 / €30–35
$40–50 JWK ⊞

This butter dish is in good condition and has an inscription. However, the cover is missing. If the dish was complete with the cover it could be worth £70–75 / €100–110 / $125–135.

Taplin's metal whisk, 1900, 11in (28cm) long.
£20–25 / €30–35
$40–50 JWK ⊞

Tailor's iron, 1910, 8½in (21.5cm) long.
£20–25 / €30–35
$40–50 JWK ⊞

Miller's compares...

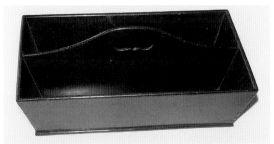

A. Pine knife box, 1910,
12½in (32cm) wide.
£25–30 / €40–45
$50–55 JWK ⊞

B. Mahogany knife box, 1900, 14½in (37cm) wide.
£50–55 / €70–80
$95–105 JWK ⊞

Item A is made from stained pine whereas
Item B is made from mahogany, which is more

appealing and desirable to collectors.
This accounts for the greater value of Item B.

Enamel teapot, decorated with flowers
and waterlilies, 1920, 4½in (11.5cm) high.
£25–30 / €40–45
$50–55 JWK ⊞

Isabella Beeton, *Mrs Beeton's
Household Management,*
published by Ward, Lock & Co,
1920, 8½in (21.5cm) high.
£35–40 / €50–60
$65–75 JWK ⊞

Stoneware preserve jar,
with label for W. Kilpatrick,
Birkenhead, 1910,
11in (28cm) high.
£25–30 / €40–45
$50–55 JWK ⊞

▶ **Victorian iron,** with a
wooden handle, the cover catch
in the form of a head,
8in (20.5cm) wide. Irons are
collectable and this is a fair price
for an example with such unusual
decoration. Irons can start as
low as £8 / €11 / $14, and it is
worth trying to collect examples
from across the price range.
£35–40 / €50–60
$65–75 HOM ⊞

Sycamore shortbread mould, late
19thC, 9in (23cm) diam. This is a nice clean
example and would be used today
for decoration rather than general use.
£35–40 / €50–60
$65–75 WeA ⊞

Booth's porcelain jug, 1900,
8in (20.5cm) high.
£50–55 / €70–80
$95–105 JWK ⊞

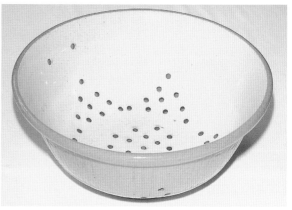

Ceramic drainer, 1900, 10½in (26.5cm) diam.
£50–55 / €70–80
$95–105 JWK ⊞

Miller's compares...

A. Copper kettle, c1910, 9in (23cm) high.
£50–55 / €70–80
$95–105 AL ⊞

B. Copper kettle, c1890, 11½in (29cm) high.
£120–135 / €175–195
$220–250 AL ⊞

Item B is larger, older and of a more elaborate shape than Item A, hence its higher price.

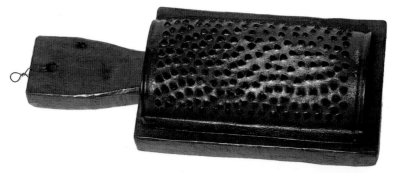

◄ **Metal grater,**
on a wooden base,
French, c1880,
12in (30.5cm) wide.
Graters can make
interesting display
pieces and a
collector can expect
to pay upwards of
£10 / €14 / $18.
£50–55 / €70–80
$95–105 Cot ⊞

Copper jelly mould, by Benham & Froud, marked, 19thC, 6in (15cm) high. This style of jelly mould was manufactured in large numbers and purchasers should look for examples of weight and with a good patina. Copper and brass moulds are currently out of fashion.
£75–90 / €105–130
$135–160 PFK ⚒

Stoneware jar, inscribed 'Meal', Scottish, c1890, 11in (28cm) high. The decorative label on this jar has increased its appeal and value.
£70–80 / €100–115
$135–155 B&R ▦

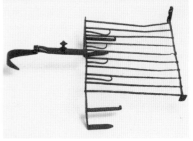

Wrought-iron griddle, c1740, 17in (43cm) wide. This griddle would make a decorative feature in the inglenook of a traditional country house.
£100–110 / €145–160
$180–200 PeN ▦

Two stoneware jars, inscribed 'PL Barley' and 'Sago', c1880, larger 10in (25.5cm) high. Decorative inscriptions and labels increase the value of storage jars.
£105–120 / €150–170
$200–230 each SMI ▦

Copeland ceramic jelly mould, with a relief of a milkmaid, c1900, 8in (20.5cm) wide. Interesting scenes on moulds increase the value. Animals are a popular subject matter and a named maker also adds value.
£105–120 / €150–170
$200–230 SMI ▦

◀ **Pine egg box,** with original paint, 1920–30, 14in (35.5cm) wide. This is a rare item, especially with its inscription. Egg-related items are very collectable.
£105–120
€150–170
$200–230 B&R ▦

Sycamore bread board, inscribed 'Our Daily Bread', c1910, 12in (30.5cm) diam. This bread board is in good condition and has a clear inscription. Prices generally start from £30 / €45 / $55 for a Victorian bread board.
£105–120 / €150–170
$200–230 SMI ▦

Ceramic jelly mould, with a relief of a lady with a milk churn, c1880, 7in (18cm) wide.
£105–120 / €150–170
$200–230 SMI ⊞

Wedgwood jelly mould, with a relief of a partridge, c1880, 5in (12.5cm) high.
£110–125 / €160–180
$200–230 SMI ⊞

Ceramic jelly mould, with a relief of a ewe and a lamb, with feet, c1850, 7in (18cm) wide. Even with slight wear and tear, a footed ceramic jelly mould will command a premium.
£135–150 / €195–220
$250–270 SMI ⊞

Sycamore bread board, inscribed 'The Staff of Life', c1880, 12in (30.5cm) wide. It is unusual to find oval bread boards, and this will make it more desirable to collectors and therefore more valuable.
£135–150 / €195–220
$250–270 SMI ⊞

◄ **Cast-iron coffee grinder,** by Kenrick & Sons, c1900, 5in (12.5cm) high.
£165–185
€240–270
$300–340 BS ⊞

Copper jelly mould, by Benham & Froud, No. 637, marked, 19thC, 6½in (16.5cm) wide.
£200–240 / €290–350
$360–430 PFK ⚒

◀ **Copper jelly mould,** by Benham & Froud, No. 57, marked, 19thC, 6¾in (17cm) wide.
£200–240
€290–350
$360–430 PFK ⚒

▶ **Cast-iron coffee grinder,** by Kenrick & Sons, c1880, 4in (10cm) diam.
£220–250
€320–360
$400–450 SMI ⊞

Kent's Patent wood and cast-iron knife polisher, with brass and enamel plaques, c1905, 23in (58.5cm) high.
£220–250 / €320–360
$400–450 SMI ⊞

Ceramic Patent Egg Beater, c1820, 4in (10cm) high.
£220–250 / €320–360
$400–450 SMI ⊞

Wrought-iron flesh fork, c1780, 21in (53.5cm) long. This flesh fork would make an attractive feature in an inglenook.
£250–280 / €360–410
$450–510 SEA ⊞

Wood spice cabinet, with 10 drawers, c1910, 19in (48.5cm) high. It is rare to find an item of this type in good condition and complete with labels.
£270–300 / €390–440
$490–550 SMI ⊞

▶ **Copper and tin chocolate mould,** in the form of a stag, c1850, 13in (33cm) high. This chocolate mould has achieved a high price due to the fact that it is made of copper as well as tin.
£400–450 / €580–650
$730–820 SMI ⊞

Lighting

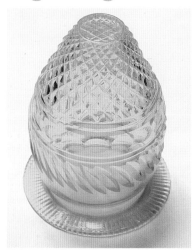

Cut-crystal glass shade,
c1810, 6in (15cm) high.
£35–40 / €50–60
$65–75 JeH ⊞

Glass fairy light, c1910.
£50–60 / €75–85
$100–115 HO ⊞

Etched glass shade, c1900,
6in (15cm) high.
£60–70 / €85–100
$115–135 JeH ⊞

Brass oil lamp, with cut-glass
reservoir, with later shade and
chimney, 19thC, 30½in (77.5cm)
high. This style of oil lamp is
currently unpopular. They are
mainly used as decorative items
and now would be a good time
to purchase.
£60–70 / €85–100
$115–135 GH ⚒

◀ **Pendant lamp,** with an etched glass shade, c1900,
8in (20.5cm) high.
£85–95 / €125–140
$165–185 JeH ⊞

▶ **Brass oil chamberstick,** engraved
'Buckingham Palace', No. 43, feet
missing, 19thC, 4½in (11.5cm) diam.
The provenance should have added more
value to this chamberstick.
£90–105 / €130–150
$165–190 G(L) ⚒

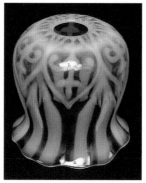

Edwardian gilt-brass desk lamp, on a marble stand, 13¼in (33.5cm) high. This is an ornate and sought-after style of desk lamp.
£100–120 / €145–170
$200–230 WW ✧

Vaseline glass shade, c1900, 5in (12.5cm) high. These glass shades are rare as few have survived in good condition.
£140–160 / €200–230
$250–280 JeH ⊞

Victorian brass oil lamp, with an earthenware reservoir and glass shade, 25¼in (64cm) high. This lamp's ornate decoration has added to the price achieved at auction.
£150–180 / €220–260
$270–320 WilP ✧

◄ **Pair of gilt-metal wall lights,** with porcelain flowers, 19thC, 6¼in (16cm) high.
£160–190 / €240–280
$290–350 SWO ✧

◄ **Victorian oil lamp,** with a glass shade and reservoir, 41in (104cm) high. This lamp was sold by an American auction house where it achieved a higher price than it would have done had it been sold in England.
£220–260
€320–380
$400–470 DuM ✧

Neo-classical-style celadon table lamp, with ormolu mounts, decorated with a maiden, Continental, late 19thC, 16in (40.5cm) high.
£220–260 / €320–380
$400–470 MCA ✧

Late Victorian cut-glass chandelier, made from parts of an earlier chandelier, 15in (38cm) high. Chandeliers are still in demand today, especially the smaller versions. This chandelier would not necessarily have achieved a higher price had it been completely original.
£270–300 / €390–440
$490–550 JPr ⊞

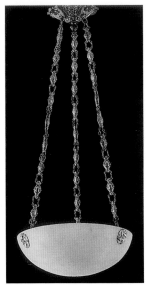

Gilt-metal-mounted celadon oil lamp, decorated with flowers, French, 19thC, 25¼in (64cm) high.
£300–360 / €430–520
$540–640 GIL ⚘

Alabaster hall light, with embossed suspension chains, Italian, c1900, 21in (53.5cm) high.
£300–360 / €430–380
$540–640 NOA ⚘

Ceramic oil lamp, by Moore Bros, moulded with flowers, the metal-mounted burner with Messenger patent, slight damage, impressed marks, late 19thC, 18¼in (46.5cm) high, with another reservoir and glass shade.
£400–480 / €580–700
$730–870 SWO ⚘

Oil lamp, by Moore Bros, with moulded and applied floral decoration, restored, printed mark, late 19thC, 17¾in (45cm) high. The elaborate designs by Moore Bros may not be to everyone's taste but this is a reasonable price for a renowned maker.
£450–540 / €650–780
$820–980 SWO ⚘

Miller's compares...

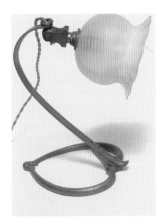

A. Brass table lamp, with a vaseline glass shade, 1890s, 10in (25.5cm) high.
£490–550 / €710–800
$890–1,000 MiW ▦

B. Brass table lamp, by W. A. S. Benson, the vaseline glass shade by James Powell, lamp signed, 1890s, 11in (28cm) high.
£810–900 / €1,150–1,300
$1,450–1,650 MiW ▦

Both Item A and Item B are desirable table lamps. However, Item B is by a named designer and is signed, and its shade was made by James Powell & Sons who were one of the most important glass-blowing companies of the period. This is why Item B is worth twice the price of Item A.

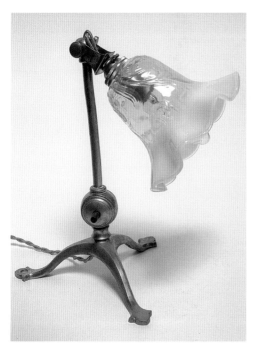

Brass table lamp, by W. A. S. Benson, the glass shade by James Powell & Sons, lamp signed, 1890s, 10in (25.5cm) high.
£720–800 / €1,000–1,150
$1,300–1,450 MiW ⊞

Regency bronze and parcel-gilt lamp, with a later glass reservoir and Hink's No.2 Duplex burner, converted for electricity, 22in (56cm) high.
£750–900
€1,100–1,300
$1,400–1,650
WW ↗

Pair of brass oil lanterns, by Davey & Co, c1880, 17in (43cm) high.
£760–850 / €1,100–1,250
$1,400–1,550 TOP ⊞

Brass three-branch ceiling lamp, c1910, 19in (48.5cm) diam.
£760–850 / €1,100–1,250
$1,400–1,550 CHA ⊞

▶ **Chrome lamp,** the base and glass shade decorated with Greek-key pattern, with a porcelain base, 1905, 23in (58.5cm) high. The unusual design and good condition of this lamp has accounted for its high price.
£800–900 / €1,150–1,300
$1,450–1,650 TOL ⊞

Regency iron lantern, with snuffers, with gilt decoration, c1830, 19in (48.5cm) high. This style of lantern is very rare making it desirable to collectors and more valuable.
£850–950 / €1,250–1,400
$1,550–1,750 HA ⊞

Metalware

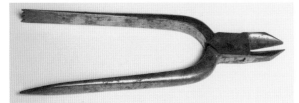

Champagne wire cutting nippers, the handle ends with a spike and a serrated edge for opening wooden crates, c1880, 7in (18cm) long.
£15–20 / €20–30
$25–35 CS ⊞

Copper milk jug, Irish, c1875, 8in (20.5cm) high. This is a reasonably-priced item that would be a good addition to a collection.
£30–35 / €45–50
$55–65 Byl ⊞

◄ **Miner's brass tobacco tin,** inscribed 'John Williams Mardy 1880', 3in (7.5cm) wide. This is a very collectable piece. Provenance is important and adds to the value. Without provenance this tin could be worth half this price.
£60–70 / €85–100
$110–125 MB ⊞

▶ **Pair of brass wick trimmers and tray,** c1780, tray 9in (23cm) wide.
£80–90 / €115–130
$145–165 F&F ⊞

Copper ale mull, c1760, 10½in (26.5cm) high. This is a very collectable item.
£90–100 / €130–145
$165–180 F&F ⊞

▶ **Brass barber's bowl,** with engraved decoration, c1870, 11in (28cm) wide. This is an unusual item with good decoration at a fair price.
£120–135
€175–195
$220–250 PeN ⊞

Britannia metal coffee pot, by James Dixon & Sons, with a wooden handle, 1860, 6in (15cm) high.
£180–200 / €260–290
$330–360 DML ⊞

Wrought-iron two-valve crusie lamp, Scottish, c1740, 10in (25.5cm) high. A crusie lamp is a simple iron lamp consisting of a saucer in which a wick of moss or wool is floated. They were frequently used in Scotland and Ireland from the 18thC.
£130–145 / €190–210
$240–270 PeN ⊞

Gilt-metal chatelaine, hung with an *etui* set with hardstone, containing a spoon, ear spoon, ivory leaf note book and pencil, the chatelaine with further clips for appendages, pencil incomplete, c1750. This is a quality collector's item with long-term investment potential.
£180–210 / €260–300
$330–380 LAY 🔨

Liberty & Co Tudric pewter biscuit barrel, decorated with a geometric pattern and blue gemstones, c1905, 4½in (11.5cm) high. This item sold at auction for a very reasonable price and would make a good investment piece.
£200–240 / €290–350
$360–430 IM 🔨

Toleware tray table, on a *faux* bamboo support, late 19thC, 26in (66cm) wide. Toleware is currently popular and this collector's piece has good colour and has sold at a very reasonable price.
£260–310 / €380–450
$470–560 G(L) 🔨

Pewter ink stand, with a wafer drawer, c1820, 3in (7.5cm) square. This is an interesting collector's piece.
£270–300 / €390–440
$490–550 PeN ⊞

Hog scraper-style candlesticks would have served two purposes; lighting and scraping the hair off hogs at butchering time. The base on the candlestick is the same as a blade and the candle stub ejector enabled the candle to be burned low.

Bronze two-handled vase, by Hattori, inlaid with silver and gold-coloured metal dragons and clouds, Japanese, 19thC, 9½in (24cm) high. This is a decorative item that would make a good investment piece. Always look for a signature on bronze wares as this increases the value.
**£300–360 / €440–520
$550–660** SWO 🔨

Liberty & Co pewter cup holder, by Archibald Knox, with a later glass liner, c1905, 5in (12.5cm) high. The Liberty name has added a premium to this piece. It is highly collectable and a good investment in the current climate.
**£310–350 / €450–510
$560–640** HABA ⊞

▶ **Figural bronze,** depicting a woman at a trough, 1900, 6in (15cm) high. This is a desirable Art Nouveau item which may have originally held a matchbox or a striker. If it had been signed it could have achieved twice this price as it would appeal to both Art Nouveau collectors and collectors of smoking items.
**£360–400 / €520–580
$660–730** MiW ⊞

Pair of steel and iron hog scraper candlesticks, 1790, 7in (18cm) high. These are unusual items, which will have added to their value.
**£400–450 / €580–650
$730–820** SEA ⊞

◀ **Pewter mirror,** with Arts and Crafts floral decoration, c1900, 9 x 11in (23 x 28cm). This is a useful size of mirror from a popular collecting period. This will have made it more desirable and therefore more valuable.
**£460–520 / €670–750
$840–950** AFD ⊞

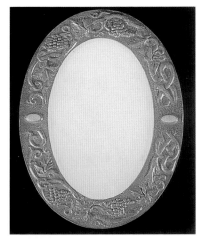

Pewter wall mirror, with Arts and Crafts embossed vine decoration and two ceramic mounts, c1900, 31½in (80cm) wide.
The ceramic mounts on this piece are a desirable feature, and this mirror would make a good collector's piece.
£480–570 / €700–830
$870–1,050 S(O) ⚒

Pewter chalice, North Country/ Scottish, c1750, 9in (23cm) high.
£480–540 / €700–780
$870–980 PeN ⊞

Liberty & Co pewter vase, designed by David Veazy, inscribed 'For Old Times Sake', c1908, 8in (20.5cm) high.
This vase would make a very attractive investment piece.
£510–570 / €740–830
$930–1,050 HABA ⊞

▶ **Late Victorian pair of cast-metal plaques,** depicting 16thC courting scenes, in rosewood frames with cast-metal corners, 23½ x 18½in (59.5 x 47cm). These are good, decorative plaques which sold in the US. They might have achieved a higher price if they had sold on the UK market.
£560–670 / €810–970
$1,000–1,200 JAA ⚒

◀ **Glasgow-style brass two-light wall sconce,** by Margaret Gilmour, embossed with a fruiting vine pattern, with spiral-twist sconces, c1905, 24in (61cm) high.
£630–700 / €900–1,000
$1,150–1,300 DAD ⊞

▶ **Pair of brass candlesticks,** on petal bases, c1740, 8in (20.5cm) high.
£800–880 / €1,150–1,300
$1,450–1,600 SEA ⊞

Rugs & Carpets

Kashmir cloth, European, c1900, 57½ x 55¼in (146 x 140cm). The term Kashmir is used to describe textiles of similar character which might be made in Kashmir and, curiously, in France, and refers more specifically to shawls. Although the market for such items has not been particularly strong in recent years, this cloth could have achieved more.
£100–120 / €150–180 $190–220 DORO ♪

Two bag faces, Turkish, 1900–20, 24¾ x 21¾in (63 x 55.5cm). Bag faces such as these, and examples made in Persia and Afghanistan appeal to collectors. Woven bags can be a good starting point for collecting as reasonably priced examples can be found. Also they take up little space and are highly decorative on walls, furniture and floors.
£130–150 / €190–220 $230–270 DORO ♪

Condition

Condition will affect the price of an antique rug or carpet, and the type of damage should be taken into consideration when making a purchase. Frayed ends and ragged side cords are considered normal wear and tear, and can easily be repaired. Wear to the pile is not too serious as long as the pattern can still be seen. However, rugs that have been cut, shortened or rejoined should be avoided as should rugs that have bald patches tinted with felt pen.

Miller's compares...

A. Rya rug, damaged, dated 1871, 78 x 63in (198 x 160cm).
£135–160 / €200–240 $240–290 BUK(F) ♪

B. Rya rug, damaged, dated 1841, 84¼ x 59in (214 x 150cm).
£280–330 / €400–480 $510–600 BUK(F) ♪

Both rugs are decorated with geometric figures which makes them desirable to collectors. However, Item A is worn and is a later example than Item B and this has reduced its value. Earlier 18th-century examples are rare and seldom appear on the market. Such early examples can achieve between **£1,500–2,000 / €2,200–2,900 / $2,800–3,650.**

Derbend rug, Caucasian, c1890, 58 x 40in (146.5 x 101.5cm). Although this rug is in poor condition, it has an unusual design which makes it more desirable.
£360–400 / €520–580
$650–720 DNo ⊞

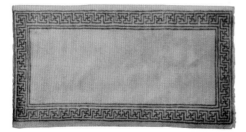

Rug, Chinese, c1900, 56 x 30in (142 x 76cm). Simple designs such as these suit the current trend for minimalism. This is a reasonable price for such an item.
£360–400 / €520–580
$650–720 DNo ⊞

Balouch rug, Afghani, c1900, 70 x 38in (178 x 96.5cm). White is used sparingly in good Balouch rugs.
£400–450 / €580–650
$730–820 DNo ⊞

Colours and dyes

Chemical dyes were introduced in rug making during the late 1860s and were used extensively from 1880 onwards, when rugs were made on a much larger commercial scale. Most pieces made after 1880 have some chemical colours present. Orange, strong red, turquoise and purple are typical chemical colours, but it is advisable to avoid these if they have been used as the main colour of the rug or carpet. Chemical colours fade and they lack the subtlety and individuality of vegetable colours. To determine whether a dye is chemical or vegetable, turn the piece over and if any of the colours are darker on the reverse than on the front, then those are chemical dyes. However, fading is often considered an attractive feature of a rug or carpet.

Rug, Anatolian, c1910, 81 x 50in (205.7 x 127cm).
£380–430 / €550–620
$690–780 DNo ⊞

Hamadan rug, west Persian, c1920, 74 x 52in (188 x 132cm). All-over designs are more popular than those displaying a central medallion, and this is a good example with contrasting colours. However, the wear to this rug has reduced its potential value by half.
£400–450 / €580–650
$730–820 DNo ⊞

Karabakh rug, Caucasian, c1900, 77 x 51½in (195.5 x 131cm). Caucasian rugs are popular in today's market. Their geometric designs are individual and decorative, and examples made 20 or 30 years earlier than this rug could achieve three or four times this price as they would have vegetable dyes. This example is likely to have chemical dyes, which are not as desirable to collectors.
£500–580 / €730–840
$910–1,050 WW ⚲

Current market trends

Like all markets, the carpet market is influenced by trends in decoration and fashion. Dense patterning is currently out of favour, as are strong colours. Pieces with both these features are generally very affordable. Types falling into this group include rugs and carpets produced in Persian and Turkish cities. Popular and therefore more expensive pieces include the use of pale colours, with open or detailed designs. Rugs and bags made by tribal groups are often sought after by collectors and therefore achieve high prices if they are in good condition.

◄ **Kashgai chenteh,** southwest Persian, late 19thC, 15 x 14in (38 x 35.5cm).
£580–650
€840–940
$1,050–1,200
SAM ▦

The look without the price

Heriz carpets are frequently found on the market and this design with a central medallion and blue, terracotta, ivory and yellow colours is typical of examples created both before and after 1900. Although older carpets tend to be technically finer and have less pattern, this later carpet represents excellent value for money, as earlier ones can achieve £2,500 / €3,650 / $4,550.

Heriz carpet, northwest Persian, c1930, 141¾ x 91¼in (360 x 232cm).
£720–860 / €1,050–1,250
$1,300–1,550 S(O) ⚲

Rug, possibly Hereke, Turkish, 1920–30, 71¼ x 45¾in (181 x 116cm). Although dense patterns are not currently as popular as simple designs, this rug represents good value for money as it is finely woven.
£750–900 / €1,100–1,300
$1,400–1,650 DORO ⚲

Jaf Kurd bag, northwest Persian, c1880, 25 x 23in (63.5 x 58.5cm). Woven bags are highly collectable and this is a good example with an attractive colour combination and good-quality workmanship.
£810–900 / €1,150–1,300
$1,450–1,650 WADS ⊞

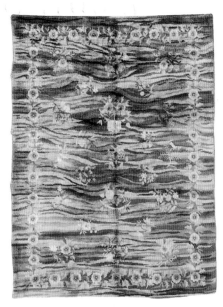

Savonnerie-style carpet, with Bessarabian Kilim decoration, c1925, 100½ x 72¾in (255.5 x 185cm). Carpets with unusual designs are hard to value but this is a reasonable price for a buyer who is looking for a particular style of decoration.
£840–1,000 / €1,250–1,450
$1,550–1,800 S(O) ⚒

◄ **Malayer runner,** northwest Persian, c1900, 196 x 45¼in (500 x 115cm). Narrow runners sell at higher prices than wider examples. However, had this runner been made with lighter colours, but still the same width, it could have achieved in the region of £1,200 / €1,750 / $2,200.
£840–1,000
€1,250–1,450
$1,550–1,800
S(O) ⚒

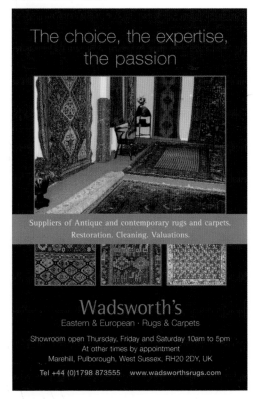

Scientific Instruments

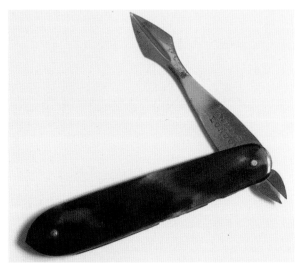

Set of brass laboratory scales, inscribed 'L. Oertling Ltd', in a glazed mahogany case, early 20thC, 20½in (52cm) high. Although this is a standard set, it is in good, clean condition and is complete with all the weights.
£75–85 / €110–125
$145–165 NSal ✯

Tortoiseshell vaccinator, by Weiss, c1825, 2½in (6.5cm) long.
£85–95 / €125–140
$165–185 FOF ⊞

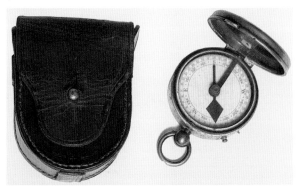

Lacquered brass light condenser,
c1860, 12in (30.5cm) high.
£90–100 / €130–145
$170–190 TOM ⊞

Verner brass Mark I British marching compass, by J. H. Steward, with original leather case, c1890, 2¼in (5.5cm) diam. The leather pouch has added to the desirability and therefore the price of this compass.
£130–145 / €190–210
$240–270 FOF ⊞

Surgeon's metal pincer, c1900, 10½in (26.5cm) long.
£135–150 / €195–220
$250–280 CuS ⊞

◀ **Brass transit theodolite,** by E. R. Watts & Son, signed, c1910, 10in (25.5cm) high, with a fitted mahogany box and wooden tripod. This is a good item and could have been expected to achieve more.
£150–180 / €220–260
$270–320 GTH ✯

Iron coffer padlock, with key, 19thC, 12in (30.5cm) long. This lock, which appears to be in working condition and complete, would be sought-after by collectors.
£155–175 / €220–250
$280–320 FST ⊞

Brass veterinary fleam, with six blades and a castrator, c1900, 4¾in (12cm) long. This type of fleam would be desirable to collectors.
£150–165 / €220–250
$270–300 FOF ⊞

▶ **Silver pedometer,** by Lion, with subsidiary register, enamel dial and steel hands, London 1898, 1½in (4cm) diam.
£200–230 / €290–330
$360–410 FOF ⊞

Tortoiseshell thumb lancet, by Evans & Co, signed, c1760, 6½in (16.5cm) long, with case. The tortoiseshell handle and the good condition of the blade has helped this lancet achieve a high value.
£175–200 / €250–280
$320–360 FOF ⊞

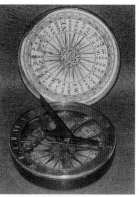

Gilt-metal pocket compass, c1800, 3in (7.5cm) diam, with a leather case. The case has added to the desirability and the value of this compass.
£240–280 / €350–410
$440–520 DN ⚒

Georgian mahogany apothecary box, the fitted interior with glass bottles, balance scales, other accessories and a drawer, 6½in (16.5cm) wide.
£260–310 / €380–450
$470–560 Bea ⚒

Brass pocket sundial and compass, with paper compass and scale, 18thC, 3½in (9cm) diam.
£300–360 / €440–520
$550–660 PF ⚒

Bronze sundial and compass, with a silvered dial, arc support and shaped gnomon, c1800, 4in (10cm) diam, with a shagreen case. The damaged case may have reduced the price of this item, as it could have sold for more.
£340–400 / €490–580
$620–730 HOLL ⚒

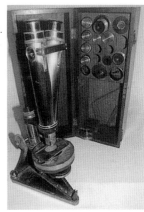

▶ **Travelling brass microscope,** by R. & J. Beck, with accessories, No. 5193, signed, c1870, 14¼in (36cm) high, in a mahogany box. Although this type of item has dropped in price recently, it is a good example complete with accessories which makes it desirable.
£380–450
€550–650
$690–820 GTH ⚒

Nairne & Blunt-style telescope, early 19thC, 17in (43cm) long, with oak case.
£420–500 / €610–730
$760–910 G(B) ⚒

◀ **Brass compound molecular microscope,** by Andrew Pritchard, No. 442, signed, c1840, 13¼in (33.5cm) high, with mahogany box containing accessories. This microscope is by a well-known sought-after maker and this has enabled it to achieve a high price at auction.
£480–570 / €700–830
$870–1,050 S ⚒

Brass sundial and compass, by G. Boelau, signed, Russian, late 18thC, 5¾in (14.5cm) diam. This sundial achieved a high price because it is signed and is in good condition.
£480–570 / €700–830
$870–1,050 S ⚒

◀ **Brass microscope,** by J. P. Cutts, Sons & Sutton, signed, c1851, 10¾in (27.5cm) high, with a mahogany case containing accessories comprising six objectives, forceps, side mirror, insect box, tweezers, bone specimen slide, instructions and key. The good maker and extensive list of accessories could have enabled this microscope to achieve more.
£500–600 / €730–870
$910–1,100 S ⚒

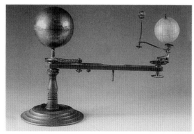

Wooden orrery, by Trippensee Manufacturing Co, with a brass sun, papier–mâché globe and wooden moon, one operating chain missing, American, c1900, 12¾in (32.5cm) high.
£560–670 / €810–970
$1,000–1,200 JDJ ➤

Brass orrery, with printed gores and engraved silver scales, the globe signed 'Lane's Pocket Globe, London 1815', 2¾in (7cm) diam.
£500–600 / €730–870
$910–1,100 GTH ➤

Mercury thermometer, compass, barometer and altimeter, with a silvered dial, c1910, 2in (5cm) diam. This set would need resilvering, a fact that would need to be taken into consideration before making a purchase.
£720–800 / €1,000–1,150
$1,300–1,450 HOM ⊞

Brass microscope, with a fitted case, stamped 'Secretan Paris', French, c1870, 6¾in (17cm) wide, with accessories.
£700–840 / €1,000–1,200
$1,250–1,500 S ➤

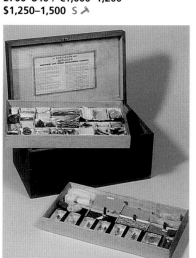

Universal equinoctial brass ring dial, engraved with the names and latitudes of European cities, 17thC, 3¼in (8.5cm) diam, with turned wood travelling case.
£840–1,000 / €1,200–1,450
$1,600–1,900 NSal ➤

◀ **Pine specimen box,** by Edward's Scientific & Educational Cabinets, with four trays and contents, 19thC, 16in (40cm) wide. This very collectable item is by a sought-after maker and in good condition. This accounts for its high price.
£960–1,150 / €1,400–1,650
$1,750–2,100 HOK ➤

Sculpture

Bronze bust of a woman, French, c1890,
7½in (19cm) high.
£200–240 / €280–330
$370–440 JAA ⚒

Painted terracotta gnome,
c1920, 22in (56cm) high.
Undamaged antique terracotta
is relatively rare but undesirable
subject matter can have a
negative effect on value.
£220–260 / €310–370
$400–470 G(L) ⚒

▶ **Carved
alabaster figural
group of a boy
and a girl,** on a
waisted socle,
19thC, 17½in
(44.5cm) high.
£220–260
€310–370
$400–470 AH ⚒

Bronzes

The great century of bronze sculpting from
1830 to 1930 saw figural work evolve from
the Classical masters through Art Nouveau
and Art Deco to the Modernism of Dalou
and Rodin. French foundries produced the
majority of the bronzes, turning art into a
successful commerce with finely finished
and detailed models.

◀ **Bronze figure,** after Jean-Antoine
Houdon, entitled 'The Arrow of Cupid', on
a marble base, signed 'Houdon', French,
25in (63.5cm) high.
£260–310 / €370–440
$470–560 NOA ⚒

The sculptor Jean-Antoine Houdon
(1741–1828) was born in Versailles.
He became famous for his busts
and statues of the great thinkers
and statesmen of the time,
including Denis Diderot, Benjamin
Franklin, Thomas Jefferson,
Napoleon, Jean-Jacques Rousseau,
Voltaire and George Washington.

Carved marble bust of Diana, Italian,
c1900, 14in (35.5cm) high.
£270–320 / €380–450
$500–600 DuM ⚒

Gilt-bronze sculpture of an armorial shield, on a marble
base, Continental, c1900, 12in (30.5cm) high.
£310–370 / €440–520
$570–680 NOA ⚒

**Carved walnut bust of a
woman,** late 17thC,
13½in (34.5cm) high.
£400–480 / €570–680
$720–870 TMA ⚒

Carved parcel-gilt figure of Louis XIV,
Austrian, Tyrol, 17thC, 12in (30.5cm) high.
£400–480 / €580–700
$730–870 G(L) ⚒

► **Bronze figure of Pan,** the
base decorated with putti,
19thC, 33½in (85cm) high.
£450–540 / €640–760
$820–980 GIL ⚒

Marble bust of a girl in a bonnet, on an enamelled wood base, Italian, Florence, 1875–1900, 28in (71cm) high.
£450–540 / €640–760
$820–980 NOA ⚒

◀ **Pair of bronze figures,** each cast as a putto, one carrying wheat, the other carrying a sickle and a fruiting vine, on Sienna marble bases, 19thC, 8½in (21.5cm) high.
£460–550 / €650–780
$840–1,000 L&E ⚒

Marble bust of a young boy, by Galli Rizzardo, signed, Italian, Milan, c1880, 17¾in (45cm) high. There are hundreds of types of marble. The difference between them is determined by mineral deposits which cause enormous variations in colour and pattern.
£460–550 / €650–780
$840–1,000 Bea ⚒

▶ **Bronze sculpture,** by Pierre Jules Cavelier, entitled 'Penelope', French, 9½in (24cm) high.
£600–710 / €850–1,000
$1,100–1,300 DuM ⚒

Marble figure of a child on a day bed, damaged, 19thC, 33in (84cm) wide.
£600–710 / €850–1,000
$1,100–1,300 PFK ⚒

Bronze figural group of Minerva and a nymph, by Felix Sanzel, signed, French, 1829–83, 17½in (44.5cm) high.
£720–860 / €1,050–1,250
$1,300–1,550 S(O) ⚒

Alabaster bust of a woman, signed
'Battiglia/Firenze', Italian, 19thC, 20½in (52cm) high.
£840–980 / €1,200–1,450
$1,500–1,800 BERN ➚

Bronze figure of a dancing girl, after Bruno Zach,
on a marble base, signed, c1925, 15in (38cm) high. Not
all bronzes are signed or stamped by either the artist or
the foundry, making signed pieces more desirable to
collectors and therefore more valuable.
£800–960 / €1,150–1,350
$1,450–1,750 G(L) ➚

Pair of bronze sculptures, in the form of satyr and
putti musicians, on marble bases, late 18thC,
7¾in (19.5cm) high.
£860–1,000 / €1,200–1,400
$1,500–1,800 Bea ➚

Carved marble figural group, late 19thC,
34in (86.5cm) high.
£960–1,150 / €1,400–1,650
$1,750–2,050 S(S) ➚

Textiles

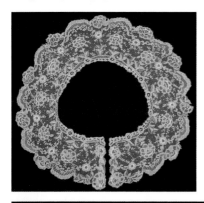

◄ **Maltese silk bobbin lace collar,** early 20thC, 19in (48.5cm) long. This is a good, usable item of lace at a reasonable price.
£30–35 / €45–50
$55–65 DHa ⊞

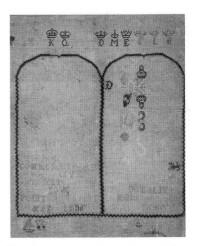

Needlework sampler, worked with the alphabet outlined by two arches, a vase of flowers flanked by a bird and a snake, dated 1710, 13 x 10½in (33 x 26.5cm), in a later frame. The lack of colour here has made the wording almost impossible to read and has kept the price of this early tablet sampler low.
£50–60 / €75–85
$100–110 DMC ⚒

◄ **Set of six cutwork and fillet lace mats,** c1900, 10in (25.5cm) square. This is a useful set of mats.
£65–75 / €95–105
$125–145 DHa ⊞

► **Chinese rank badge bag,** with hand-embroidered decoration, Chinese, late 19thC, 14in (35.5cm) long. Chinese rank badges are worn by officials on the front of the robe to show what level of bureacracy is held by the wearer. These badges are always more popular and valuable than simple needlework pictures.
£110–125
€160–180
$200–230 JPr ⊞

Needlework sampler, by Isabella Anderson, worked with the alphabet above flowering plants, a peacock and initials, dated 1842, 13 x 8½in (33 x 21.5cm).
£130–155 / €190–220
$240–290 PFK ⚒

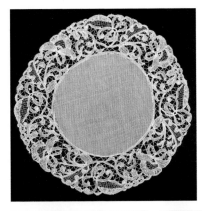

◄ **Set of 12 placemats,** with Bruges lace borders, Belgian, 1900, 12in (30.5cm) diam. This is a very useful set of mats.
£135–150
€195–220
$240–270 DHa ⊞

Victorian needlework sampler, by Isabelle Parker, Galgate, worked with a religious verse above flowering plants and berries, 19thC, 16½ x 17in (42 x 43cm), in a later frame. The date on this vanity sampler has been unpicked for some reason. The lack of a full date can deter purchasers from buying, and this has kept the price of this sampler low. Nevertheless, it was still a good buy at auction.
£140–165 / €200–240
$250–300 PFK ♪

Child's hat, with embroidered decoration, Chinese, late 19thC, 8in (20.5cm) wide.
£135–150 / €195–220
$240–270 JCH ⊞

Needlework sampler, by Maryah Colls, worked with the alphabet, dated 1825, 12 x 8½in (30.5 x 21.5cm), with later frame. The lack of colour or pictorial image has kept the price of this sampler low.
£180–210 / €260–310
$330–390 JDJ ♪

Woolwork sampler, by Ann Brewster, worked with the alphabet, royal crest, anchor and foliage, within a border of strawberries, dated 1888, 16½in (42cm) square, framed. The value of this sampler lies in the fact that it has good decoration.
£210–250 / €300–360
$380–450 DD ♪

Child's headdress, Chinese, 1920s, 6½in (16.5cm) wide.
£200–230 / €290–330
$360–420 JCH ⊞

◄ **Silk sampler,** by Anne Campion worked on gauze with a scene and a verse, dated 1833, 16 x 12in (40.5 x 30.5cm), framed. This is a classic sampler, but the lack of colour has kept the price low.
£210–250 / €300–360
$380–450 GAK ♪

Needlework sampler, by Eliza Wise, worked with a hymn and country house decoration, dated December 1840, 16 x 12in (40.5 x 30.5cm). This is fine work with a good image, but the line of dirt caused by the glass having been broken has kept the price down. Without the stain this sampler could have achieved £900–1,000 / €1,300–1,450 / $1,650–1,800.
£300–360 / €440–520
$550–660 Mal(O) 🪡

Three printed silk day dresses, one with green and white floral print and chemical lace trim, another sapphire blue with white spots, the third red with white stripes, c1905.
£300–360 / €440–520
$550–660 KTA 🪡

Sa Ni cotton rainbow hat, Chinese, Yunnan Province, Shi Lin County, early 20thC. In the Chinese ethnic group Sa Ni, the rainbow hat is worn by un-married girls. Wearing it gives the girl permission to meet potential marriage partners.
£250–280 / €360–410
$460–510 Wai ⊞

Silk sampler, by Elizabeth James, worked with a verse, a house with memorial country garden, windmill, cottage, dovecote and motifs, within a strawberry border, dated 1824, 17 x 13in (43 x 33cm), framed. This sampler was an extremely good buy at auction; it could have achieved as much as £1,400 / €2,000 / $2,500.
£400–480 / €580–700
$730–870 G(L) 🪡

Needlework sampler, by Fanny Brough, worked with an alphabet and numbers, a church, trees, birds and a verse, dated 1871, 25 x 24½in (63.5 x 62cm). This sampler has a pleasing image. If it had been dated earlier and worked in silk it could have been worth a great deal more.
£320–380 / €460–550
$580–690 Mit 🪡

◄ **Silk sampler,** worked with the alphabet, dated 1671, 13½ x 7in (34.5 x 18cm). This very early sampler has lost its colour and has possibly been cut down from a larger piece of work. These faults have kept the price low; however, it was still a good buy at auction.
£310–370 / €450–540
$560–670 DD 🪡

Satin bridal gown, the pleated panel bodice *à la Greque*, with matching pelerine cape edged with bobbin lace and a gauze bonnet trimmed with bows, 1840–45.
£400–480 / €580–700
$730–870 KTA ⚒

► **Silk sampler,** by Fanny A. Gibbs, worked with trees, figures, animals and flowers within a floral border, dated 1865, 15 x 15¾in (38 x 40cm). This is a good sampler with interesting spot motifs and was a good buy at auction.
£480–570
€700–830
$870–1,050 M ⚒

Puzzle sampler, entitled 'God is Love', worked with motifs and lettering including the days of the week and months, dated 1900, 22 x 20in (56 x 51cm). Unusual samplers such as this are good investment pieces as they are increasingly rare and hard to find.
£720–800 / €1,000–1,150
$1,300–1,450 HIS ⊞

Needlework sampler, by Sarah Shute, worked with a country house with birds, trees and flowers, a stanza and the alphabet, dated 1817, 18½ x 17in (47 x 43cm), in an ebonized frame.
£700–840 / €1,000–1,200
$1,250–1,500 AH ⚒

► **Silk panel,** decorated with gold thread, Indian, 19thC, 50 x 24in (127 x 61cm).
£760–850 / €1,100–1,250
$1,400–1,550 MGa ⊞

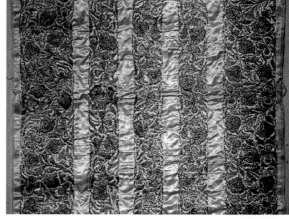

Wooden Antiques

Wooden mouse trap, c1850, 11in (28cm) wide.
£25–30 / €40–45
$50–55 HO ⊞

Tunbridge ware napkin ring, c1880, 3in (15cm) diam.
£30–35 / €45–50
$55–65 MB ⊞

▶ **Boxwood needle case,**
c1880, 3in (7.5cm) long.
£30–35 / €45–50
$55–65 MB ⊞

Tunbridge ware brush, c1860, 6in (15cm) wide.
£30–35 / €45–50
$55–65 MB ⊞

Anri bottle stopper, carved
in the form of a French man,
c1930, 4in (10cm) high. This
item would be sought after by
bottle stopper collectors and
Anri collectors.
£35–40 / €50–60
$65–75 CAL ⊞

▶ **Boxwood box,**
1860, 2½in (6.5cm)
diam. This box
could command a
higher price if sold
in the USA.
£45–50 / €65–75
$85–95 MB ⊞

Tunbridge ware box, 1830,
2½in (6.5cm) diam.
£50–60 / €75–85
$100–115 MB ⊞

Mauchline ware thimble holder, depicting a view of Ryde Pier,
slight damage, 1870, 2in (5cm) long. It is important to take into
consideration the quality of decoration when making a purchase.
£50–60 / €75–85
$100–115 MB ⊞

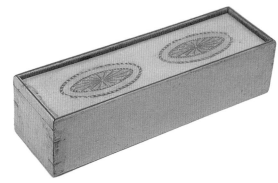

Sycamore pen box, c1815,
8in (20.5cm) long.
£60–70 / €85–100
$115–135 MB ⊞

For more examples of
Boxes see (pages 238–243)

Tunbridge ware box, 1880, 3½in (9cm)
wide. This is a popular Tunbridge ware
pattern which is sought after by collectors.
When buying Tunbridge ware items it is
best to avoid examples where the surface is
rough or there are parts missing. However,
restoration can be undertaken by experienced
craftsmen and this is worth taking into
consideration when making a purchase.
£75–85 / €110–125
$145–165 MB ⊞

Sycamore nut cracker,
carved in the form of Lord
Kitchener's head, early 20thC,
11in (28cm) long. Despite the
obvious woodworm damage to
this item, it would be sought
after by collectors.
£90–105 / €130–150
$170–200 TMA ⚒

Mahogany stationery tray, c1830, 9in (23cm) wide.
£135–150 / €195–220
$240–270 F&F ⊞

Carved wood inkwell, in the form of a bear, Swiss, late 19thC, 8in (20.5cm) long.
£190–220 / €280–320
$350–400 G(B) ⚒

Mauchline ware stamp box, inscribed 'Made of Dunkeld Wood, Dunkeld, McLean & Son, Publishers', c1880, 1¾in (4.5cm) diam. The presence of a picture or an inscription can add value to an item as this enables the piece to be dated more easily.
£260–290 / €380–420
$470–530 GAU ⊞

Walnut door porter, c1810, 9in (23cm) high.
£230–270 / €330–390
$420–490 PeN ⊞

▶ **Wooden spoon,** with pierced decoration, c1880, 14in (35.5cm) long.
£250–280 / €360–410
$460–510 PeN ⊞

Oak wall hanging box, c1780, 17¼in (44cm) high. This box could have been used to store candles.
£350–390 / €510–570
$640–710 F&F ⊞

Miller's compares...

A. Oak wall hanging cutlery box, c1790, 18¼in (46.5cm) high.
£350–390 / €510–570
$640–710 F&F ⊞

B. Mahogany-banded wall hanging cutlery box, c1780, 18in (45.5cm) high.
£390–440 / €570–640
$710–800 F&F ⊞

Item B is older and is made of banded mahogany which makes it more desirable and more valuable than Item A.

Tunbridge ware spinning top, c1860, 3½in (9cm) high. This spinning top would be desirable to both collectors of Tunbridge ware items and toys.
£470–530 / €680–770
$860–960 AMH ⊞

Alder and sycamore feather-jointed luggie, Scottish, mid-19thC, 7in (18cm) diam. A luggie is a Scottish bowl with a handle at each side. The individual staves are joined by feathering the edges – these slivers fit together to form a watertight seal.
£490–550 / €710–800
$890–1,000 NEW ⊞

◄ **Tunbridge ware blotter,** depicting a view of Eridge Castle, c1845, 11½in (29cm) wide. This is a popular Tunbridge ware subject.
£710–800 / €1,050–1,200
$1,300–1,450 AMH ⊞

Beech adjustable stool, in the form of a mermaid holding a shell, Italian, c1880, 27in (68.5cm) high.
£800–960 / €1,150–1,350
$1,500–1,750 G(B) 🖉

Glossary

We have defined here some of the terms that you will come across in this book. If there are any terms or technicalities you would like explained or you feel should be included in future, please let us know.

abrashed: A slight shift in colour tone caused by the weaver running out of one batch of yarn and continuing with another: each batch of a natural dye will differ slightly from others.

armorial: A full coat-of-arms. Also a term used for any object decorated with the owner's coat-of-arms, especially silver or silver plate.

astragal: Moulding into which are set the glass panes of a cabinet or bookcase.

bergère: Originally any armchair with upholstered sides, now more often used to describe a chair with a square or round caned back and sides.

bevelled glass: Where a slope is cut at the edge of a flat surface. Usually associated with the plate glass used in mirrors.

boteh: The Paisley motif which may also be found in stylized form. It probably represents a leaf.

bright-cut engraving: Whereby the metal surface is cut creating facets that reflect the light.

cabriole leg: Tall curving leg subject to many designs and produced with club, pad, paw, claw-and-ball, and scroll feet.

canapé: A large settee with upholstered back and arms.

cartouche: A decorative frame, surrounded by scrollwork and foliage, often bearing an inscription, monogram or coat-of-arms.

chanteh: a small bag, pouch or satchel.

chasing: Method of decorating using hammers and punches to push metal into a relief pattern – the metal is displaced, not removed.

corbel: Projecting moulding at the top of tall cabinet furniture.

coromandel: Yellow- and black-striped wood from South America which is used mainly for crossbanding.

credenza: Elaborately decorated Victorian side cabinet, sometimes with rounded ends, and often with glazed or solid doors.

doucai: Decoration on Chinese porcelain using five colours.

enamel: Coloured glass, applied to metal, ceramic or glass in paste form and then fired for decorative effect.

field: The large area of a rug or carpet usually enclosed by borders.

finial: An ornament, often carved in many forms from animal figures to obelisks, and used to finish off any vertical projection.

fleam: A type of lancet, popular from the beginning of the 18thC, for making an incision into the vein of an animal for blood letting.

gesso: Composition of plaster of Paris and size which was used as a base for applying gilding and usually moulded in bas relief.

incuse: A mark or design stamped or hammered onto an object (usually a coin).

intaglio: Incised gemstone, often set in a ring, used in antiquity and during the Renaissance as a seal. Any incised decoration; the opposite of carving in relief.

kilim: A simple, pileless rug or carpet.

KPM: Königliche Porzellan Manufactur. Mark used on Berlin porcelain 1832–1957.

libation cup: used in drinking the honour of a deity.

lithography: Method of polychrome printing in which a design is drawn in ink on a stone surface and transferred to paper. Lithographic prints were also used to decorate ceramics.

manchineel: a poisonous tree which grows around the Caribbean. The wood is occasionally used in furniture making.

marotte: Doll on a stick which plays a tune when spun round.

marquetry: Design formed from different coloured woods veneered onto a carcase to give a decorative effect. Many early examples are Dutch.

meiping: Chinese for cherry blossom. A term referring to a tall vase, with high shoulders, small neck and narrow mouth, used to display flowering branches.

mon: A Japanese crest, or coat-of-arms.

monopodia: Furniture leg carved as an animal's limb with a paw, usually found on console or pier tables.

nacreous: Made from mother-of-pearl, or having the lustre of, mother-of-pearl.

naos or cella: The inner room of a temple housing the statue of a deity.

ogee: Double curved shape which is convex at the top and becomes concave at the bottom. It is often found on the feet of Georgian furniture. Also known as *cyma reversa*.

orrery: mechanical model of the solar system.

papier-mâché: Paper pulp usually combined with a glue and moulded into boxes, trays and ornaments, painted or japanned. Also used to make furniture building up layers of paper with pitch and oil over an iron frame.

parquetry: Decorative veneers laid in a geometric pattern.

patera: Small flat circular ornament, often in the form of an open flower or rosette, used as a ceiling or furniture ornament.

patina: Surface colour of genuinely old wood resulting from the layers of grease, dirt and polish built up over the years, and through handling. Differs from wood to wood and difficult to fake.

pilaster: Decorative flat-faced column projecting from a wall.

porter: A dark sweet ale brewed from black malt.

pricket: A sharp metal spike on which to stick a candle.

prie-dieu: Chair with a low seat and a tall back. They were made during the 19th century and were designed for prayer.

purdonium: Form of coal box patented by a Mr A. Purdon, with slots for matching shovels, often highly ornate.

putti: Cupids or cherubs used as decoration.

retipping: Replacing the tips of chair legs.

salt glaze: Hard translucent glaze used on stoneware and achieved by throwing common salt into the kiln at high temperatures. Produces a silky, pitted appearance like orange peel.

scratchweight: A note made of the weight of a silver article at assay, usually inscribed on the base. It may show how many items were in a set and, by a change in weight, if a piece has been altered. The weights are expressed as troy ounces (oz), pennyweights (dwt) and grains (gr).

skiver: Thin skin of leather used as a writing surface on desks etc.

socle: Another name for a plinth.

spelter: Zinc treated to look like bronze. An inexpensive substitute used in Art Nouveau appliqué ornament and Art Deco figures.

spigot: A stopper or tap, usually wood, and fitted to a cask.

splat: Central upright in a chair back.

strapwork: Repeated carved decoration suggesting plaited straps. Originally used in the 16th and 17th centuries and revived in the 19th century.

tamper: An instrument for packing down tobacco in a pipe.

tine: The prong of a fork; early ones have two, later ones three.

tôle peinte: French 18th-century method of varnishing sheet iron vessels so that the surface could be painted upon. And by derivation, painted metal panels applied to furniture.

troy ounce: A measurement used to express the weight of a piece of silver. One troy ounce comprises 20 pennyweights.

Tunbridge ware: Objects decorated with wooden inlay made of bundles of coloured wood cut into sections; usually simple geometric designs, but sometimes whole scenes; mid-17th to late 19th century.

verdigris: Greenish or blueish patina formed on copper, bronze or brass.

wrought-iron: A pure form of iron often used for decorative purposes.

wucai: Type of five-colour Chinese porcelain decoration.

Directory of Specialists

If you wish to be included in next year's directory, or if you have a change of address or telephone number, please contact Miller's Advertising Department on +44 (0)1580 766411 by July 2006. We advise readers to make contact by telephone before visiting a dealer, therefore avoiding a wasted journey.

ANTIQUITIES
Dorset
Ancient & Gothic, P.O. Box 5390, Bournemouth, BH7 6XR Tel: 01202 431721 *Antiquities from before 300,000 BC to about 1500 AD*

Lancashire
Millennia Antiquities Tel: 01204 690175 or 07930 273998 www.AncientAntiquities.co.uk

Leicestershire
Ancient & Oriental Ltd Tel: 01664 812044 alex@antiquities.co.uk

London
Helios Gallery, 292 Westbourne Grove, W11 2PS Tel: 077 11 955 997 www.heliosgallery.com

ARCHITECTURAL ANTIQUES
Gloucestershire
Olliff's Architectural Antiques, 19–21 Lower Redland Road, Redland, Bristol, BS6 6TB Tel: 0117 923 9232 www.olliffs.com

Surrey
Drummonds Architectural Antiques Ltd, The Kirkpatrick Buildings, 25 London Road (A3), Hindhead, GU26 6AB Tel: 01428 609444 www.drummonds-arch.co.uk

ARMS & MILITARIA
Nottinghamshire
Michael D Long Ltd, 96-98 Derby Road, Nottingham, NG1 5FB Tel: 0115 941 3307 www.michaeldlong.com

East Sussex
The Lanes Armoury, 26 Meeting House Lane, The Lanes, Brighton, BN1 1HB Tel: 01273 321357 www.thelanesarmoury.co.uk

U.S.A.
Faganarms, Box 425, Fraser, MI 48026 Tel: 586 465 4637 www.faganarms.com

BOXES & TREEN
Berkshire
Mostly Boxes, 93 High Street, Eton, Windsor, SL4 6AF Tel: 01753 858470

East Sussex
June & Tony Stone, Fine Antique Boxes, P.O. Box 106, Peacehaven, BN10 8AU Tel: 01273 579333 www.boxes.co.uk

CLOCKS
Devon
Carnegie Paintings & Clocks, 15 Fore Street, Yealmpton, Plymouth, PL8 2JN Tel: 01752 881170 www.paintingsandclocks.com

Essex
Bellhouse Antiques Tel: 01268 710415 Bellhouse.Antiques@virgin.net

Somerset
Kembery Antique Clocks Ltd, George Street Antique Centre, 8 Edgar Buildings, George Street, Bath, BA1 2EH Tel: 0117 956 5281 www.kdclocks.co.uk

DECORATIVE ARTS
Hertfordshire
Caniche Decorative Arts, P.O. Box 350, Watford, WD19 4ZX Tel: 01923 251 206

Kent
The Design Gallery 1850–1950, 5 The Green, Westerham, TN16 1AS Tel: 01959 561234 www.thedesigngalleryuk.com

London
Mike Weedon, 7 Camden Passage, Islington, N1 8EA Tel: 020 7226 5319 or 020 7609 6826 www.mikeweedonantiques.com

Oxfordshire
Hall-Bakker Decorative Arts at Heritage, 6 Market Place, Woodstock, OX20 1TA Tel: 01993 811332

Republic of Ireland
Mitofsky Antiques, 8 Rathfarnham Road, Terenure, Dublin 6 Tel: 492 0033 www.mitofskyantiques.com

Scotland
decorative arts @ doune, Scottish Antique & Arts Centre, By Doune, Stirling, FK16 6HD Tel: 01786 834401 www.decorative-doune.com

Worcestershire
Art Nouveau Originals, The Bindery Gallery, 69 High Street, Broadway, WR12 7DP Tel: 01386 854645 www.artnouveauoriginals.com

DOLLS
Kent
Barbara Ann Newman Tel: 07850 016729

London
Glenda - Antique Dolls, A18-A19 Grays Antique Market, Davies Mews, W1Y 2LP Tel: 020 8367 2441/020 7629 7034 www.glenda-antiquedolls.com

FURNITURE
Peter Norden Antiques, 61 Long Street, Tetbury, GL8 8AA Tel: 01666 503 854 www.peter-norden-antiques.co.uk *17th and 18th century early oak, walnut, mahogany, country furniture, carvings and paintings, treen, pewter, arms and armour, metalware, glass & pottery*

Kent
Langton Green Antiques, Langton Green, Langton Green, Tunbridge Wells, TN3 0HP Tel: 01892 862004 www.langtongreenantiques.co.uk

Swan Antiques, Stone Street, Cranbrook, TN17 3HF Tel: 01580 712720

Middlesex
Phelps Antiques, 133-135 St Margaret's Road, Twickenham, TW1 1RG Tel: 020 8892 1778 www.phelps.co.uk

Oxfordshire
The Country Seat, Huntercombe Manor Barn, Henley-on-Thames, RG9 5RY Tel: 01491 641349 www.thecountryseat.com

Dorchester Antiques, 3 High Street, Dorchester- on- Thames, OX10 7HH Tel: 01865 341 373 *Georgian furniture, country pieces*

Hallidays, The Old College, Dorchester-on-Thames, OX10 7HL Tel: 01865 340028/68 www.hallidays.com *18th–19th century furniture, upholstery, ceramics*

Scotland
Georgian Antiques, 10 Pattison Street, Leith Links, Edinburgh, EH6 7HF Tel: 0131 553 7286 www.georgianantiques.net

Somerset
Mary Cruz Antiques, 5 Broad Street, Bath, BA1 5LJ Tel: 01225 334174 *18th–19th century English and French furniture, 18th–20th century paintings, bronze and marble statues*

East Sussex
Wish Barn Antiques, Wish Street, Rye, TN31 7DA Tel: 01797 226797 *19th century pine and country furniture, 19th century mahogany furniture*

U.S.A.
One Of A Kind Antiques, 36D Plains Road, Essex, CT 06426 www.oneofakindantiques.com

RJG Antiques, P.O. Box 60, Rye, NH 03870 Tel: 603 433 1770 *Specialists in American furniture, accessories and decoys in their original paint*

Warwickshire
Apollo Antiques Ltd, The Saltisford, Birmingham Road, Warwick, CV34 4TD Tel: 01926 494746/494666 mynott@apolloantiques.com *English 18th–19th century furniture, sculpture, paintings, decorative items, Arts & Crafts, Gothic revival*

West Midlands
Martin Taylor Antiques, 323 Tettenhall Road, Wolverhampton, WV6 0JZ Tel: 01902 751166 www.mtaylor-antiques.co.uk

Worcestershire
Fenwick & Fenwick, 88-90 High Street, Broadway, WR12 7AJ Tel: 01386 853227/841724 *17th–early 19thc oak, mahogany, walnut furniture and works of art. Treen, boxes, pewter, lace bobbins, Chinese porcelain, corkscrews, early metalware*

GLASS
London
Jeanette Hayhurst Fine Glass, 32a Kensington Church Street, W8 4HA Tel: 020 7938 1539

Carol Ketley Antiques, P.O. Box 16199, NW1 7WD Tel: 020 7359 5529 *Glassware, mirrors and decorative antiques*

JEWELLERY
London
Shapiro & Co, Stand 380, Gray's Antique Market, 58 Davies Street, W1Y 5LP Tel: 020 7491 2710 *Jewellery, silver, objets d'art*

Republic of Ireland
Courtville Antiques, Powerscourt Townhouse Centre, South William Street, Dublin 2 Tel: 01 679 4042 courtville@eircom.net *Victorian and Art Deco jewellery, silver, paintings, decorative items*

Somerset
Excalibur Antiques, Taunton Antique Centre, 27-29 Silver Street, Taunton, TA13DH Tel: 01823 289327 www.excaliburantiques.com

KITCHENWARE
Gloucestershire
Cottage Collectibles, Long Street Antiques, 14 Long Street, Tetbury, G18 8AQ Tel: 01666 500850 sheila@cottagecollectibles.co.uk

Kent
Wenderton Antiques Tel: 01227 720295 (by appointment only)

Lincolnshire
Skip & Janie Smithson Antiques Tel: 01754 810265 or 07831 399180 smithsonantiques@hotmail.com

East Sussex
Jane Wicks Kitchenalia, Country Ways, Strand Quay, Rye, TN31 7AY Tel: 01424 713635 Janes_kitchen@hotmail.com

Warwickshire
Bread & Roses Tel: 01926 817342

LIGHTING
Gloucestershire
Jennie Horrocks, Top Banana Antiques Mall, 1 New Church Street, Tetbury, GL8 8DS Tel: 07836 264896 artnouveaulighting.co.uk *Art Nouveau lighting.*

London
Turn On Lighting, Antique Lighting Specialists, 116/118 Islington High St, Camden Passage, Islington, N1 8EG Tel: 020 7359 7616

U.S.A.
Chameleon Fine Lighting, 223 East 59th Street, New York, NY 10022 Tel: 212 355 6300 www.chameleon59.com

MARKETS & CENTRES
Derbyshire
Ashbourne Antiques Centre, 28A Church Street, Ashbourne, DE6 1AF Tel: 01335 300 820 barbara@acres120.freeserve.co.uk

Chappells Antiques Centre - Bakewell, King Street, Bakewell, DE45 1DZ Tel: 01629 812496 www.chappellsantiquescentre.com

Gloucestershire
The Top Banana Antiques Mall,
1 New Church Street, Tetbury,
GL8 8DS Tel: 0871 288 1102
www.topbananaantiques.com
Decorative antiques and interiors

London
Northcote Road Antique Market,
155a Northcote Road, Battersea,
SW11 6QB Tel: 020 7228 6850
www.spectrumsoft.net/nam.htm

Northamptonshire
The Brackley Antique Cellar,
Drayman's Walk, Brackley,
NN13 6BE Tel: 01280 841841
antiquecellar@tesco.net
*Ceramics, porcelain, clocks,
glass, books, dolls, jewellery,
militaria, linen, lace, Victoriana,
kitchenalia and furniture*

Nottinghamshire
Newark Antiques Warehouse
Ltd, Old Kelham Road, Newark,
NG24 1BX Tel: 01636 674869
www.newarkantiques.co.uk

Oxfordshire
Heritage, 6 Market Place,
Woodstock, OX20 1TA Tel:
01993 811332/0870 4440678
www.atheritage.co.uk

East Sussex
The Brighton Lanes Antique
Centre, 12 Meeting House Lane,
Brighton, BN1 1HB
Tel: 01273 823121
www.brightonlanes-antique
centre.co.uk

U.S.A.
The Brass Armadillo Des Moines,
701 NE 50th Avenue,
Des Moines, Iowa 50313
Tel: 515 282 0082 or
800 775 2140
www.brassarmadillo.com

Colonial Antique Mall, 890 Lake
Ave, Woodstock, IL 60098
Tel: 815 334 8960
www.colonialantiquemall.com

The Williamsburg Antique Mall,
500 Lightfoot Road,
Williamsburg, VA 23188
Tel: 757 565 3422
www.antiqueswilliamsburg.com

Worcestershire
Worcester Antiques Centre,
Reindeer Court, Mealcheapen
Street, Worcester, WR1 4DF
Tel: 01905 610680
WorcsAntiques@aol.com

METALWARE
Warwickshire
David Moulson, The Gorralls,
Cold Comfort Lane, Alcester,
B49 5PU Tel: 01789 764092
dmoulson@hotmail.com
Antique pewter

OAK & COUNTRY
Cambridgeshire
Mark Seabrook Antiques,
P.O. Box 396, Huntingdon,
PE28 0ZA Tel: 01480 861935
www.markseabrook.com

Oxfordshire
Key Antiques of Chipping
Norton, 11 Horsefair, Chipping
Norton, OX7 5AL
Tel: 01608 644992/643777
www.keyantiques.com

ORIENTAL
Anglesey
Peter Wain, Mor Awel,
Marine Terrace, Camaes Bay,
LL67 0ND Tel: 01407 710077
peterwain@supanet.com

London
Jocelyn Chatterton,
126 Grays, 58 Davies St,
W1Y 2LP
Tel: 020 7629 1971
www.cixi.demon.co.uk

*Professional lecturer, textile
consultant, antique oriental
textiles and Chinese social history*
Guest & Gray, 1-7 Davies Mews,
W1K5 AB Tel: 020 7408 1252
www.chinese-porcelain-art.com
Chinese porcelain

U.S.A.
The Wyndham Gallery, Lafayette
Antiques Center, 401E 110th
Street, New York
Tel: 212 722 8400
john_cullis@hotmail.com

PAPERWEIGHTS
Cheshire
Sweetbriar Gallery Paperweights
Ltd, 56 Watergate Street,
Chester, CH1 2LA
Tel: 01244 329249
www.sweetbriar.co.uk
www.sweetbriarartglass.co.uk

U.S.A.
The Dunlop Collection,
P.O. Box 6269, Statesville,
NC 28687
Tel: 704 871 2626 or Toll Free
Telephone (800) 227 1996

PINE
Gloucestershire
Cottage Farm Antiques,
Stratford Road, Aston Subedge,
Chipping Campden, GL55 6PZ
Tel: 01386 438263
www.cottagefarmantiques.co.uk

Nottinghamshire
Harlequin Antiques, 79-81
Mansfield Road, Daybrook,
Nottingham, NG5 6BH
Tel: 0115 967 4590
www.antiquepine.net

POTTERY & PORCELAIN
Buckinghamshire
Helen Girton Antiques, P.O. Box
2022, Buckingham, MK18 4ZH
Tel: 01280 815012

Gillian Neale Antiques, P.O. Box
247, Aylesbury, HP20 1JZ
Tel: 01296 423754
www.gilliannealeantiques.co.uk
*English blue printed pottery
1780–1900*

Dorset
Greystoke Antiques, 4 Swan Yard,
(off Cheap Street), Sherborne,
DT9 3AX Tel: 01935 812833
*Georgian and Victorian, English
blue transfer printed pottery
1800–1850*

Gloucestershire
Peter Scott Tel: 0117 986 8468
or 07850 639770
*Blue & white transferware
pottery*

Hampshire
Millers Antiques Ltd,
Netherbrook House, 86
Christchurch Road, Ringwood,
BH24 1DR Tel: 01425 472062
www.millers-antiques.co.uk
19thc Majolica, Quimper

Kent
Serendipity, 125 High Street,
Deal, CT14 6BB
Tel: 01304 369165/
01304 366536
dipityantiques@aol.com
*English and continental ceramics
1750–1900*

London
Diana Huntley Antiques,
8 Camden Passage, Islington,
N1 8ED Tel: 020 7226 4605
www.dianahuntleyantiques.com
19thc porcelain

Rogers de Rin, 76 Royal Hospital
Road, SW3 4HN
Tel: 020 7352 9007
www.rogersderin.co.uk
*Wemyss, Staffordshire, collectors
items*

Oxfordshire
John Howard at Heritage,
6 Market Place, Woodstock,
OX20 1TA Tel: 0870 4440678
www.antiquepottery.co.uk
British 18th–19th century pottery

Key Antiques of Chipping
Norton, 11 Horsefair,
Chipping Norton, OX7 5AL
Tel: 01608 644992/643777
www.keyantiques.com

Scotland
Sandra D Deas
Tel: 01333 360 214 or
07713 897 482
*Scottish ceramics, including
Wemyss, Cumnock*

Glebe Antiques, Scottish Antique
Centre, Doune, FK16 6HG
Tel: 01259 214559
rrglebe@aol.com

Surrey
Judi Bland Antiques
Tel: 01276 857576 or
01536 724145
18th & 19th century Toby jugs

U.S.A.
Karen Michelle Antique Tiles,
PMB 243, 1835 US 1 South
#119, St Augustine, FL 32084
Tel: 904 471 3226
www.antiquetiles.com

Carlson's Antiques, Blake
Antiques, 901 Main St, Hopkins,
MN 55343 Tel: 952 9300477
www.carlsonsantiques.com
*Roseville pottery, Fiesta ware,
Flow Blue and Haviland china*

Danish Porcelain Imports, 214
West F Street, Joplin, MO 64801
Tel: 866 228 9374 or
417 624 1798
www.danishporcelain.com

Rufus Foshee Antiques, P.O. Box
839, Camden, ME 04843
Tel: 207 236 2838
www.rufusfosheeantiques.com
*American & English 18th &
19thc pottery*

Jerry S. Hayes, P.O. Box 18483,
Oklahoma City, OK 73154
Tel: 405 843 8999
www.jerryshayes.com
Majolica specialist

Wales
West Wales Antiques,
18 Mansfield Road, Murton,
Swansea, SA3 3AR
Tel: 01792 234318/
01639 644379
www.westwalesantiques.co.uk
Swansea and Nantgarw

Wiltshire
Andrew Dando, 34 Market
Street, Bradford on Avon,
BA15 1LL Tel: 01225 865444
www.andrewdando.co.uk
Pottery and porcelain 1750–1870

Typically English Antiques
Tel: 01249 721721 or
07818 000704
typicallyeng@aol.com
English pottery and porcelain

London
Aurea Carter, P.O. Box 44134,
SW6 3YX Tel: 020 7731 3486
www.englishceramics.com
*18th–early 19th century English
pottery and porcelain*

RUGS & CARPETS
Kent
Desmond & Amanda North,
The Orchard, 186 Hale Street,
East Peckham, TN12 5JB
Tel: 01622 871353
Oriental rugs and carpets

Scotland
Samarkand Galleries,
16 Howe Street, Edinburgh,

EH3 6TD Tel: 0131 225 2010
www.samarkand.co.uk
*Antique rugs from near east &
central Asia*

West Sussex
Wadsworth's, Marehill,
Pulborough, RH20 2DY
Tel: 01798 873555
www.wadsworthsrugs.com

SCIENTIFIC INSTRUMENTS
Cambridgeshire
Fossack & Furkle, P.O. Box 733,
Abington, CB1 6BF
Tel: 01223 894296
www.fossackandfurkle.
freeservers.com

Cheshire
Charles Tomlinson, Chester
Tel: 01244 318395
charlestomlinson@tiscali.co.uk

Somerset
Richard Twort Tel: 01934 641900
or 07711 939789

SILVER
Gloucestershire
Corner House Antiques and Ffoxe
Antiques, Gardners Cottage,
Broughton Poggs, Filkins,
Lechlade-on-Thames, GL7 3JH
Tel: 01367 252007
www.corner-house-antiques.co.uk
*Antique silver, jewellery, country
furniture, porcelain, objets d'art*

London
Daniel Bexfield, 26 Burlington
Arcade, W1J 0PU
Tel: 020 7491 1720
www.bexfield.co.uk
*Fine quality silver, jewellery and
objects of vertu dating from
17th–20thc*

Lyn Bloom & Jeffrey Neal, Vault
27, The London Silver Vaults,
Chancery Lane, WC2A 1QS
Tel: 0207 242 6189
www.bloomvault.com

U.S.A.
Alter Silver Gallery Corp, Gallery
49A & 50, 1050 Second Avenue,
New York, NY10022
Tel: 212 750 1928/917 848
1713 altersilvergallery@mac.com

TEXTILES
London
Diane Harby Antique Lace &
Linen, Grays Antique Market,
Davies Street, W1Y 2LP
Tel: 020 7629 5130

Erna Hiscock & John Shepherd,
Chelsea Galleries, 69 Portobello
Road, W11 Tel: 01233 661407
www.ernahiscockantiques.com
Antique samplers

Somerset
Joanna Proops Antique Textiles
& Lighting, 34 Belvedere,
Lansdown Hill, Bath, BA1 5HR
Tel: 01225 310795
www.antiquetextiles.co.uk

Suffolk
Marilyn Garrow - By appointment
only Tel: 01728 648671 or
07774 842074
www.antiquesweb.co.uk/
marilyngarrow

TUNBRIDGE WARE
London
Amherst Antiques, Monomark
House, 27 Old Gloucester Street,
WC1N 3XX Tel: 01892 725552
www.amherstantiques.co.uk
*Tunbridge ware, 19thc English
ceramics, glass, silver*

WINE ANTIQUES
Buckinghamshire
Christopher Sykes, The Old
Parsonage, Woburn, Milton
Keynes, MK17 9QM
Tel: 01525 290259
www.sykes-corkscrews.co.uk

Directory of Auctioneers

Auctioneers who hold frequent sales should contact us on +44 (0)1580 766411 by July 2006 for inclusion in the next edition.

UK & IRELAND

Bedfordshire
W&H Peacock, 26 Newnham Street, Bedford, MK40 3JR
Tel: 01234 266366

Berkshire
Dreweatt Neate, Donnington Priory, Donnington, Newbury, RG14 2JE
Tel: 01635 553553
www.dnfa.com/donnington

Law Fine Art Tel: 01635 860033
www.lawfineart.co.uk

Special Auction Services, Kennetholme, Midgham, Reading, RG7 5UX
Tel: 0118 971 2949
www.antiquestradegazette.com/sas

Cambridgeshire
Cheffins, Clifton House, 1 & 2 Clifton Road, Cambridge, CB1 7EA
Tel: 01223 271966 www.cheffins.co.uk

Cornwall
David Lay (ASVA), Auction House, Alverton, Penzance, TR18 4RE
Tel: 01736 361414

Cumbria
Mitchells, Fairfield House, Station Road, Cockermouth, CA13 9PY Tel: 01900 827800
info@mitchellsfineart.com

Penrith Farmers' & Kidd's plc, Skirsgill Salerooms, Penrith, CA11 0DN
Tel: 01768 890781
www.pfkauctions.co.uk

Thomson, Roddick & Medcalf Ltd, Coleridge House, Shaddongate, Carlisle, CA2 5TU Tel: 01228 528939
www.thomsonroddick.com

Devon
Bearnes, St Edmund's Court, Okehampton Street, Exeter, EX4 1DU
Tel: 01392 207000
www.bearnes.co.uk

S.J. Hales, 87 Fore Street, Bovey Tracey, TQ13 9AB Tel: 01626 836684

Dorset
Charterhouse, The Long Street Salerooms, Sherborne, DT9 3BS
Tel: 01935 812277
www.charterhouse-auctions.co.uk

Hy Duke & Son, The Dorchester Fine Art Salerooms, Weymouth Avenue, Dorchester, DT1 1QS Tel: 01305 265080
www.dukes-auctions.com

Essex
Ambrose, Ambrose House, Old Station Road, Loughton, IG10 4PE
Tel: 020 8502 3951

Sworders, 14 Cambridge Road, Stansted Mountfitchet, CM24 8BZ
Tel: 01279 817778 www.sworder.co.uk

Gloucestershire
Dreweatt Neate, St John's Place, Apsley Road, Clifton, Bristol, BS8 2ST
Tel: 0117 973 7201 www.dnfa.com/bristol

Tayler & Fletcher, London House, High Street, Bourton-on-the-Water, Cheltenham, GL54 2AP
Tel: 01451 821666
www.taylerfletcher.com

Herefordshire
Brightwells Fine Art, The Fine Art Saleroom, Easters Court, Leominster, HR6 0DE Tel: 01568 611122
www.brightwells.com

Hertfordshire
Tring Market Auctions, The Market Premises, Brook Street, Tring, HP23 5EF Tel: 01442 826446
www.tringmarketauctions.co.uk

Kent
Bentley's Fine Art Auctioneers, The Old Granary, Waterloo Road, Cranbrook, TN17 3JQ Tel: 01580 715857
www.bentleysfineartauctioneers.co.uk

The Canterbury Auction Galleries, 40 Station Road West, Canterbury, CT2 8AN Tel: 01227 763337
www.thecanterburyauctiongalleries.com

Mervyn Carey, Twysden Cottage, Scullsgate, Benenden, Cranbrook, TN17 4LD Tel: 01580 240283

Dreweatt Neate, The Auction Hall, The Pantiles, Tunbridge Wells, TN2 5QL Tel: 01892 544500
www.dnfa.com/tunbridgewells

Lambert & Foster, 102 High Street, Tenterden, TN30 6HT
Tel: 01580 762083
www.lambertandfoster.co.uk

Orpington Sale Rooms Ltd, Unit 7 Tripes Farm, Chelsfield Lane, Orpington, BR6 7RS Tel: 01689 896678 www.orpsalerooms.co.uk

Leicestershire
Gilding's Auctioneers and Valuers, 64 Roman Way, Market Harborough, LE16 7PQ Tel: 01858 410414
www.gildings.co.uk

London
Sotheby's, 34-35 New Bond Street, W1A 2AA Tel: 020 7293 5000
www.sothebys.com

Norfolk
Keys, Off Palmers Lane, Aylsham, NR11 6JA Tel: 01263 733195
www.aylshamsalerooms.co.uk

Oxfordshire
Holloway's, 49 Parsons Street, Banbury, OX16 5NB
Tel: 01295 817777
www.hollowaysauctioneers.co.uk

Mallams, Bocardo House, 24 St Michael's Street, Oxford, OX1 2EB
Tel: 01865 241358
oxford@mallams.co.uk

Republic of Ireland
James Adam & Sons, 26 St Stephen's Green, Dublin 2
Tel: 676 0261 www.jamesadam.ie/

Hamilton Osborne King, 4 Main Street, Blackrock, Co. Dublin
Tel: 288 5011 www.hok.ie

Mealy's, Chatsworth Street, Castle Comer, Co Kilkenny Tel: 564 441 229
www.mealys.com

Scotland
Lyon & Turnbull, 33 Broughton Place, Edinburgh, EH1 3RR
Tel: 0131 557 8844 or 07714699802
info@lyonandturnbull.com

Thomson, Roddick & Medcalf Ltd, 43/44 Hardengreen Business Park, Eskbank, Edinburgh, EH22 3NX
Tel: 0131 454 9090
www.thomsonroddick.com

Shropshire
Halls Fine Art Auctions, Welsh Bridge, Shrewsbury, SY3 8LA
Tel: 01743 231212

Somerset
Lawrences Fine Art Auctioneers, South Street, Crewkerne, TA18 8AB
Tel: 01460 73041 www.lawrences.co.uk

Gardiner Houlgate, The Bath Auction Rooms, 9 Leafield Way, Corsham, Nr Bath, SN13 9SW Tel: 01225 812912
www.invaluable.com/gardiner-houlgate

Greenslade Taylor Hunt Fine Art, Magdelene House, Church Square, Taunton, TA1 1SB
Tel: 01823 332525

Staffordshire
Potteries Specialist Auctions, 271 Waterloo Road, Cobridge, Stoke on Trent, ST6 3HR
Tel: 01782 286622
www.potteriesauctions.com

Wintertons Ltd, Lichfield Auction Centre, Fradley Park, Lichfield, WS13 8NF Tel: 01543 263256
www.wintertons.co.uk

Suffolk
Diamond Mills & Co, 117 Hamilton Road, Felixstowe, IP11 7BL
Tel: 01394 282281

Olivers, Olivers Rooms, Burkitts Lane, Sudbury, CO10 1HB Tel: 01787 880305
oliversauctions@btconnect.com

Surrey
Dreweatt Neate, Baverstock House, 93 High Street, Godalming, GU7 1AL
Tel: 01483 423567
www.dnfa.com/godalming

Ewbank, Burnt Common Auction Rooms, London Road, Send, Woking, GU23 7LN Tel: 01483 223101
www.ewbankauctions.co.uk

John Nicholson, The Auction Rooms, Longfield, Midhurst Road, Fernhurst, GU27 3HA Tel: 01428 653727
sales@johnnicholsons.com

East Sussex
Dreweatt Neate, 46-50 South Street, Eastbourne, BN21 4XB
Tel: 01323 410419
www.dnfa.com/eastbourne

Gorringes Auction Galleries, Terminus Road, Bexhill-on-Sea, TN39 3LR
Tel: 01424 212994
www.gorringes.co.uk

Gorringes inc Julian Dawson, 15 North Street, Lewes, BN7 2PD
Tel: 01273 478221
www.gorringes.co.uk

Wallis & Wallis, West Street Auction Galleries, Lewes, BN7 2NJ
Tel: 01273 480208
www.wallisandwallis.co.uk

West Sussex
John Bellman Auctioneers, New Pound Business Park, Wisborough Green, Billingshurst, RH14 PAZ
Tel: 01403 700858
hbeves@bellmans.co.uk

Rupert Toovey & Co Ltd, Spring Gardens, Washington, RH20 3BS
Tel: 01903 891955
www.rupert-toovey.com

Sotheby's Sussex, Summers Place, Billingshurst, RH14 9AD
Tel: 01403 833500
www.sothebys.com

Wales
Peter Francis, Curiosity Sale Room, 19 King Street, Carmarthen, SA31 1BH
Tel: 01267 233456
www.peterfrancis.co.uk

Warwickshire
Locke & England, 18 Guy Street, Leamington Spa, CV32 4RT
Tel: 01926 889100
www.auctions-online.com/locke

West Midlands
Fellows & Sons, Augusta House, 19 Augusta Street, Hockley, Birmingham, B18 6JA Tel: 0121 212 2131
www.fellows.co.uk

Wiltshire
Finan & Co, The Square, Mere, BA12 6DJ Tel: 01747 861411
www.finanandco.co.uk

Netherhampton Salerooms, Salisbury Auction Centre, Netherhampton, Salisbury, SP2 8RH Tel: 01722 340 041

Woolley & Wallis, Salisbury Salerooms, 51-61 Castle Street, Salisbury, SP1 3SU
Tel: 01722 424500/411854
www.woolleyandwallis.co.uk

Yorkshire
David Duggleby, The Vine St Salerooms, Scarborough, YO11 1XN
Tel: 01723 507111
www.davidduggleby.com

Andrew Hartley, Victoria Hall Salerooms, Little Lane, Ilkley, LS29 8EA
Tel: 01943 816363
www.andrewhartleyfinearts.co.uk

Morphets of Harrogate, 6 Albert Street, Harrogate, HG1 1JL Tel: 01423 530030

Tennants, The Auction Centre, Harmby Road, Leyburn, DL8 5SG
Tel: 01969 623780
www.tennants.co.uk

Wilkinson's Auctioneers Ltd, The Old Salerooms, 28 Netherhall Road, Doncaster, DN1 2PW Tel: 01302 814884
www.wilkinsons-auctioneers.co.uk

East Yorkshire
Dee, Atkinson & Harrison, The Exchange Saleroom, Driffield, YO25 6LD
Tel: 01377 253151
www.dahauctions.com

South Yorkshire
BBR, Elsecar Heritage Centre, Elsecar, Barnsley, S74 8HJ
Tel: 01226 745156
www.onlinebbr.com

AUSTRALIA
Leonard Joel Auctioneers, 333 Malvern Road, South Yarra, Victoria 3141
Tel: 03 9826 4333 www.ljoel.com.au

Shapiro Auctioneers, 162 Queen Street, Woollahra, Sydney NSW 2025
Tel: 612 9326 1588

AUSTRIA
Dorotheum, Palais Dorotheum, A-1010 Wien, Dorotheergasse 17, 1010 Vienna Tel: 515 60 229
client.services@dorotheum.at

BELGIUM
Bernaerts, Verlatstraat 18-22, 2000 Antwerpen/Anvers
Tel: (+)3 248 19 21
www.auction-bernaerts.com

CANADA
Ritchies Inc., Auctioneers & Appraisers of Antiques & Fine Art, 288 King Street East, Toronto, Ontario M5A 1K4
Tel: (416) 364 1864
www.ritchies.com

NETHERLANDS
Sotheby's Amsterdam, De Boelelaan 30, Amsterdam 1083 HJ
Tel: 31 20 550 2200
www.sothebys.com

SWEDEN
Bukowskis, Arsenalsgatan 4, Stockholm
Tel: +46 (8) 614 08 00 ww.bukowskis.se

U.S.A.
Bertoia Auctions, 2141 DeMarco Drive, Vineland, New Jersey 08360
Tel: 856 692 1881
www.bertoiaauctions.com

Bloomington Auction Gallery, 300 East Grove St, Bloomington, Illinois 61701 Tel: 309 828 5533
www.joyluke.com

Du Mouchelles, 409 East Jefferson, Detroit, Michigan 48226
Tel: 313 963 6255

Leslie Hindman, Inc., 122 North Aberdeen Street, Chicago, Illinois 60607 Tel: 312 280 1212
www.lesliehindman.com

Jackson's International Auctioneers & Appraisers of Fine Art & Antiques, 2229 Lincoln Street, Cedar Falls, IA 50613
Tel: 319 277 2256/800 665 6743
www.jacksonsauction.com

James D Julia, Inc., PO Box 830, Rte.201, Skowhegan Road, Fairfield, ME 04937 Tel: 207 453 7125
www.juliaauctions.com

New Orleans Auction Galleries, Inc., 801 Magazine Street, AT 510 Julia, New Orleans, Louisiana 70130
Tel: 504 566 1849

R. O. Schmitt Fine Art, Box 1941, Salem, New Hampshire 03079
Tel: 603 893 5915
www.antiqueclockauction.com

Skinner Inc., The Heritage On The Garden, 63 Park Plaza, Boston, MA 02116 Tel: 617 350 5400

Skinner Inc., 357 Main Street, Bolton, MA 01740 Tel: 978 779 6241

Sotheby's, 1334 York Avenue at 72nd St, New York, NY 10021
Tel: 212 606 7000
www.sothebys.com

Key to Illustrations

Each illustration and descriptive caption is accompanied by a letter code. By referring to the following list of auctioneers (denoted by ➤) and dealers (⊞), the source of any item may be immediately determined. Inclusion in this edition no way constitutes or implies a contract or binding offer on the part of any of our contributors to supply or sell the goods illustrated, or similar articles, at the prices stated. Advertisers in this year's directory are denoted by †.

If you require a valuation, it is advisable to check whether the dealer or specialist will carry out this service and if there is a charge. Please mention Miller's when making an enquiry. A valuation by telephone is not possible. Most dealers are willing to help you with your enquiry; however, they may be very busy and consideration of the above points would be welcomed.

A&O ⊞ Ancient & Oriental Ltd Tel: 01664 812044 alex@antiquities.co.uk

AFD ⊞ Afford Decorative Arts Tel: 01827 330042 or 07831 114909 afforddecarts@fsmail.net

AH ➤† Andrew Hartley, Victoria Hall Salerooms, Little Lane, Ilkley, Yorkshire, LS29 8EA Tel: 01943 816363 info@andrewhartleyfinearts.co.uk www.andrewhartleyfinearts.co.uk

AL ⊞ Ann Lingard, Ropewalk Antiques, Rye, East Sussex, TN31 7NA Tel: 01797 223486 ann-lingard@ropewalkantiques.freeserve.co.uk

AMB ➤ Ambrose, Ambrose House, Old Station Road, Loughton, Essex, IG10 4PE Tel: 020 8502 3951

AMH ⊞† Amherst Antiques, Monomark House, 27 Old Gloucester Street, London, WC1N 3XX Tel: 01892 725552 info@amherstantiques.co.uk www.amherstantiques.co.uk

ANG ⊞† Ancient & Gothic, P.O. Box 5390, Bournemouth, Dorset, BH7 6XR Tel: 01202 431721

ANO ⊞ Art Nouveau Originals, The Bindery Gallery, 69 High Street, Broadway, Worcestershire, WR12 7DP Tel: 01386 854645 cathy@artnouveauoriginals.com www.artnouveauoriginals.com

APO ⊞ Apollo Antiques Ltd, The Saltisford, Birmingham Road, Warwick, CV34 4TD Tel: 01926 494746/494666 mynott@apolloantiques.com

AUC ⊞ Aurea Carter, P.O. Box 44134, London, SW6 3YX Tel: 020 7731 3486 aureacarter@englishceramics.com www.englishceramics.com

B&R ⊞ Bread & Roses Tel: 01926 817342

BaN ⊞ Barbara Ann Newman Tel: 07850 016729

BBA ➤ Bloomsbury, Bloomsbury House, 24 Maddox Street, London, W1S 1PP Tel: 020 7495 9494 info@bloomsburyauctions.com www.bloomsburyauctions.com

Bea ➤ Bearnes, St Edmund's Court, Okehampton Street, Exeter, Devon, EX4 1DU Tel: 01392 207000 enquiries@bearnes.co.uk www.bearnes.co.uk

BeFA ➤ Bentley's Fine Art Auctioneers, The Old Granary, Waterloo Road, Cranbrook, Kent, TN17 3JQ Tel: 01580 715857 BentleysKent@aol.com www.bentleysfineartauctioneers.co.uk

BELL ⊞ Bellhouse Antiques, Chelmsford, Essex Tel: 01268 710415 Bellhouse.Antiques@virgin.net

BERN ➤ Bernaerts, Verlatstraat 18-22, 2000 Antwerpen/Anvers, Belgium Tel: (0)3 248 19 21 www.auction-bernaerts.com

Bert ➤ Bertoia Auctions, 2141 DeMarco Drive, Vineland, New Jersey 08360, U.S.A. Tel: 856 692 1881 bill@bertoiaauctions.com www.bertoiaauctions.com

BEV ⊞ Beverley, 30 Church Street, Marylebone, London, NW8 8EP Tel: 020 7262 1576 or 07776136003

BEX ⊞† Daniel Bexfield Antiques, 26 Burlington Arcade, London, W1J 0PU Tel: 020 7491 1720 antiques@bexfield.co.uk www.bexfield.co.uk

BLm ⊞ Lyn Bloom & Jeffrey Neal, Vault 27, The London Silver Vaults, Chancery Lane, London, WC2A 1QS Tel: 0207 242 6189 bloomvault@aol.com www.bloomvault.com

BRT ⊞ Britannia, Grays Antique Market, Stand 101, 58 Davies Street, London, W1Y 1AR Tel: 020 7629 6772 britannia@grays.clara.net

BS ⊞ Below Stairs, 103 High Street, Hungerford, Berkshire, RG17 0NB Tel: 01488 682317 hofgartner@belowstairs.co.uk www.belowstairs.co.uk

BUK ➤ Bukowskis, Arsenalsgatan 4, Stockholm, Sweden Tel: 46 (8) 614 08 00 info@bukowskis.se www.bukowskis.se

BUK(F) ➤ Bukowskis, Horhammer, Iso Roobertink, 12 Stora Robertsg, 00120 Helsinki Helsingfors, Finland Tel: 358 9 668 9110 www.bukowskis.fi

BWL ➤ Brightwells Fine Art, The Fine Art Saleroom, Easters Court, Leominster, Herefordshire, HR6 0DE Tel: 01568 611122 fineart@brightwells.com www.brightwells.com

Byl NO LONGER TRADING

CAL ⊞ Cedar Antiques Ltd, High Street, Hartley Wintney, Hampshire, RG27 8NY Tel: 01252 843222 or 01189 326628

CANI ➤ Caniche Decorative Arts, P.O. Box 350, Watford, Hertfordshire, WD19 4ZX Tel: 01923 251 206 or 07860 833 170

CGC ➤ Cheffins, Clifton House, 1 & 2 Clifton Road, Cambridge, CB1 7EA Tel: 01223 271966 www.cheffins.co.uk

CHA ⊞ Chislehurst Antiques, 7 Royal Parade, Chislehurst, Kent, BR7 6NR Tel: 020 8467 1530

CHTR ➤ Charterhouse, The Long Street Salerooms, Sherborne, Dorset, DT9 3BS Tel: 01935 812277 enquiry@charterhouse-auctions.co.uk www.charterhouse-auctions.co.uk

COF ⊞ Cottage Farm Antiques, Stratford Road, Aston Subedge, Chipping Campden, Gloucestershire, GL55 6PZ Tel: 01386 438263 info@cottagefarmantiques.co.uk www.cottagefarmantiques.co.uk

CoHA ⊞ Corner House Antiques and Ffoxe Antiques, Gardners Cottage, Broughton Poggs, Filkins, Lechlade-on-Thames, Gloucestershire, GL7 3JH Tel: 01367 252007 jdhis007@btopenworld.com enquiries@corner-house-antiques.co.uk www.corner-house-antiques.co.uk

Cot ⊞ Cottage Collectibles, Long Street Antiques, 14 Long Street, Tetbury, Gloucestershire, G18 8AQ Tel: 01666 500850/07967 713512 sheila@cottagecollectibles.co.uk

CPC ⊞ Carnegie Paintings & Clocks, 15 Fore Street, Yealmpton, Plymouth, Devon, PL8 2JN Tel: 01752 881170 info@paintingsandclocks.com www.paintingsandclocks.com

CRU ⊞ Mary Cruz Antiques, 5 Broad Street, Bath, Somerset, BA1 5LJ Tel: 01225 334174

CS ⊞ Christopher Sykes, The Old Parsonage, Woburn, Milton Keynes, Buckinghamshire, MK17 9QM Tel: 01525 290259 www.sykes-corkscrews.co.uk

CVA ⊞ Courtville Antiques, Powerscourt Townhouse Centre, South William Street, Dublin 2, Republic of Ireland Tel: 01 679 4042 courtville@eircom.net

DA ➤† Dee, Atkinson & Harrison, The Exchange Saleroom, Driffield, East Yorkshire, YO25 6LD Tel: 01377 253151 info@dahauctions.com www.dahauctions.com

DAD ⊞ decorative arts @ doune, Scottish Antique & Arts Centre, By Doune, Stirling, FK16 6HD, Scotland Tel: 01786 834401 decorativearts.doune@btinternet.com www.decorative-doune.com

DAN ⊞ Andrew Dando, 34 Market Street, Bradford on Avon, Wiltshire, BA15 1LL Tel: 01225 865444 andrew@andrewdando.co.uk www.andrewdando.co.uk

DD ➤ David Duggleby, The Vine St Salerooms, Scarborough, Yorkshire, YO11 1XN Tel: 01723 507111 auctions@davidduggleby.com www.davidduggleby.com

DEB ⊞ Debden Antiques, Elder Street, Debden, Saffron Walden, Essex, CB11 3JY Tel: 01799 543007 info@debden-antiques.co.uk www.debden-antiques.co.uk

DHa ⊞ Diane Harby Antique Lace & Linen, Grays Antique Market, Davies Street, London, W1Y 2LP Tel: 020 7629 5130

DIA ⊞ Mark Diamond London Tel: 020 8508 4479 mark.diamond@dial.pipex.com

DLP ⊞ The Dunlop Collection, P.O. Box 6269, Statesville, NC 28687, U.S.A. Tel: 704 871 2626 or Toll Free Telephone (800) 227 1996

DMC ➤ Diamond Mills & Co, 117 Hamilton Road, Felixstowe, Suffolk, IP11 7BL Tel: 01394 282281

DML ⊞ David Moulson, The Gorralls, Cold Comfort Lane, Alcester, Warwickshire, B49 5PU Tel: 01789 764092 dmoulson@hotmail.com

DN ➤ Dreweatt Neate, Donnington Priory, Donnington, Newbury, Berkshire, RG14 2JE Tel: 01635 553553 donnington@dnfa.com www.dnfa.com/donnington

DN(BR) ➤ Dreweatt Neate, The Auction Hall, The Pantiles, Tunbridge Wells, Kent, TN2 5QL Tel: 01892 544500 tunbridgewells@dnfa.com www.dnfa.com/tunbridgewells

DN(HAM) ➤ Dreweatt Neate, Baverstock House, 93 High Street, Godalming, Surrey, GU7 1AL Tel: 01483 423567 godalming@dnfa.com www.dnfa.com/godalming

DNO ⊞ Desmond & Amanda North, The Orchard, 186 Hale Street, East Peckham, Kent, TN12 5JB Tel: 01622 871353

DNW ➤ Dix-Noonan-Webb, 16 Bolton Street, London, W1J 8BQ Tel: 020 7016 1700 coins@dnw.co.uk medals@dnw.co.uk www.dnw.co.uk

DOA ⊞ Dorchester Antiques, 3 High Street, Dorchester-on-Thames, Oxfordshire, OX10 7HH Tel: 01865 341 373

DORO ➤ Dorotheum, Palais Dorotheum, A-1010 Wien, Dorotheergasse 17, 1010 Vienna, Austria Tel: 515 60 229 client.services@dorotheum.at

DRU ⊞ Drummonds Architectural Antiques Ltd, The Kirkpatrick Buildings, 25 London Road (A3), Hindhead, Surrey, GU26 6AB Tel: 01428 609444 www.drummonds-arch.co.uk

DuM ➤ Du Mouchelles, 409 East Jefferson, Detroit, Michigan 48226, U.S.A. Tel: 313 963 6255

E ➤ Ewbank, Burnt Common Auction Rooms, London Road, Send, Woking, Surrey, GU23 7LN Tel: 01483 223101 antiques@ewbankauctions.co.uk www.ewbankauctions.co.uk

EXC ⊞ Excalibur Antiques, Taunton Antique Centre, 27-29 Silver Street, Taunton, Somerset, TA13DH Tel: 01823 289327/07774 627409 pwright777@btopenworld.com www.excaliburantiques.com

F&C ➤ Finan & Co, The Square, Mere, Wiltshire, BA12 6DJ Tel: 01747 861411 post@finanandco.co.uk www.finanandco.co.uk

F&F ⊞ Fenwick & Fenwick, 88-90 High Street, Broadway, Worcestershire, WR12 7AJ Tel: 01386 853227/841724

FAC ⊞ Faganarms, Box 425, Fraser, MI 48026, U.S.A. Tel: 586 465 4637 info@faganarms.com www.faganarms.com

FHF ➤ Fellows & Sons, Augusta House, 19 Augusta Street, Hockley, Birmingham, West Midlands, B18 6JA Tel: 0121 212 2131 info@fellows.co.uk www.fellows.co.uk

FOF ⊞ Fossack & Furkle, P.O. Box 733, Abington, Cambridgeshire, CB1 6BF Tel: 01223 894296 fossack@btopenworld.com www.fossackandfurkle.freeservers.com

FST ⊞ Frank Scott-Tomlin, The Old Ironmongers Antiques Centre, 5 Burford St, Lechlade, Gloucestershire, GL7 3AP Tel: 01367 252397

G(B) ➤ Gorringes Auction Galleries, Terminus Road, Bexhill-on-Sea, East Sussex, TN39 3LR Tel: 01424 212994 bexhill@gorringes.co.uk www.gorringes.co.uk

G(L) ➤ Gorringes inc Julian Dawson, 15 North Street, Lewes, East Sussex, BN7 2PD Tel: 01273 478221 clientservices@gorringes.co.uk www.gorringes.co.uk

G&G ⊞ Guest & Gray, 1-7 Davies Mews, London, W1K 5AB Tel: 020 7408 1252 info@chinese-porcelain-art.com www.chinese-porcelain-art.com

GAK ➤ Keys, Off Palmers Lane, Aylsham, Norfolk, NR11 6JA Tel: 01263 733195 www.aylshamsalerooms.co.uk

GAU ⊞ Becca Gauldie Antiques, The Old School, Glendoick, Perthshire, PH2 7NR, Scotland Tel: 01738 860 870 becca@scottishantiques.freeserve.co.uk

GEO ⊞ Georgian Antiques, 10 Pattinson Street, Leith Links, Edinburgh, EH6 7HF, Scotland Tel: 0131 553 7286 info@georgianantiques.net JDixon7098@aol.com www.georgianantiques.net

GGD ⊞ Great Grooms Antiques Centre, 51/52 West Street, Dorking, Surrey, RH4 1BU Tel: 01306 887076 dorking@greatgrooms.co.uk www.greatgrooms.co.uk

GH ➤ Gardiner Houlgate, The Bath Auction Rooms, 9 Leafield Way, Corsham, Nr Bath, Somerset, SN13 9SW Tel: 01225 812912 www.invaluable.com/gardiner-houlgate

GIL ➤ Gilding's Auctioneers and Valuers, 64 Roman Way, Market Harborough, Leicestershire, LE16 7PQ Tel: 01858 410414 sales@gildings.co.uk www.gildings.co.uk

GIR ⊞ Helen Girton Antiques, P.O. Box 2022, Buckingham, MK18 4ZH Tel: 01280 815012

GLB ⊞ Glebe Antiques, Scottish Antique Centre, Doune, FK16 6HG, Scotland Tel: 01259 214559 rrglebe@aol.com

GLEN ⊞ Glenda - Antique Dolls, A18-A19 Grays Antique Market, Davies Mews, London, W1Y 2LP Tel: 020 8367 2441/020 7629 7034 glenda@glenda-antiquedolls.com www.glenda-antiquedolls.com

GN ⊞ Gillian Neale Antiques, P.O. Box 247, Aylesbury, Buckinghamshire, HP20 1JZ Tel: 01296 423754/07860 638700 gillianneale@aol.com www.gillinnealeantiques.co.uk

GRe ⊞ Greystoke Antiques, 4 Swan Yard, (off Cheap Street), Sherborne, Dorset, DT9 3AX Tel: 01935 812833

GTH ⚒ Greenslade Taylor Hunt Fine Art, Magdelene House, Church Square, Taunton, Somerset, TA1 1SB Tel: 01823 332525

HA ⊞ Hallidays, The Old College, Dorchester-on-Thames, Oxfordshire, OX10 7HL Tel: 01865 340028/68 antiques@hallidays.com www.hallidays.com

HABA ⊞ Hall-Bakker Decorative Arts at Heritage, 6 Market Place, Woodstock, Oxfordshire, OX20 1TA Tel: 01993 811332

Hal ⚒ Halls Fine Art Auctions, Welsh Bridge, Shrewsbury, Shropshire, SY3 8LA Tel: 01743 231212

HEL ⊞ Helios Gallery, 292 Westbourne Grove, London, W11 2PS Tel: 077 11 955 997 info@heliosgallery.com www.heliosgallery.com

HIS ⊞ Erna Hiscock & John Shepherd, Chelsea Galleries, 69 Portobello Road, London, W11 Tel: 01233 661407 or 0771 562 7273 erna@ernahiscockantiques.com www.ernahiscockantiques.com

HO ⊞ Houghton Antiques Tel: 01480 461887 or 07803 716842

HOK ⚒ Hamilton Osborne King, 4 Main Street, Blackrock, Co. Dublin, Republic of Ireland Tel: 288 5011 blackrock@hok.ie www.hok.ie

HOLL ⚒ Holloway's, 49 Parsons Street, Banbury, Oxfordshire, OX16 5NB Tel: 01295 817777 enquiries@hollowaysauctioneers.co.uk www.hollowaysauctioneers.co.uk

HOM ⊞ Home & Colonial, 134 High Street, Berkhamsted, Hertfordshire, HP4 3AT Tel: 01442 877007 homeandcolonial@btinternet.com www.homeandcolonial.co.uk

HOW ⊞ John Howard at Heritage, 6 Market Place, Woodstock, Oxfordshire, OX20 1TA Tel: 0870 4440678 john@johnhoward.co.uk www.antiquepottery.co.uk

HRQ ⊞ Harlequin Antiques, 79-81 Mansfield Road, Daybrook, Nottingham, NG5 6BH Tel: 0115 967 4590 sales@antiquepine.net www.antiquepine.net

HTE ⊞ Heritage, 6 Market Place, Woodstock, Oxfordshire, OX20 1TA Tel: 01993 811332/0870 4440678 dealers@atheritage.co.uk www.atheritage.co.uk

HUN ⊞ The Country Seat, Huntercombe Manor Barn, Henley-on-Thames, Oxfordshire, RG9 5RY Tel: 01491 641349 wclegg@thecountryseat.com www.thecountryseat.com

HYD ⚒ Hy Duke & Son, The Dorchester Fine Art Salerooms, Weymouth Avenue, Dorchester, Dorset, DT1 1QS Tel: 01305 265080 www.dukes-auctions.com

IM ⚒ Ibbett Mosely, 125 High Street, Sevenoaks, Kent, TN13 1UT Tel: 01732 456731 auctions@ibbettmosely.co.uk www.ibbettmosely.co.uk

JAA ⚒ Jackson's International Auctioneers & Appraisers of Fine Art & Antiques, 2229 Lincoln Street, Cedar Falls, IA 50613, U.S.A. Tel: 319 277 2256/800 665 6743 sandim@jacksonsauctions.com www.jacksonsauction.com

JAd ⚒ James Adam & Sons, 26 St Stephen's Green, Dublin 2, Republic of Ireland Tel: 676 0261 www.jamesadam.ie/

JAK ⊞ Clive & Lynne Jackson Tel: 01242 254375 or 0410 239351

JBe ⚒ John Bellman Auctioneers, New Pound Business Park, Wisborough Green, Billingshurst, West Sussex, RH14 PAZ Tel: 01403 700858 hbeves@bellmans.co.uk

JBL ⊞ Judi Bland Antiques Tel: 01276 857576 or 01536 724145

JCH ⊞ Jocelyn Chatterton, 126 Grays, 58 Davies St, London, W1Y 2LP Tel: 020 7629 1971 or 07798 804 853 jocelyn@cixi.demon.co.uk www.cixi.demon.co.uk

JDJ ⚒ James D Julia, Inc., P.O. Box 830, Rte. 201 Skowhegan Road, Fairfield ME 04937, U.S.A. Tel: 207 453 7125 www.juliaauctions.com

JeH ⊞ Jennie Horrocks, Top Banana Antiques Mall, 1 New Church Street, Tetbury, Gloucestershire, GL8 8DS Tel: 07836 264896 info@artnouveaulighting.co.uk www.artnouveaulighting.co.uk

JHa ⊞ Jeanette Hayhurst Fine Glass, 32a Kensington Church Street, London, W8 4HA Tel: 020 7938 1539

JNic ⚒ John Nicholson, The Auction Rooms, Longfield, Midhurst Road, Fernhurst, Surrey, GU27 3HA Tel: 01428 653727 sales@johnnicholsons.com

JOR ⊞ John Rogers Tel: 01643 863170 or 07710 266136 johnrogers024@btinternet.com

JPr ⊞ Joanna Proops Antique Textiles & Lighting, 34 Belvedere, Lansdown Hill, Bath, Somerset, BA1 5HR Tel: 01225 310795 antiquetextiles@aol.co.uk www.antiquetextiles.co.uk

JTS ⊞ June & Tony Stone Fine Antique Boxes, P.O. Box 106, Peacehaven, East Sussex, BN10 8AU Tel: 01273 579333 www.boxes.co.uk

JUN ⊞ Junktion, The Old Railway Station, New Bolingbroke, Boston, Lincolnshire, PE22 7LB Tel: 01205 480068/480087 junktionantiques@hotmail.com

JUP ⊞ Jupiter Antiques, P.O. Box 609, Rottingdean, East Sussex, BN2 7FW Tel: 01273 302865

JWK ⊞ Jane Wicks Kitchenalia, Country Ways, Strand Quay, Rye, East Sussex, TN31 7AY Tel: 01424 713635 Janes_kitchen@hotmail.com

K&D ⊞ Kembery Antique Clocks Ltd, George Street Antique Centre, 8 Edgar Buildings, George Street, Bath, Somerset, BA1 2EH Tel: 0117 956 5281 kembery@kdclocks.co.uk www.kdclocks.co.uk

K&M ⊞ K & M Antiques, 369-370 Grays Antique Market, 58 Davies Street, London, W1K 5LP Tel: 020 7491 4310 Kandmantiques@aol.com

KET ⊞ Carol Ketley Antiques, P.O. Box 16199, London, NW1 7WD Tel: 020 7359 5529

KEY ⊞ Key Antiques of Chipping Norton, 11 Horsefair, Chipping Norton, Oxfordshire, OX7 5AL Tel: 01608 644992/643777 info@keyantiques.com www.keyantiques.com

KTA ⚒ Kerry Taylor Auctions, in Association with Sotheby's, St George Street Gallery, Sotheby's, New Bond Street, London, W1A 2AA Tel: 07785 734337 fashion.textiles@sothebys.com

L ⚒ Lawrences Fine Art Auctioneers, South Street, Crewkerne, Somerset, TA18 8AB Tel: 01460 73041 www.lawrences.co.uk

L&E ⚒ Locke & England, 18 Guy Street, Leamington Spa, Warwickshire, CV32 4RT Tel: 01926 889100 info@leauction.co.uk www.auctions-online.com/locke

L&T ⚒ Lyon & Turnbull, 33 Broughton Place, Edinburgh, EH1 3RR, Scotland Tel: 0131 557 8844 info@lyonandturnbull.com www.lyonandturnbull.com

LAY ⚒ David Lay (ASVA), Auction House, Alverton, Penzance, Cornwall, TR18 4RE Tel: 01736 361414

LBr ⊞ Lynda Brine - By appointment only lyndabrine@yahoo.co.uk www.scentbottlesandsmalls.co.uk

LFA ⚒ Law Fine Art Tel: 01635 860033 info@lawfineart.co.uk www.lawfineart.co.uk

Lfo ⊞ Lorfords, 57 Long Street, Tetbury, Gloucestershire, GL8 8AA Tel: 01666 505111 toby@lorfordsantiques.co.uk www.lorfordsantiques.co.uk

LGr ⊞ Langton Green Antiques, Langton Road, Langton Green, Tunbridge Wells, Kent, TN3 0HP Tel: 01892 862004 antiques@langtongreen.fsbusiness.co.uk www.langtongreenantiques.co.uk

LHA ➤ Leslie Hindman, Inc., 122 North Aberdeen Street, Chicago, Illinois 60607, U.S.A. Tel: 312 280 1212 www.lesliehindman.com

M ➤ Morphets of Harrogate, 6 Albert Street, Harrogate, North Yorkshire, HG1 1JL Tel: 01423 530030

MAL ➤ Mallams, 26 Grosvenor Street, Cheltenham, Gloucestershire, GL52 2SG Tel: 01242 235712

Mal(O) ➤ Mallams, Bocardo House, 24 St Michael's Street, Oxford, OX1 2EB Tel: 01865 241358 oxford@mallams.co.uk

MB ⊞ Mostly Boxes, 93 High Street, Eton, Windsor, Berkshire, SL4 6AF Tel: 01753 858470

MCA ➤ Mervyn Carey, Twysden Cottage, Scullsgate, Benenden, Cranbrook, Kent, TN17 4LD Tel: 01580 240283

MDL ⊞ Michael D Long Ltd, 96-98 Derby Road, Nottingham, NG1 5FB Tel: 0115 941 3307 sales@michaeldlong.com www.michaeldlong.com

MEA ➤ Mealy's, Chatsworth Street, Castle Comer, Co Kilkenny, Republic of Ireland Tel: 564 441 229 info@mealys.com www.mealys.com

MGa ⊞ Marilyn Garrow - By appointment only Tel: 01728 648671 or 07774 842074 marogarrow@aol.com www.antiquesweb.co.uk/marilyngarrow

MIL ⊞ Millennia Antiquities Tel: 01204 690175 or 07930 273998 millenniaant@aol.com www.AncientAntiquities.co.uk

Mit ➤ Mitchells, Fairfield House, Station Road, Cockermouth, Cumbria, CA13 9PY Tel: 01900 827800 info@mitchellsfineart.com

MiW ⊞ Mike Weedon, 7 Camden Passage, Islington, London, N1 8EA Tel: 020 7226 5319 or 020 7609 6826 info@mikeweedonantiques.com www.mikeweedonantiques.com

MLL ⊞ Millers Antiques Ltd, Netherbrook House, 86 Christchurch Road, Ringwood, Hampshire, BH24 1DR Tel: 01425 472062 mail@millers-antiques.co.uk www.millers-antiques.co.uk

MTay ⊞ Martin Taylor Antiques, 323 Tettenhall Road, Wolverhampton, West Midlands, WV6 0JZ Tel: 01902 751166/07836 636524 enquiries@mtaylor-antiques.co.uk www.mtaylor-antiques.co.uk

NAW ⊞ Newark Antiques Warehouse Ltd, Old Kelham Road, Newark, Nottinghamshire, NG24 1BX Tel: 01636 674869/07974 429185 enquiries@newarkantiques.co.uk www.newarkantiques.co.uk

NEW ⊞ Newsum Antiques, 2 High Street, Winchcombe, Gloucestershire, GL54 5HT Tel: 01242 603446/ 07968 196668 mark@newsumantiques.co.uk www.newsumantiques.co.uk

NOA ➤ New Orleans Auction Galleries, Inc., 801 Magazine Street, AT 510 Julia, New Orleans, Louisiana 70130, U.S.A. Tel: 504 566 1849

NSal ➤ Netherhampton Salerooms, Salisbury Auction Centre, Netherhampton, Salisbury, Wiltshire, SP2 8RH Tel: 01722 340 041

NWE ⊞ North Wilts Exporters, Farm Hill House, Brinkworth, Wiltshire, SN15 5AJ Tel: 01666 510876 mike@northwilts.demon.co.uk www.northwiltsantiqueexporters.com

OLA ⊞ Olliff's Architectural Antiques, 19–21 Lower Redland Road, Redland, Bristol, Gloucestershire, BS6 6TB Tel: 0117 923 9232 marcus@olliffs.com www.olliffs.com

Oli ➤ Olivers, Olivers Rooms, Burkitts Lane, Sudbury, Suffolk, CO10 1HB Tel: 01787 880305 oliversauctions@btconnect.com

PeN ⊞ Peter Norden Antiques, 61 Long Street, Tetbury, Gloucestershire, GL8 8AA Tel: 01666 503 854 peternorden_antiques@lineone.net www.peter-norden-antiques.co.uk

Penn ⊞ Penny Fair Antiques Tel: 07860 825456

PF ➤ Peter Francis, Curiosity Sale Room, 19 King Street, Carmarthen, SA31 1BH, Wales Tel: 01267 233456 nigel@peterfrancis.co.uk www.peterfrancis.co.uk

PFK ➤ Penrith Farmers' & Kidd's plc, Skirsgill Salerooms, Penrith, Cumbria, CA11 0DN Tel: 01768 890781 info@pfkauctions.co.uk www.pfkauctions.co.uk

Pott ➤† Potteries Specialist Auctions, 271 Waterloo Road, Cobridge, Stoke on Trent, Staffordshire, ST6 3HR Tel: 01782 286622 www.potteriesauctions.com

PT ⊞ Pieces of Time, 1-7 Davies Mews, London, W1K 5AB Tel: 020 7629 2422 info@antique-watch.com www.antique-watch.com

QA ⊞ Quayside Antiques, 9 Frankwell, Shrewsbury, Shropshire, SY3 8JY Tel: 01743 360490 www.quaysideantiques.co.uk www.quaysideantiquesshrewsbury.co.uk

QM ⊞ The Wyndham Gallery, Lafayette Antiques Center, 401E 110th Street, New York, U.S.A. Tel: 212 722 8400 john_cullis@hotmail.com

RdeR ⊞ Rogers de Rin, 76 Royal Hospital Road, London, SW3 4HN Tel: 020 7352 9007 rogersderin@rogersderin.co.uk www.rogersderin.co.uk

ReN ⊞ Rene Nicholls, 56 High Street, Malmesbury, Wiltshire, SN16 9AT Tel: 01666 823089

RPh ⊞ Phelps Antiques, 133-135 St Margaret's Road, Twickenham, Middlesex, TW1 1RG Tel: 020 8892 1778 antiques@phelps.co.uk www.phelps.co.uk

RTo ➤ Rupert Toovey & Co Ltd, Spring Gardens, Washington, West Sussex, RH20 3BS Tel: 01903 891955 auctions@rupert-toovey.com www.rupert-toovey.com

RTW ⊞ Richard Twort Tel: 01934 641900 or 07711 939789

S ➤ Sotheby's, 34-35 New Bond Street, London, W1A 2AA Tel: 020 7293 5000 www.sothebys.com

S(Am) ➤ Sotheby's Amsterdam, De Boelelaan 30, Amsterdam 1083 HJ, Netherlands Tel: 31 20 550 2200

S(NY) ➤ Sotheby's, 1334 York Avenue at 72nd St, New York, NY 10021, U.S.A. Tel: 212 606 7000

S(O) ➤ Sotheby's Olympia, Hammersmith Road, London, W14 8UX Tel: 020 7293 5555

S(P) ➤ Sotheby's France SA, 76 rue du Faubourg, Saint Honore, Paris 75008, France Tel: 33 1 53 05 53 05

S(S) ➤ Sotheby's Sussex, Summers Place, Billingshurst, West Sussex, RH14 9AD Tel: 01403 833500

SaH ⊞ Sally Hawkins Tel: 01636 636666 sallytiles@aol.com

SAM ⊞ Samarkand Galleries, 16 Howe Street, Edinburgh, Scotland, EH3 6TD Tel: 0131 2252010 howe@samarkand.co.uk www.samarkand.co.uk

SAS ➤ Special Auction Services, Kennetholme, Midgham, Reading, Berkshire, RG7 5UX Tel: 0118 971 2949 www.antiquetradegazette.com/sas

SAT ⊞ The Swan at Tetsworth, High Street, Tetsworth, Nr Thame, Oxfordshire, OX9 7AB Tel: 01844 281777 antiques@theswan.co.uk www.theswan.co.uk

SCO ⊞ Peter Scott Tel: 0117 986 8468 or 07850 639770

SDD ⊞ Sandra D Deas Tel: 01333 360 214 or 07713 897 482

SEA ⊞ Mark Seabrook Antiques, P.O. Box 396, Huntingdon, Cambridgeshire, PE28 0ZA Tel: 01480 861935 enquiries@markseabrook.com www.markseabrook.com

SER ⊞ Serendipity, 125 High Street, Deal, Kent, CT14 6BB Tel: 01304 369165/01304 366536 dipityantiques@aol.com

SHa ⊞ Shapiro & Co, Stand 380, Gray's Antique Market, 58 Davies Street, London, W1Y 5LP Tel: 020 7491 2710

SJH ↗ S.J. Hales, 87 Fore Street, Bovey Tracey, Devon, TQ13 9AB Tel: 01626 836684

SK ↗ Skinner Inc., The Heritage On The Garden, 63 Park Plaza, Boston, MA 02116, U.S.A. Tel: 617 350 5400

SK(B) ↗ Skinner Inc., 357 Main Street, Bolton, MA 01740, U.S.A. Tel: 978 779 6241

SMI ⊞ Skip & Janie Smithson Antiques Tel: 01754 810265 or 07831 399180 smithsonantiques@hotmail.com

SWA ⊞ S.W. Antiques, Newlands (road), Pershore, Worcestershire, WR10 1BP Tel: 01386 555580 catchall@sw-antiques.co.uk www.sw-antiques.co.uk

SWB ⊞† Sweetbriar Gallery Paperweights Ltd, 56 Watergate Street, Chester, CH1 2LA Tel: 01244 329249 sales@sweetbriar.co.uk www.sweetbriar.co.uk www.sweetbriarartglass.co.uk

SWN ⊞ Swan Antiques, Stone Street, Cranbrook, Kent, TN17 3HF Tel: 01580 712720

SWO ↗ Sworders, 14 Cambridge Road, Stansted Mountfitchet, Essex, CM24 8BZ Tel: 01279 817778 auctions@sworder.co.uk www.sworder.co.uk

TDG ⊞ The Design Gallery 1850–1950, 5 The Green, Westerham, Kent, TN16 1AS Tel: 01959 561234 sales@thedesigngalleryuk.com www.thedesigngalleryuk.com

TEN ↗ Tennants, The Auction Centre, Harmby Road, Leyburn, Yorkshire, DL8 5SG Tel: 01969 623780 enquiry@tennants-ltd.co.uk www.tennants.co.uk

TLA ⊞ The Lanes Armoury, 26 Meeting House Lane, The Lanes, Brighton, East Sussex, BN1 1HB Tel: 01273 321357 enquiries@thelanesarmoury.co.uk www.thelanesarmoury.co.uk

TOM ⊞ Charles Tomlinson, Chester Tel: 01244 318395 charlestomlinson@tiscali.co.uk

TMA ↗† Tring Market Auctions, The Market Premises, Brook Street, Tring, Hertfordshire, HP23 5EF Tel: 01442 826446 sales@tringmarketauctions.co.uk www.tringmarketauctions.co.uk

TMi ⊞ T. J. Millard Antiques, 59 Lower Queen Street, Penzance, Cornwall, TR18 4DF Tel: 01736 333454 chessmove@btinternet.com

TOL ⊞ Turn On Lighting, Antique Lighting Specialists, 116/118 Islington High St, Camden Passage, Islington, London, N1 8EG Tel: 020 7359 7616

TOP ⊞† The Top Banana Antiques Mall, 1 New Church Street, Tetbury, Gloucestershire, GL8 8DS Tel: 0871 288 1102 info@topbananaantiques.com www.topbananaantiques.com

TRM(C) ↗ Thomson, Roddick & Medcalf Ltd, Coleridge House, Shaddongate, Carlisle, Cumbria, CA2 5TU Tel: 01228 528939 www.thomsonroddick.com

TRM(E) ↗ Thomson, Roddick & Medcalf Ltd, 43/44 Hardengreen Business Park, Eskbank, Edinburgh, EH22 3NX, Scotland Tel: 0131 454 9090

TYE ⊞ Typically English Antiques Tel: 01249 721721 or 07818 000704 typicallyeng@aol.com

WAA ⊞ Woburn Abbey Antiques Centre, Woburn, Bedfordshire, MK17 9WA Tel: 01525 290666 antiques@woburnabbey.co.uk www.discoverwoburn.co.uk

WAC ⊞ Worcester Antiques Centre, Reindeer Court, Mealcheapen Street, Worcester, WR1 4DF Tel: 01905 610680 WorcsAntiques@aol.com

WADS ⊞† Wadsworth's, Marehill, Pulborough, West Sussex, RH20 2DY Tel: 01798 873555 info@wadsworthsrugs.com www.wadsworthsrugs.com

Wai ⊞ Peter Wain, Mor Awel, Marine Terrace, Camaes Bay, Anglesey, LL67 0ND Tel: 01407 710077 or 07860 302945 peterwain@supanet.com

WAL ↗ Wallis & Wallis, West Street Auction Galleries, Lewes, East Sussex, BN7 2NJ Tel: 01273 480208 auctions@wallisandwallis.co.uk grb@wallisandwallis.co.uk www.wallisandwallis.co.uk

WeA ⊞ Wenderton Antiques - By appointment only Tel: 01227 720295

WEBB ↗ Webb's, 18 Manukau Rd, Newmarket, P.O. Box 99251, Auckland, New Zealand Tel: 09 524 6804 auctions@webbs.co.nz www.webbs.co.nz

WeW ⊞ West Wales Antiques, 18 Mansfield Road, Murton, Swansea, SA3 3AR, Wales Tel: 01792 234318/ 01639 644379 info@westwalesantiques.co.uk www.westwalesantiques.co.uk

WiB ⊞ Wish Barn Antiques, Wish Street, Rye, East Sussex, TN31 7DA Tel: 01797 226797

WILK ↗ Wilkinson's Auctioneers Ltd, The Old Salerooms, 28 Netherhall Road, Doncaster, Yorkshire, DN1 2PW Tel: 01302 814884 sid@wilkinsons-auctioneers.co.uk www.wilkinsons-auctioneers.co.uk

WilP ↗ W&H Peacock, 26 Newnham Street, Bedford, MK40 3JR Tel: 01234 266366

WL ↗ Wintertons Ltd, Lichfield Auction Centre, Fradley Park, Lichfield, Staffordshire, WS13 8NF Tel: 01543 263256 Tel: 01283 762813 enquiries@wintertons.co.uk www.wintertons.co.uk Photos: Courtesy of Crown Photos

WW ↗ Woolley & Wallis, Salisbury Salerooms, 51-61 Castle Street, Salisbury, Wiltshire, SP1 3SU Tel: 01722 424500/411854 enquiries@woolleyandwallis.co.uk www.woolleyandwallis.co.uk

Index to Advertisers

Amherst Antiques 281
Ancient & Gothic ....*back jacket*
Ashbourne Antiques 65
Daniel Bexfield 145
Dee Atkinson
& Harrison ....*front of book*
Andrew Hartley 75
Lambert & Foster 43
Orpington Sales Room 49
Sweetbriar Gallery 183
Top Banana 93
Tring Market Auctions 161
Wadsworth's 265
West Street Antiques 235

Index

Bold numbers refer to information boxes.

A

Admiral Fitzroy barometers 216
Afghani rugs 263
African antiquities 222
alabaster
  clocks 200, 201
  sculpture 273
Alcock, Samuel 98
Aldridge, Edward 144
Aldwinkle & Slater 151
ale glasses 174
ale mulls 258
Allen, Thomas 151
Amelung, John Frederick 178
American
  bedroom suites 15
  boxes 241
  chests 30
  chests of drawers 32
  clocks 205, 207
  glass 169, 178, 181, 186
  money boxes 244
  scientific instruments 269
  silver 144, 151, 155, 161
  sofas 48
  stands 50
  watches 208–11
amphorae 220, 221
Anatolian rugs 263
Anderson, Isabella 274
Angell, Joseph 147
Anglo-Indian chests 31
Anglo-Saxon antiquities 221
animals
  ceramic 84–6
  cows 85
  dogs 84, 86, 89, 245
  horses 245–7
  lions 86, 231
  zebras 88
Anri 278
antiquities 219–23
  authenticity **222**
  fakes **219**
apothecary boxes 267
Appleton, Nathaniel 154
architectural antiques 224–33
Arita 126, 127
armchairs 19–28
  carvers 24
  child's 20
  library 24
  Windsor 23
  wing 20, 21
armoires 40
arms and armour 234–7
Art Nouveau
  cabinets 42
  metalware 260
Arts and Crafts
  metalware 260–1
  stands 50
  stools 51
  tables 55, 56
asparagus servers 129

asparagus tongs 152
Asprey & Co 159
Atkins Bros 149
Austrian
  ceramics 67, 72–4, 85
  glass 189–90
  sculpture 271
  silver 143
axes 223, 235
Ayres, F.H. 247

B

Baccarat **180**, 180, 183
bag faces 262
Bagnall, William 164
bags
  Chinese 274
  woven 265
Balerna, L. 211
Balouch rugs 263
barber's bowls 258
Barbienne le Jeune 212
Barlow, Florence 75
Barnard, Edward & Sons
  157, 158
Barnard, John 158
Barnard, Messrs 134, 162
Barnard, William James 158
Barnett 237
barometers **214**, 214–17,
  216, **217**, 269
baskets
  ceramic 65–6
  silver 134
Bateman, Hester 146, **153**,
  153
Bavarian arms and armour 235
Bayreuth 65
beakers
  ceramic 71
  glass 173, 176, 177, 180
  silver 147, 148
Beck, R. & J. 268
bedroom suites 15
beds 15
bedside cabinets 38, 39, 42
Beeton, Isabella 249
Belgian
  arms and armour 237
  lace 275
Bellarmine jugs 111
benches 16, 233
Benham & Froud 251–3
Bennett 205
Benson, W.A.S. 256, 257
bergère lounge suites 49
Berlin porcelain 114
bible boxes 243
Biedermeier sofas 48
biscuit barrels 259
black basalt
  jugs 110
  plaques 115
blanc de Chine 85
blanket chests 30

blotters 281
Boelau, G. 268
Bohemian
  ceramics 96, 115
  glass 173, 176, 177,
    188–90
bonbon dishes 133
bonheurs du jour 43
bookcases 17–18
  bureau 44
books, kitchenware 249
boot scrapers 225
boot stands 50
bottle stoppers 164, 278
bottles
  ceramic 129
  glass 170
  see also scent bottles
Bovet, Fleurier 212
Bow
  baskets 66
  bowls 80
  cups 71
  dishes 77, 83
  mugs 72
  plates 103
  sauce boats 112
bowls
  barber's 258
  ceramic 75–83
  glass 167–8
  silver 133–5
box mirrors 46
boxes 238–43
  ceramic 65–6
  silver 136–40
  wooden 238–43, 278–81
Boyce 206
Boyton, Charles 156, 182
bracelets, antiquities 221
bracket clocks 193–4
Bradbury, J. 160
Bradbury, Thomas & Sons
  135, 142
brandy saucepans 134
Brannam Pottery 111
brass
  architectural antiques
    224–6, 231–3
  bowls 258
  candlesticks 261
  clocks 195–7, 204, 207
  lighting 256, 257
  scientific instruments 266–9
  tins 258
  wick trimmers 258
bread boards 248, 251, 252
breakfast tables 54, 57, 58
Breguet 210
Bretby 106
Brewster, Ann 275
brick inserts 224
bridal gowns 277
brilliant cutting, glass **186**, 186
Bristol delft 92, 103

Bristol glass 172
Britannia metal 259
Britannia standard silver **138**,
  146, 163
Broad, John 107
Broadway, W.I. & Co 141
bronze
  antiquities 219–21
  figures 260
  sculpture **270**, 270–3
  vases 260
brooches, antiquities 219
Brooke Ltd 51
Brough, Fanny 276
Brown, Westhead & Moore 76
brushes 278
buckets, coal 232
buckles, antiquities 219–20
buffets 56, 61
Bunn 210
bureau bookcases 44
bureaux 43–5, **44**
Burridge, Frederick Augustus
  143
busts
  porcelain 131
  sculpture 270–3
butler's trays 62
Butt, A.W. 208
butter dishes 134, 135, 248

C

cabinet cups 69
cabinet plates 95, 99
cabinets 38–42
  bedside 38, 39, 42
  cigar 38
  display 41, 42
  music 41
  pier 41
  side 39, 55, 58, 60, 61
  spice 253
  stationery 38, 42
  table 38, 39
  wall 38
Cabrier, Charles 211
caddy spoons 150, 151, 153
Cafe, John 141
cake stands 50
cameo glass 190
Cameron, R. 214
campaign furniture
  bookcases 18
  chests of drawers 34
Campion, Anne 275
candelabra
  ceramic 67, 68
  silver 141, 142
candle boxes 241
candle snuffers 165
candlestands 50
candlesticks
  brass 261
  ceramic 67–8
  hog scraper **260**, 260

silver 141–2
caneware 112
canisters, ceramic 108
Cantagalli 128
canterburies 63
Cantonese ceramics 90
card cases 136, 140
card tables 53–6, **54**, 58, 61
Carey 161
Carlton Ware 119
carpet boules 130
carpets *see* rugs and carpets
carriage clocks 195–7, **196**
cars, toy 246
Cartlidge, George 122
carvers 24
cast iron *see* iron
Castman, Arvid 145
Caucasian rugs 263, 264
Caughley 70, 83
Cavelier, Pierre Jules 272
Celtic antiquities 219
centre tables 61
ceramics 64–101
   antiquities 219–23, **220**
   baskets and boxes 65–6
   candlesticks 67–8
   cups, mugs and tea bowls 69–74
   dishes and bowls 75–83
   figures 84–9
   flatware 90–105
   jardinières 106–7
   jars and canisters 108
   jugs and ewers 109–13
   kitchenware 248–53
   plaques 114–15
   services 116–17
   stands 118
   tea and coffee pots 119–21
   tiles 122–3
   vases 124–8
chairs 19–28
   child's 20, **27**, 27
   dining 19, 22, 23, 25, 26, 28
   elbow 19, 22, 23, 25, 28
   garden 229
   hall 22, 28
   library 25
   low 26
   nursing 26
   rocking 19, 20, 27
   side 19, 20
   tub 27
chalices 261
Chalon 205
chamber pots 129
Chamberlain's Worcester 72, 81
chambersticks 67, 254
Champagne glasses 179
chandeliers 255
Channel Islands silver 148
chargers 75, 77, 93, 97, 104
Chartier, John 165
chatelaines 259
cheese domes 131
cheese stands 118
Chelsea
   baskets 65
   dishes 80
   plates 100
cheroot cases 137
chess sets 246, 427

chesterfield sofas **48**, 48
chests 29–31
chests of drawers 32–7, **34**
chests-on-chests 37
cheval mirrors 47
Chiesa Keizer & Co 215
chiffoniers 52, 54, 59, 60
children's
   ceramics 69, 91, 94–5, 97
   chairs 20, **27**, 27
   hats 275
   sleighs 230
chimney pots 229
Chinese
   cabinets 39
   rugs 263
   silver 138, 165
   tables 53
   textiles 274–6
Chinese ceramics
   cups 105
   dishes 102
   plates 99, 100, 103
   soup plates 95
   supper sets 131
   tea caddies 130
   teapots 120, 121
   vases 124
Chippendale style
   chairs 19, 21
   tables 55
chocolate cups 73
chocolate moulds 253
Choisy Le Roi 92
christening mugs 146, 147
cigar boxes 241
cigar cabinets 38
cigar cases 137
cigarette boxes 240
clamps 228
Clare, Thos. 211
claret jugs 154, 155, 181, 182
Clichy 183–4
clocks 192–207
   bracket 193–4
   carriage 195–7, **196**
   longcase **198**, 198–9
   mantel 200–4, **201**
   wall 205–6
clothes presses 40
coal buckets 232
coal scuttles 231
Coalbrookdale 230
Coalport 107, 125
coffee cans 72
coffee grinders 252, 253
coffee pots
   Britannia metal 259
   ceramic 119–21
   silver 158–9
coffee services 116, 158
coffers 29–31
Colefax, Sibyl 20
collars, lace 274
Colls, Maryah 275
colours, rugs and carpets **263**
commemorative jugs 112
commodes 34, 36
compacts 137
compasses 217, 266, 267–9
Comtoise clocks 198, 206
Comyns, William 139, 165, 187
condiments, silver 143–5

Consular style commodes 36
Continental
   ceramics 65
   chests 30
   chests of drawers 36
   desks 45
   lighting 255
   sculpture 271
   silver 136, 149, 150, 161
   tea caddies 243
   watches 208
Copeland
   busts 131
   dessert services 116
   figures 85, 89
   jelly moulds 251
   plates 95, 99
Copeland & Garrett 86
copper
   ale mulls 258
   kitchenware 250–3
   milk jugs 258
cordial glasses 174, 175
Cork Glass Co 172
corner cupboards 40, 41
costume 276, 377
Cowlishaw, J.Y. 150
cradles 15
cranberry glass 188
cream boats 113
cream jugs
   ceramic 110, 111
   silver 154–5
creamware
   beakers 71
   coffee pots 120
   jugs 74, 112
   mugs 70, 73
   plates 93, 98
   sauce boats 113
   teapots 120, 121
Crown Derby 116
Crown Staffordshire 130
cruets
   glass 191
   silver 143–5
crusie lamps 259
cuckoo clocks 205
Cuhna, Jose de 96
cup holders 260
cupboards 38–42
   corner 40, 41
   cupboards-on-stands 40, 42
   night 40
   smoker's 42
cups
   antiquities 219
   ceramic 69–74, 105
   silver 146–8
custard cups 69, 72
cut glass 167–9, 171
cutlery, silver 149–53
cutlery boxes 280
Cutts, J.P., Sons & Sutton 268
Cypriot antiquities 220–1

D
Daniell, Thomas & Jabez 143, 145
Danish ceramics 114
Daum 167
Davenport 129
davenports 45

Davey & Co 257
Davis, Joseph & Co 217
Day, Louis F. 122
Day, Thomas 48
day beds 48
De Morgan, William 123
decanter labels 163
decanter sets 170
decanters 169–72, 191
delft
   bowls 78, 81, 82
   chargers 77, 93
   dishes 77, 81, 82, 94
   drug jars 108
   flower bricks 131
   plates 92, 96–8, 102, 103
Derby
   candlesticks 68
   figures 84
   inkstands 118
   plates 95
   sauce boats 113
   tea bowls 72
   tureens 78
desk lamps 255
desks 43–5, **44**
dessert services 116, 117
Dewdney, James 111
Dicks, Thomas 162
dining chairs 19, 22, 23, 25, 26, 28
dining tables 61
dinner services 117
dish rings 135
dishes
   antiquities 221
   ceramic 75–83, 94, 102
   silver 133–5
display cabinets 41, 42
display tables 54
Dixon, James & Sons 141, 259
Doccia 100, 101, 120
Dogon antiques 225
dolls 244–7
dolls' houses 246
Don Pottery 92
door furniture 224, 225, 228
door porters 280
Doulton
   bowls 75
   jardinières 106, 107
   services 117
drainers 250
Dresden porcelain 68, 124
Dresser, Christopher 125
dresses 276
dressing-table boxes 241
Drew & Son 171
drinking glasses 173–80
drop-leaf tables 56, 58, 59
drug jars 108
dumb waiters 63
Durtnall, Beatrice M. 106
Dutch
   cabinets 42
   ceramics 123
   chairs 20
   glass 185
   silver 137
Dutch Delft
   chargers 77
   dishes 82, 83
   drug jars 108

plates 96, 102
Duverdry & Bloquel 197
dyes, rugs and carpets **263**

E
earrings, antiquities 219, 222
earthenware *see* ceramics
East Anglian antiquities 219
Eastern European chests of
drawers 33
Ebel 213
écuelles 74
Edward, David and George
163
Edwards' Scientific and
Educational Cabinets 269
egg beaters 253
egg boxes 251
egg cruets 164
eggs, ceramic 131
Egyptian antiquities 223
elbow chairs 19, 22, 23, 25, 28
Eley, William 151
Elgin National Watch Co
209, 210
Emes, John 148
Empire style
clocks 201, 207
sofas 48
enamel
kitchenware 249
watches 212
English delft 103
étagères 62
Ethiopian arms and armour 234
Evans, John 147
Evans, William 144
Evans & Co 267
ewers, ceramic 111–13

F
Fagerroos, Johan Edvard 158
faïence
baskets 65
plates 103
fakes, antiquities **219**
famille rose 70, 130
famille vert 131
Favell, Rupert 142
Fearn, William 151
Federal-style stands 50
fenders 226, 233
Fife Pottery 75
figures
antiquities 222, 223
bronze 260
ceramic 84–9
sculpture 270, 271
finials, gate post 226, 228,
230
Finnish silver 158
fire dogs 225, 232, 233
fire irons 231
fire screens 229
fire surrounds 231, 232
firearms 234–7
fish servers 150, 151
flagons, antiquities 222
flasks
antiquities 222, 223
spirit 191
flatware, ceramic 90–105
flower bricks 131

fob watches 208, 209
footbaths 76
footstools 51
forks
kitchenware 253
silver 150, 151
four-poster beds 15
Fowler, John 20
frames 46–7
photograph 165
Francis, Catherine 106
François, Paris 204
French
architectural antiques 226,
228, 229, 232, 233
armoires 40
arms and armour 236, 237
beds 15
boxes 243
buffets 61
cabinets 61
canterburies 63
ceramics 67, 69, 92, 101,
106, 109, 115, 118
clocks 194–8, 200–7
commodes 36
glass 167, 180, 183–4,
190, 191
kitchenware 250
lighting 256
mirrors 46
scientific instruments 269
sculpture 270, 272
silver 135, 142, 155, 157
sofas 49
stools 51
tables 61
watches 210–12
fruit knives, silver 149, 150
funnels, wine 165
furniture 14–63
furniture mounts 227

G
Gallé, Emile 179, 190
Gamage, A.W. Ltd 244
Gamble, James 122
games compendiums 247
Ganthony 212
garden furniture 227, 229–31
Gardener, Henry 152
garnitures, clock 204
Garratt 235
gas water heaters 230
gate post finials 226, 228, 230
Gatward 199
German
arms and armour 234, 235
boxes 239
chests 31
dolls 244, 247
glass 182
silver 139, 145
German ceramics
Bellarmine jugs 111
boxes 65
candlesticks 68
dinner services 117
écuelles 74
figures 85–9
plaques 114, 115
plates 93, 99, 101
tea canisters 108

vases 124, 128
wall brackets 68
Gibbs, Fanny A. 277
Gilbert Clock Co 205, 207
Giles, James 185
Gilmour, Margaret 261
gin glasses 175
girandoles 46
glass 166–91
antiquities 222, 223
baskets, bowls and dishes
167–8
bottles and decanters
169–72
brilliant cutting **186**, 186
drinking glasses 173–80
18th-century coloured glass
173
jugs 181–2
lighting 254–7
Mary Gregory glass **188**,
189
paperweights 183–4, **184**
Russian pattern **169**, 169
scent bottles **185**, 185–7
stained glass windows
226, 228
Vaseline glass **188**, 188, 189
vases 188–90
Gloster, James 137
gnomes, terracotta 270
goblets
glass 173–4, 178–80
silver 146, 148
gold
antiquities 222
watches 208–13
Goldsmiths & Silversmiths Co
141, 146, 161, 162
Goodfellow, Thomas 145
Gorham Manufacturing Co
155, 155
Gosselin 194
Gothic revival
armchairs 21
chairs 22, 28
Grainger's Worcester 71
graters 250
grates 231, 232
Graydon-Stannus, Elizabeth
171
Greek antiquities **221**, 221–3
Gresley, C. 127
griddles 251
Grinsell, John & Sons 153
guggle jugs 110
Guillaume, Berfleur 237
Guilmet 207
guns 234–7

H
Hadley, James 86, 88
Hall, Ralph 82
Hall, William 154
hall benches 16
hall chairs 22, 28
Hamadan rugs 263
Hamilton & Diesinger 158
Hamilton & Inches 144
hammers 223
hanging shelves 18
Harley, Thomas 120
Harris, Charles Stewart 138

Harrison, G. 160
Hatfield, Charles 156
hats 275, 276
Hattori 260
Heater, Geo. C. 198
heaters, water 230
Heath, J. 159
Heitzman & Son 202
Hellenistic antiquities 223
helmets, military 234–6
Hemming, Henry 149
Henderson, J. 160
Hennell, Richard 160
Hennell, Robert 133
Hepplewhite style
chairs 28
wardrobes 42
Heriz carpets 264
Hience, Antoine 155
highchairs 27
Hispano-Moresque pottery 83
hitching posts 225
hob grates 232
Hodges, George 151
Hoffman, Wilhelm 176
hog scraper candlesticks
260, 260
Holdcroft, Joseph 118, 128
Hollamby, Richard 281
horn snuff boxes 242
horses, rocking 247
Horton Allday 186
hot water jugs 154, 158
Houdon, Jean-Antoine **270**,
270
Hugo, E. 135
Hung Chong 165
Hungarian ceramics 113
Hutton, William & Sons 133,
152, 187

I
ice buckets 79
Iker, K.B. 205
Imari 75, 97, 125, 126
Imperial Porcelain
Manufactory 68
Indian
arms and armour 237
silver 160
textiles 277
writing slopes 43
inkstands
ceramic 118
pewter 259
silver 161–2
inkwells
ceramic 130
silver 161, 162
wooden 280
Irish
ceramics 131
glass 168, 169, 171, **172**,
172
metalware 258
silver 152, 154, 157
iron
architectural antiques 224,
225, 230–3
kitchenware 251–3
money boxes 244
toys 245
irons 248, 249

Ironstone
  services 116
  vases 127
Italian
  armchairs 28
  mirrors 47
  sculpture 271–3
Italian ceramics
  dishes 83
  ewers 112
  jugs 109
  plates 98, 101, 102, 104, 105
  vases 126, 128
ivory
  boxes 240
  chess sets 427
  clamps 228
  tea caddies 242

J
Jackson, Joseph 157
Jackson, Joshua 148
Jackson, W.H. 208
Jacot, Henri 197
James, Elizabeth 276
Japanese
  boxes 240
  cabinets 38
  ceramics 97, 126, 127, 130
  metalware 260
japanned writing tables 45
Japy Frères 202
Jaques 246
jardinière stands 118
jardinières, ceramic 106–7
jars
  ceramic 108
  glass 168, 191
  kitchenware 249, 251
jasper ware 119
Jefferys & Ham 212
jelly moulds 251–3
jewellery, antiquities 219, 221, 222
jewellery boxes 139, 239
jigsaws 244
Jones, George 118
Joyce, Richard 104
Jücht, J.C. 89
jugs
  antiquities 220, 222
  ceramic 74, 109–13
  copper 258
  glass 181–2
  kitchenware 250
  silver 154–5
  Toby jugs 112, 113
Juvenia 213

K
Kalabergo, G. 216
Kämmer & Reinhardt 247
Kändler, J.J. 87
Karabakh rugs 264
Kashgai rugs 264
Kashmir cloth 262
Keating, Michael 152
Kenrick & Sons 252, 253
kettles, copper 250
Kirkcaldy Pottery 91
kitchenware 248–53
kneehole desks 45

knife boxes 249
knife polishers 253
Knight, Elkin & Co 90
knives, silver 149–51, 164
knockers 224
Knox, Archibald 260
Kocks, Pieter Adriaensz 82
Kohn, J. & J. 51
Kornilov 102
koros 130
Kosta 178
Kothgasser, Anton 173
Kullberg, Victor 212

L
labels, decanter 163
laboratory scales 266
lace 274, 275
lacquer
  boxes 241, 242
  tables 53
ladles
  ceramic 129
  silver 151–3
Lambeth 98
lamps *see* lighting
Langlands, Dorothy 146
lanterns, garden 229
lavatory pans 233
Le Roy & Fils 203
Leeds Pottery 90
Lépine 211
Leroy 210
Lewis & Son 202
libation cups 71
Liberty & Co
  pewter 259–61
  tables 55
library furniture
  chairs 24, 25
  tables 52
lighting 254–7
Lillja, Adolf 135
Linthorpe 125
Lion 267
Lione, J. 216
liqueur sets 191
Liverpool delft 91
Llanelli Pottery 98, 102
locks 224, 228
Lodi 105
Löetz 190
longcase clocks **198**, 198–9
Longchamps 98
lounge suites 49
loving cups 71
low chairs 26
Lowestoft pottery 77, 119
luggies 281
lustre ware 97, 114
Luvate, D. 215

M
McDonald, Phillip **169**
McLaren, Andrew & Co 231
McLean & Son 280
maiolica
  plates 98, 102, 104, 105
  saucers 105
  vases 128
majolica
  cheese stands 118
  dishes 75, 83

ewers 111–12
jardinières 106, 107
oyster plates 98
tiles 122
vases 128
Maltese lace 274
Mann, Thomas 152
mantel clocks 200–4, **201**
Mappin & Webb 163
marble
  benches 233
  sculpture 271–3
Marc, Henri 204
Margaine 197
Marieberg 72
marine barometers 214, **217**, 217
marquetry
  boxes 239
  cabinets 39
  chests of drawers 36
  chiffoniers 59
  clocks 203
  tables 59
marrow spoons 152
Martin Hall & Co 134, 147, 149
Mary Gregory glass **188**, 189
Mason, William 94
Mason & Parker 246
Mason's Ironstone
  mugs 69, 71
  vases 127
mats, lace 274, 275
Mauchline ware
  boxes 238, 280
  thimble holders 279
Measham ware **119**, 119, 121
measures, spirit 191
meat platters 79, 94, 104
medical instruments 266, 267
Meissen
  boxes 65
  dinner services 117
  dishes 79
  écuelles 74
  figures 85–9
  mirrors 130
  plates 99, 101
  vases 128
  wall brackets 68
Meriton, Samuel 134
metalware 258–61
  antiquities 219–20
Methven Pottery 76
Mewburn, John 159
microscopes 268, 269
Middleton, J. 159
Minter, George 24
Minton
  birds 89
  candelabra 68
  cups 73
  figures 88
  jardinières 106, 107
  meat platters 104
  plates 94, 96
  spittoons 131
  tiles 122, 123
  trios 73
  vases 127, 128
mirrors 46–7, 130, 165, 260–1
Mitchell & Son 150

Mohn family 173
money boxes 240, 244
Moore 210
Moore & Co 116
Moore Bros 256
Moralee 217
Mordan, Sampson & Co 161
Morel & Co 157
Moser **190**, 190
mote spoons 151
mother-of-pearl boxes 242, 243
moulds, kitchenware 249, 251–3
mouse traps 278
Moustier 109
Moyr Smith, John 122, 123
mugs
  ceramic 69–74
  glass 176
  silver 146–8
mule chests 31
Muller, Bernard 133
music cabinets 41
music stools 51
muskets 237
mustard pots 143, 144–5
mystery clocks 207

N
Nailsea glass 181
Nairne & Blunt 268
Nantgarw 104
napkin rings 163, 278
Nasmyth, James & Co 136
needle cases 278
needlework 274–7
New Bremen Glassworks 178
newel posts 229
night cupboards 40
nursery ceramics 69, 91, 94–5, 97
nursing chairs 26
nut crackers 279

O
occasional tables 52, 56–9
Oertling, L. 266
oil bottles 129
oil lamps 254–7
Orchies 106
ormolu
  clocks 203, 204
  vases 127
orreries 269
Osler, F. & C. **168**, 168

P
padlocks 224, 267
Paillard Watch Co 208
Pairpoint, John and Frank 165
Palissy 96
paper knives 164
paperweights 183–4, **184**
papier-mâché
  snuff boxes 241
  tables 61
  toys 245
Parian figures 85, 88, 89
Paris porcelain 69, 115, 125
Parker, Isabelle 275
parquetry
  boxes 239

stands 50
patch boxes, silver 140
pearlware
  boxes 66
  figures 88
  mugs 70
  plates 92, 99
  tea caddies 129
  teapots 120
pedometers 267
Pemberton, Samuel 137, 140
Pembroke tables 55, 57
pen boxes 279
pencils, silver 161, 162
pens, silver 161
pepper pots
  ceramic 129
  silver 143, 144
Perry, H. 99
Persian
  bags 265
  rugs and carpets 263–5
Peruvian antiquities 222
pewter 182, 259–61
Phipps & Robinson 163
photograph frames, silver 165
Piaget 213
piano stools 51
pier cabinets 41
pier mirrors 46
Piercy, Robert 157
Pilkington, Robert 153
Pilkington's Royal Lancastrian 104, 124
pill boxes 138
pillar tables 57
pin cushions 164
pinchbeck watches 210
pistols 234, 236, 237
plaques
  ceramic 114–15
  metalware 261
plates 90–105
platters 77, 79, 82, 90, 94
pocket watches 208–12
pole screens 63
pomanders, silver 139
porcelain see ceramics
Portuguese ceramics 96
post boxes 243
pottery see ceramics
powder compacts 137
Powell 188
Powell, James 256, 257
Pratt, Christopher 58
Prattware 84, 129
preserve pots 130
Pritchard, Andrew 268
punch bowls 82, 168
Purnell, Frederic 186
purses, silver 140

R

Randell, Emily 106
rapiers 234
rattles, silver 163
Rawlings, C.L. 139
reading stands 50
Red-Figure painting 221
redware
  antiquities 222
  mugs 73

Regina 208
Reily & Storer 135
Rhodes, Ackroyd 146
Richards, Henry 236
Richardson's 169
Ridgway 79, 117
rifles 235, 236
Riley, J. & R. 118
Rimavesi Bros 214
Rizzardo, Galli 272
Robertson, Ann 155
rock crystal snuff bottles 187
rocking chairs 19, 20, 27
rocking horses 247
Rolex 213
Roman antiquities 219–22
Romer, Emick 142
Rörstrand 103
Royal Copenhagen 114
Royal Crown Derby 73, 127
Royal Doulton 114
Royal Worcester
  ewers 125
  plates 101
  scent bottles 129
  vases 128
Rugg, Richard 156
rugs and carpets 262–5, 264
  colours and dyes 263
rummers 176
Rundell, Philip 159
runners 265
Russell, Thomas & Sons 209
Russian
  boxes 241, 242
  ceramics 68, 102
  scientific instruments 268
  silver 137, 140, 147, 153
Russian pattern, glass 169, 169

S

sabres 234, 235
St Louis 183, 184
salad servers 153
salt-glazed stoneware 111, 121
salts
  glass 167
  silver 144, 144, 145
salvers, silver 156–7
samplers 274–7
Samson 67, 125
Sangamo Special 209
Sanzel, Felix 272
Satsuma ware 124, 130
sauce boats
  ceramic 112–13
  silver 155
sauce tureens 78
saucers 105
Savoie 109
Savona 104, 105
Savonnerie carpets 265
scales, laboratory 266
scent bottles
  ceramic 129
  glass 185, 185–7
  silver 164
Schwaber, Heinrich 85
scientific instruments 266–9
Scott, James 152
Scottish

kitchenware 251
metalware 259, 261
silver 150
wood 281
Scottish ceramics
  bowls 75, 81
  chamber pots 129
  dishes 83
  jardinières 106, 107
  mugs 69
  plates 91, 97, 100, 101
  preserve pots 130
  vases 127, 128
screens
  fire 229
  pole 63
sculpture 270, 270–3
sealing wax holders 161
seats, garden 231
secretaire chests 35
secrétaires à abattant 45
services 116–17
settees 49
Sèvres
  candlesticks 67
  clocks 203
  coffee services 116
  cups 74
  jardinières 107
  plates 95, 101
  vases 127
  writing stands 118
shabti figures 223
Shaw, John 138
Shaw, William 148
Sheffield plate 133, 164
shelves 17–18
Sheraton revival
  cabinets 60
  desks 45
Sherwin & Cotton 122
shields 234
ship's decanters 172
Shoolbred, James & Co 44
shortbread moulds 249
Shute, Sarah 277
side cabinets 39, 55, 58, 60, 61
side chairs 19, 20
side furniture 52–5, 58–61
side tables 52, 53, 58–60
sideboards 53, 55, 59
silk samplers 275–7
silver 132–65
  antiquities 219, 221, 223
  barometers 217
  baskets, bowls and dishes 133–5
  boxes and cases 136–40
  Britannia standard silver 138, 146, 163
  candlesticks and chambersticks 141–2
  claret jugs 181, 182
  clocks 207
  condiments and cruets 143–5
  cups, mugs and tankards 146–8
  cutlery and serving implements 149–53
  jugs and sauce boats 154–5

salvers and trays 156–7
scent bottles 185–7
  tea, coffee and chocolate pots 158–9
  toast racks 160
  watches 208, 210–12
  writing equipment 161–2
Simon & Halbig 244, 246
Sitzendorf 67
sleigh beds 15
sleighs 230
slipware 82
Smith, Ann 154
Smith, George 149
smoker's cupboards 42
snuff bottles, rock crystal 187
snuff boxes
  ceramic 66
  horn 242
  papier-mâché 241
  silver 136–40
  Tunbridge ware 238
Sobey, William R. 153
sofas 48–9
  chesterfield 48, 48
soup bowls 78
soup plates 91, 95
sovereign cases 137
Spanish ceramics 83
specimen boxes 269
spelter clocks 200, 201
spice cabinets 253
spice pots 144, 145
spill vases 84
spinning tops 281
spirit flasks 191
spirit measures 191
spittoons 131
Spode
  chambersticks 67
  dessert services 116
  jugs 110
  plates 94, 99
  platters 79
spongeware
  bowls 75, 76
  chamber pots 129
spoons
  silver 149–53
  wooden 280
Staffordshire
  animals 84–6, 88, 89
  bowls 82
  dishes 78–81
  eggs 131
  figures 84, 87–9
  jugs 110
  mugs 73
  plates 96
  platters 90
  teapots 121
  vases 126
stained glass windows 226, 228
stamp boxes 280
stands 50, 233
  ceramic 118
  silver 157
Star, Marcus 144
stationery boxes 240, 243
stationery cabinets 38, 42
stationery trays 279

statues, stone 227
Staunton 246
Steiff 245
Steiner 244
Stettinger & Wondrich 214
Stevens & Williams 181
Steward, J.H. 215, 217, 266
stick barometers **214**, 214–17
stick stands 50, 233
stirrup flasks 222
stone statues 227
stoneware
　kitchenware 249, 251
　mugs 72
　salt-glazed 111, 121
　see also ceramics
stools 51, 281
Stourbridge 181
Straham & Co 25
sugar bowls, silver 133, 135
sugar casters, silver 163–5
sugar tongs 149–51
suites
　bedroom 15
　lounge 49
Summers, W. 139
sundials 267–8
Superior Silver Co 141
supper sets 131
surveying instruments 266
Sutherland tables 52, 53, 59
Swansea pottery
　bowls 79
　jugs 109, 110
　plates 91, 93, 99
Swedish
　ceramics 102
　glass 178
　silver 135, 145, 148
Swiss
　boxes 243
　chests 29
　watches 211, 212
　wood 280
swords 234–7

T
table cabinets 38, 93
table lamps 255–7
tables 52–61
　breakfast 54, 57, 58
　card 53–6, **54**, 58, 61
　centre 61
　dining 61
　display 54
　drop-leaf 56, 58, 59
　library 52
　occasional 52, 56–9
　Pembroke 55, 57
　pillar 57
　side 52, 53, 58–60
　Sutherland 52, 53, 59
　tea 57, 60
　tilt-top 54, 61
　two-tier 55
　wine 56
　work 54, 60
　writing 55, 56
tankards, silver 147, 148
tantaluses 171
tapersticks 141
Taylor & Perry 139

tazzas 191
tea bowls 70, 72
tea caddies 241–3
　ceramic 108, 129, 130
　silver 138
tea caddy bowls 167
tea services
　ceramic 116, 117
　silver 158, 159
tea tables 57, 60
teapots
　ceramic 119–21
　kitchenware 249
　silver 158–9
teddy bears 245
telescopes 268
terracotta
　antiquities 222
　architectural antiques 228–30
　sculpture 270
Teste 217
textiles 274–7
　rugs and carpets 262–5
theodolites 266
thermometers 269
thimble holders 279
Thomas, Francis Borne 158
Thomson, George 208
Thornhill, W. & Co 163
Thornycroft, Mary 131
Tiffany & Co
　clocks 195, 196
　silver 148, 151
Tiffany-style boxes 241
tiles 122–3, 221
tilt-top tables 54, 61
toast racks, silver 160
tobacco tins 258
Toby jugs 112, 113
toleware 259
tongs, silver 149–52
Tooth, Henry 125
tortoiseshell tea caddies 242
toys 244–7
Traies, William 152
trays 63
　butler's 62
　ceramic 130
　silver 156–7
　toleware 259
trinket trays 130
trios 73
Trippensee Manufacturing Co 269
tub chairs 27
Tudor 213
tumblers 177
Tunbridge ware
　blotters 281
　boxes 238, 239, 243, 279, 281
　brushes 278
　napkin rings 278
　panels 281
　spinning tops 281
tureens
　ceramic 77, 78, 80
　silver 133
Turkish
　arms and armour 237
　bag faces 262
　rugs 264

Turner 110
Turvey 234
two-tier tables 55

U
urns
　garden 230
　silver 165

V
Valanterio, G. 217
Van Dyke rims, glass bowls 167
Vaseline glass **188**
　lighting 255, 256
　vases 188, 189
vases
　bronze 260
　ceramic 124–8
　glass 188–90
　pewter 261
Veazy, David 261
Venice, ceramics 105
vesta pots 133
veterinary instruments 267
Vienna porcelain
　figures 85
　plaques 114
　tureens 80
　vases 126
Vienna wall clocks 206
vinaigrettes 138, 140
Vincenti & Cie 196
Viners & Co 203
Volkstedt 108

W
waiters, silver 156, 157
Walker & Hall 149, 158
wall brackets 68
wall cabinets 38
wall clocks 205–6
wall mirrors 46
wall sconces 261
Walsh, John Walsh 189
Waltham 209, 211
Walton 88
Walton, John 146
wardrobes 42
Warner, Edith 117
washstands 228
watch stands 50
watches 208–13
　pocket 208–12
　wristwatches 213
water heaters 230
Waterford 168
Watts, E.R. & Son 266
weapons 234–7
Webb, Thomas 169, 181
Wedgwood
　cheese domes 131
　cups 69
　dishes 80
　jelly moulds 252
　jugs 110
　plaques 115
　services 117
　teapots 119
　tiles 122
Weiss 266
Wellington chests 35
Welsh ceramics

bowls 79
jugs 109, 110
plates 94, 98, 99, 102, 104
platters 82
Wemyss
　bowls 81
　candlesticks 68
　dishes 83
　jardinières 106, 107
　plates 97, 100, 101
　preserve pots 130
　vases 127–8
whatnots 62
wheel barometers 214–16, **216**
Whieldon 88
Whipham, Thomas 145
whisks 248
Whitford, Samuel 146
wick trimmers 258
Wilkins Toy Co 245
Wilkinson, Henry & Co 146, 162, 191
Wilmore, Joseph 136, 151
windows, stained glass 226, 228
Windsor armchairs 23
wine coolers 164
wine funnels 165
wine glasses 173, 175–80
wine tables 56
wing chairs 20, 21
Wise, Eliza 276
WMF 182
Wood, Samuel 143
Wood, Thomas 198
wooden antiques 278–81
　boxes 238–43
　sculpture 271
Worcester
　baskets 66
　bowls 81
　cream boats 113
　cups 72
　dishes 81
　figures 86, 88
　jugs 111
　loving cups 71
　mugs 70, 74
　plates 105
　tea canisters 108
　teapots 120
work boxes 243
work tables 54, 60
wristwatches 213
writing equipment, silver 161–2
writing slopes 43
writing stands 118
writing tables 44, 45, 55, 56
wrought iron see iron

Y
Yapp & Woodward 163
Ynysmedw pottery 94
Yorkshire Pottery 90

Z
Zach, Bruno 273
Zarribeitia, Jose 216
Zimmerman, Johan 148
Zsolnay 113